My Testimony

ANATOLY MARCHENKO

My Testimony

Translated by
MICHAEL SCAMMELL

Introduction by
MAX HAYWARD

A DELTA BOOK

A DELTA BOOK

Published by
Dell Publishing Co., Inc.
750 Third Avenue, New York, N. Y. 10017

First published in the United States of America by
E. P. Dutton & Co., Inc.

2/73

CONTENTS

INTRODUCTION

On March 27, 1968, *Literary Gazette* published a long 'Letter to a Reader' by its editor-in-chief, Alexander Chakovsky. A few months previously, in November 1967, Chakovsky had come to London to debate with Malcolm Muggeridge in a BBC television studio the sentence on the Soviet writers Sinyavsky and Daniel. Just as he had then hotly defended the proceedings taken against them, so he now justified in a reply to a Soviet reader the trial in Moscow in January 1968 of two more young Soviet intellectuals, Ginzburg and Galanskov, one of whose offences, in the eyes of their prosecutors, was to have circulated detailed information about the case of Sinyavsky and Daniel. This has now become a familiar pattern in the Soviet Union—one trial inevitably leads to another in a chain reaction of protest and reprisal.

The general policy of the Soviet press has been to ignore the great numbers of written protests (in the form of open letters to the Soviet authorities and newspapers) that circulate in typescript in the country, and Chakovsky's long statement in *Literary Gazette* was the first public response of any importance. While angrily condemning the victims of the trials and those who protest on their behalf, Chakovsky nevertheless affected to be personally in disagreement with the policy of sentencing young rebels to forced labor and suggested, in what was clearly a rhetorical flourish, that they be sent abroad to join the writer Tarsis and thus be maintained at the expense of the foreign tax payer instead of 'being fed . . . at public expense in [Soviet] prisons or corrective labor colonies'.

The same day that Chakovsky's article appeared in *Literary Gazette*, Anatoly Marchenko, a young worker and the author of the present book, who had been released after six years' hard labor in 1966, wrote an open letter in reply. It has, needless to say, never been published in the Soviet Union, but it has circulated widely in the country. He pointed out that for the prisoners in the hard labor camps where he and a number of imprisoned intellectuals (including Sinyavsky and Daniel) served their sentences, the daily food ration was 2,400 calories a day—sufficient for a child of seven to eleven, but scarcely enough for an adult expected to do a full day's work. In his book Marchenko goes into much greater detail and shows what a mockery it is to speak of Soviet prisoners being fed 'at public expense'. The camps are in fact maintained at the expense of the prisoners themselves. They are paid a normal wage, of which 50 per cent is deducted for their 'upkeep' and the rest kept in an account from which they are paid only on their release. More than this, the 'public' exploits them in classical Marxist terms, since the State sells at enormous profit the product of their labor (furniture in the case of Marchenko and his fellow prisoners).

It is possible that Chakovsky was genuinely ignorant of these facts. One thing that has definitely not changed since Stalin's time is official reticence, unparalleled in any modern state, about the penal system. In the whole of the Soviet period no figure has ever been given for the number of political prisoners held at any one time in prisons or hard labor camps. Conditions in Soviet penal institutions have always been carefully hidden not only from the outside world, but from the Soviet public too. Occasional glimpses of 'model' prisons (such as the famous Bolshevo near Moscow), accorded to a handful of privileged visitors from abroad, were cynical attempts—often successful—to give the impression that there is not a great deal of difference between a Soviet prison and a sanatorium. After Stalin's death there was for the first time some public admission of the existence of slave labor camps—the vast numbers of people returning from them under amnesty during 1954–1956 in any case made further concealment pointless—but there still has not been any official data on the numbers of people involved.

The publication of Solzhenitsyn's *One Day in the Life of Ivan Denisovich* in 1962, which appeared thanks to a squabble between Khrushchev and his colleagues, was the first and only occasion on which something of the truth about conditions in Stalin's camps was allowed to reach Soviet readers. But Solzhenitsyn's even more revealing work on the subject, *The First Circle*, is banned inside Russia and for several years now there has been a party instruction to the censorship forbidding anything on the 'camp theme' to appear in print. There has never been anything at all about the development of the Soviet penal system after Stalin. The importance of Anatoly Marchenko's book is that it is the first detailed and completely unvarnished report on conditions in Soviet camps today by someone who knows them at first hand.

It is therefore now possible for the first time to make some comparisons between the system as it was under Stalin, and as it is today. It immediately becomes apparent that the change is mainly a quantitive one. While the prisoners under Stalin were numbered in millions, they are now numbered in tens (or hundreds?) of thousands. In the absence of official figures, or reliable estimates based on a study of all the materials, it is impossible to be more precise than this. It is quite likely that in the 'peak' years after the war there may have been as many as twenty million people doing forced labor, or condemned to permanent exile in the most remote and inhospitable areas of the country. As Solzhenitsyn shows in *One Day in the Life of Ivan Denisovich* and in *The First Circle*, whole sections of the Soviet populations were automatically suspect and were sent in large numbers, quite indiscriminately, to concentration camps—these included many of the millions of Soviet prisoners of war who returned home (it is a little known fact that about a third of a million stayed in the West, knowing that they would be victimized if they returned home), and people who had lived temporarily under German rule in the occupied territories.

Then there were mass deportations from the Baltic states, the Western Ukraine and the exiling to Siberia and Central Asia of several small peoples *in toto:* the Chechens and Ingush, the Karachai, Balkhars, Kalmyks and the Crimean Tartars (who are still not allowed to go back home, because their lands were given to Ukranian settlers). As Stalin's paranoia worsened during the years before his death, many non-Russian people living in border areas were also transported to Central Asia or Siberia—this happened, for instance, to the Greek colonies along the Black Sea coast. From the late forties until Stalin's death, a great many Jews were arrested and sent to the camps —in Stalin's eyes, particularly after the creation of the State of Israel, they were a natural fifth column. For most 'political' prisoners during the postwar years maximum sentences of twenty-five years were standard (the much publicized abolition of the death penalty was meant for foreign consumption: in August 1952, all the leading Yiddish-language writers were shot on one day, a fact still not admitted in the Soviet press, even though each of the victims has been posthumously 'rehabilitated'.)

In all the revelations of recent years attention has been

focused on the large camps in Siberia and the Arctic, where prisoners were employed in mining, lumbering and the general economic development of the most inaccessible and the bleakest areas of this great land mass—on the maps Alaska looks like a small, severed rump to it. People died like flies of cold and hunger, and intolerable conditions of work. It is less well known that there was under Stalin an extraordinary system of 'local' forced labor which meant that many, if not all factories and construction sites were run partly by forced labor. As a result of the labor laws passed by Stalin just before the war, workers could be sentenced to short periods (six months or so for a first offence) of forced labor *at their places of work* for being more than twenty minutes late for work, and other infringements of the 'labor code'.

In 1948, on the way to Tolstoy's estate at Yasnaya Polyana, I remember seeing the stockade adjacent to the large steel works in Tula. It was almost as large as the works themselves and at intervals along the high barbed wire fence there were characteristic watch towers, with armed guards looking inwards. In the same year, going by rail through the industrial suburbs of Tbilisi in Georgia, I noticed several similar prison camps.

It is clear from Marchenko's book that nothing on this scale now exists. There are no longer whole categories of the population behind barbed wire, and although there is still a hard core of 'political' prisoners from Stalin's times, the people now undergoing forced labor have been sentenced individually, not as members of suspect categories, but on specific criminal or 'political' charges.

Since Marchenko himself was sentenced on political grounds most of what he has to say deals with political prisoners who now fall into three main groups: intellectuals accused of anti-Soviet propaganda (the cases of only a few of those who stood trial in Moscow, such as Sinyavsky, Daniel, Ginzburg and Galanskov, have become known to the outside world); nationalists, that is people charged with advocating some degree of autonomy (mainly cultural) for non-Russian parts of the USSR such as the Ukraine; religious believers, particularly Baptists and sectarians who have actively stood up for their faith or opposed state interference with it. It is difficult to tell what the proportion of common criminals to political prisoners is, but it seems certain that, just as in Stalin's time, conditions are much harsher for the 'politicals', though they are no longer confined together with criminals and terrorized by them.

The great reduction in numbers of prisoners means, of course, that they no longer play a key part in the Soviet economy. In Stalin's day there were huge areas, (such as North Kazakhstan, equal in size to France) where the factories, mines, and even the farms were run largely by forced labor. This no longer appears to be true, though there are rumored to be 'death camps' in one or two very remote areas (uranium mines near Norilsk, and rocket installations in the Arctic) to which it is not easy to attract 'free' labor by the lure of high wages. Marchenko's book confirms the impression that most important political prisoners are now sent to the cluster of camps in the neighborhood of Potma, about 500 kilometers east of Moscow. It is by no means the only camp for political prisoners (the names and location of about ninety others distributed all over Soviet territory are known and Marchenko refers to the continued existence of camps in the traditional areas of Vorkuta and Kazakhstan), but it would seem that major political offenders, including foreigners such as Gary Powers and Gerald Brooke, are sent to Potma. Foreigners are, however, treated somewhat differently—on the whole better—than Soviet citizens. Here most of them are employed in making furniture, cabinets for television sets and—as in Brooke's case—chessmen. They work a forty-eight hour week and are expected to fulfil the usual high 'production norms'. This is not easy on a full stomach—and impossible on a semi-starvation diet, with its lack of fat and vitamins. In this respect the camps are as bad as, if not worse than, they were under Stalin.

It is also clear from Marchenko's account (as from others that have filtered out in recent years) that this inadequate diet is now used as a deliberate means of pressure on political prisoners. Those who are 'uncooperative', e.g. refuse to act as informers, are not allowed to receive parcels from their relatives and have no hope of a remission of their sentences. This is probably the main respect in which the camps are now worse than they were under Stalin. In many other ways they are much the same: the physical lay-out, the guards and punishment cells are all more or less as described in Solzhenitsyn's *One Day in the Life of Ivan Denisovich*. Even the name of the Potma camp area, Dubrovlag, is a sinister relic from Stalin's day: in 1947, Stalin personally ordered the setting-up of special camps with bucolic-sounding code names—Ozerlag ('lake camp'), Rechlag ('river camp'), Dubrovlag ('oak forest camp') in which he wished to concentrate all political prisoners to facilitate their speedy liquidation in case of a new war.

Not much is known about Marchenko except what he states about himself in his book. He was born in the small western Siberian town of Barabinsk, where both his parents were railway workers. He left school after eight classes, that is, two years short of a full secondary education, and went to work on the Novosibirsk hydro-electric station, and then on similar projects all over Siberia and Kazakhstan. His troubles began in 1960, when he was twenty-two years old, as the result of a fight in a workers' hostel. In typical fashion the police indiscriminately arrested the innocent and the guilty, and Marchenko was sent with all the others involved to a camp near Karaganda (also a relic of Stalin's time—it is the camp described from his own experiences by Solzhenitsyn in *One Day in the Life of Ivan Denisovich*). After escaping from this camp, Marchenko made his way down to Ashkhabad on the Iranian frontier where he was arrested while trying to leave the country. He was charged with 'treason' and sentenced to six years imprisonment.

After his release in 1966 he was subjected to all the usual restrictions applied to former political prisoners, that is, he was not allowed to take up residence in the capital or in any other major city. There were also the usual difficulties about getting work (and since 'there is no unemployment in the Soviet Union', there are also no unemployment benefits). After nearly a year, however, he was at last permitted to live in the small town of Alexandrov, not far from Moscow. From May 1968 he began work in Moscow as a loader though he was still forced by the regulations to live outside the city limits in Alexandrov. It was here, during 1967, that he wrote this book. After writing the book, which he could not hope to get published in the Soviet Union, he wrote a number of open letters, addressed to the President of the Soviet branch of the Red Cross, and to several Soviet writers. In one of them he said: 'The present day Soviet camps for political prisoners are just as terrible as under Stalin. In some things they are better, but in others they are worse. It is essential that everybody should know about this—both those who want to know the truth . . . and those who do not wish to know it, [preferring] to close their eyes and ears so that one day they will again be able to absolve themselves ('O God, we didn't know'). I would like this testimony of mine about Soviet camps and prisons for political prisoners to become known to the humanitarians and progressive people of other countries, to those who speak up in defence of political prisoners in Greece, Portugal, South Africa and Spain. . . .'

These activities of Marchenko were, needless to say, highly 'inconvenient' to the Soviet authorities, and they soon found a pretext to silence him. On July 22, 1968, Marchenko wrote another open letter, this time addressed to the people of Czechoslovakia. In it he welcomed the signs of restoration of freedom and democracy for the Czechs and Slovaks, protested against the systematic misrepresentation of events in Czechoslovakia in the Soviet press and said that any attempt to interfere would be nothing less than criminal. Seven days after sending this letter, on July 29, Marchenko was arrested.

Larissa Daniel described the circumstances of his arrest in her open letter of August 1, 1968:

'Why should the authorities set the machine of arbitrary power in motion against *him*? It's easy to guess the answer when you have read the appeal of Anatoly Marchenko's friends.

'His book, in which he tells the truth about the camps for political prisoners, aroused such hatred for him in the KGB that they began to bait him like a hare. KGB agents followed on his heels for months on end—I've spotted them so often that I know many of them by sight. And not only in Moscow, where he works, and in Alexandrov, where he lives: he went to visit relations in Ryazan but wasn't allowed to leave the train and had to return to Moscow. He was seized on the street almost as soon as he had been discharged from hospital; his face was smashed up as he was being pushed into a car when he came to Moscow for a literary evening. Marchenko's open letter to *Rude Pravo* and other papers evidently infuriated the KGB to such an extent that they couldn't wait any longer to put this Marchenko behind bars by any means and on any pretext. On the morning of July 29 he was picked up in the street on his way to work and now he's in prison again.'

With characteristic disingenuousness the authorities charged him not on political grounds, but for the technical offence of allegedly having infringed the regulations on residence permits which debarred him from living in Moscow. Since he had in fact established residence outside the city limits, this charge too was trumped up. For his 'offence' he has been sentenced by a Moscow court to a year's imprisonment in a 'strict regime' camp, this time in the region of Perm. He is known to have been sent there in December 1968 to begin serving his sentence.

According to some reports in the Western press (see *The Observer*, July 6, 1969) he has since been retried once more, presumably on account of his book having been published abroad in Russian, and sentenced to a further three years.

The arrest of Marchenko caused great indignation in Moscow intellectual circles. An open letter in his defense was signed by Larissa Daniel (whose husband Marchenko had met in Potma), Pavel Litvinov, General Grigorenko, and others. They pointed out that his arrest was a breach of Soviet law— it had taken place on the day of his arrival in Moscow from Alexandrov, though as a non-resident he would have been entitled under the regulations to spend three days in the city.

Larissa Daniel and Pavel Litvinov were themselves arrested in August for organizing a demonstration on Red Square against the invasion of Czechoslovakia, and have been deported to remote places in Siberia after a closed trial. General Grigorenko was arrested in Tashkent at the beginning of May 1969. Also arrested in August 1968, for having in her possession copies of the petition on behalf of Marchenko, was a young woman engineer, Irina Belgorodskaya, who is reported to be the daughter of a retired colonel of the KGB. In February 1969 she was sentenced to one year in a labor camp for 'slander'.

Finally, a word about Marchenko as a writer. What immediately strikes one is the soberness of his account, and the care with which he distinguishes between what he has witnessed himself and hearsay evidence. He does not harangue or preach, but just tries to tell us in a straightforward way the things that we want to know. He also succeeds, incidently—though this was not his conscious intention—in giving very revealing glimpses of Soviet life in general. Not only is there a wealth of information about social habits (including sexual mores), but the reader is given the 'feel' of real life at the humbler levels of existence in the Soviet Union. Marchenko introduces us to the vast submerged reality which few foreigners or even educated Russians ever see.

Despite his relative lack of formal education, he writes in good literate Russian, yet avoids the temptation to treat his material in an obviously 'literary' way. He is clearly a person of great natural gifts, integrity and will-power. Despite all the odds he has made his voice heard. It is heartening that there are still such people in Russia.

Max Hayward

Note: All the footnotes to Marchenko's text have been provided by the translator.

Surely we will be joined by all free minds and all passionate hearts?

Let them join together, let them write and speak out! Let them try together with us to enlighten public opinion and all those poor and humble people who are now being lashed into a frenzy by poisonous propaganda! The soul of our fatherland, its energy and its greatness, can be expressed only in its justice and magnanimity.

I am concerned with one thing only, and that is that the light of truth should be spread as far and as quickly as possible. A trial behind closed doors after a secret investigation will prove nothing. The real trial will only begin then, for one must speak out, since silence would mean complicity.

What madness to think you can stop history being written! No, it will be written, and then no one, however small his responsibility, will escape retribution.

Emile Zola: *Letter to France*
(Pamphlet, Fasquelle, 1898)

. . . . Guards and sentries check their watches,
The tail of the column winds through the gates,
Ten o'clock sharp in the camp—lights out
Is tolled over the palisades.

Rail thumps hard against rail—lights out!
The con hurries back to his hut—lights out!
Icy railings of tempered steel
Lull Kolymá with their Angelus peal.

It's your turn now, Igarka and Taishet!
Wrap up warm in your jackets, Karaganda!
The chiming rails of the rusty timepiece
Toll out the weeks and the years.

The shadow is half way over now,
The shadow's crept over the Urals. . . .
Dubrovlag in its turn comes in
To swell the bedtime chorus.

Songs that didn't get born—lights out!
Stars that have slipped out of sight—lights out!
I cannot sleep in the Moscow calm:
Reveille's in an hour at Kolymá.

Song of the Time Zones, 1967

(*Kolyma, Igarka, Taishet, Karaganda and Dubrovlag are prison camps spread over the Soviet Union. The prisoners' day is punctuated by the clanging of a rail on a rail which calls him to work and sends him to bed.*)

My Testimony

AUTHOR'S PREFACE

When I was locked up in Vladimir Prison I was often seized by despair. Hunger, illness, and above all helplessness, the sheer impossibility of struggling against evil, provoked me to the point where I was ready to hurl myself upon my jailers with the sole aim of being killed. Or to put an end to myself in some other way. Or to maim myself as I had seen others do.

One thing alone prevented me, one thing alone gave me the strength to live through that nightmare: the hope that I would eventually come out and tell the whole world what I had seen and experienced. I promised myself that for the sake of this aim I would suffer and endure everything. And I gave my word on this to my comrades who were doomed to spend many more years behind bars and barbed wire.

I wondered how to carry out this task. It seemed to me that in our country, with its conditions of cruel censorship and KGB* control over every word uttered, such a thing would be impossible. And also pointless: our people are so oppressed by fear and enslaved by the harsh conditions of life that nobody even wants to know the truth. Therefore, I thought, I will have to flee abroad in order to leave my evidence at least as a document, as a small contribution to history.

A year ago my imprisonment ended. I emerged into freedom. And I realized that I had been mistaken, that my

* Soviet secret police. The initials stand for Committee for State Security.

1

testimony is needed by my countrymen. The people want to know the truth.

The main aim of these notes is to tell the truth about today's camps and prisons for political prisoners—to those who wish to hear it. I am convinced that publicity is the sole effective means of combating the evil and lawlessness that is rampant in my country today.

In recent years a number of fictional and documentary works have appeared in print on the subject of the camps. In many other works, furthermore, this subject is mentioned either in passing or by implication. Lastly it has been very fully and powerfully covered in a number of productions disseminated by 'Samizdat'—typed and duplicated manuscripts circulated illegally. Thus Stalin's camps have been exposed; and even though the exposures have still not reached all readers, they will, of course, in time. All this is good. But it is also bad—and dangerous. For the impression involuntarily arises that all these descriptions refer only to the past, that such things do not and cannot exist nowadays. Once they are even written about in our press, then everything is sure to have changed here already, everything is in order again, and all the perpetrators of these terrible crimes have been punished and all the victims rewarded.

It's a lie! How many victims have been 'rewarded' posthumously, how many of them even now languish forgotten in our camps, how many new ones continue to join them. And how many of those who condemned, who interrogated and tortured them, are still occupying their posts or living peacefully on their well-earned pensions, bearing not one iota of moral responsibility for their acts! Whenever I ride in a Moscow suburban train the coaches are filled with benevolent, peaceable old pensioners. Some of them are reading newspapers, others are taking a basket of strawberries somewhere, while still others are keeping an eye on grandson. . . . Maybe these are doctors, workers, engineers now on a pension after long years of strenuous work; maybe that old man over there with the steel teeth lost his others from the 'application of physical methods' or in the mines of Kolyma. But in each such peaceful old pensioner I see rather the interrogator himself, who was himself responsible for knocking out people's teeth.

Because I myself have seen plenty of them—*just the same*—in our present camps. Because today's Soviet camps for political prisoners are just as horrific as in Stalin's time. A few things are better, a few things worse. But everybody must know about it.

Everybody must know, including those who would like to know the truth and instead are given lying, optimistic newspaper articles, designed to lull the public conscience; and also including those who don't wish to know, who close their eyes and stuff up their ears in order to be able at some future date to justify themselves and to emerge from the dirt with their noses clean: 'Good heavens, and we never knew. . . .' If they have a single particle of civic conscience or genuine love for their country they will stand up in its defence, just as the true sons of Russia have always done.

I would like this evidence of mine concerning the Soviet camps and prisons for political prisoners to come to the attention of humanists and progressive people in other countries—those who stick up for political prisoners in Greece and Portugal and in Spain and South Africa. Let them ask their Soviet colleagues in the struggle against inhumanity: 'And what have you done in your own country to stop political prisoners from being, say, "reformed" by starvation?'

I don't consider myself a writer, these notes are not a work of art. For six whole years I tried only to see and to memorize.

In these notes of mine there is not a single invented personage nor a single invented incident. Wherever there is a danger of harming others I have omitted names or remained silent about certain episodes and circumstances. But I am prepared to answer for the truth of every detail recounted here. Each incident, each fact can be confirmed by dozens and sometimes by hundreds or even thousands of witnesses and their comrades in the camps. They could also of course, cite horrific facts that I have not included.

It seems a likely supposition that the authorities will try to be revenged on me and to escape the truth that I have told in these pages by an unprovable accusation of 'slander'. Let me declare, therefore, that I am prepared to answer for it at a public trial, provided that the necessary witnesses are invited and that interested representatives of public opinion and the press are allowed to be present. And if instead we are given yet another masquerade known as a 'public trial', where representatives of the KGB stand at the entrance in order to repel ordinary citizens and secret policemen dressed up in civvies are used as the 'public', and where the correspondents of all foreign newspapers (including communist ones) are forced to hang around outside, unable to get any information—as happened at the trials of the writers Sinyavsky and Daniel, Khaustov and Bukovsky and the others—then that will merely confirm the justice of what I have written.

One day our company officer, Captain Usov, said to me:

'You, Marchenko, are always dissatisfied, nothing suits you. But what have you ever done to make things better? All you wanted to do was run away and nothing more!'

If, after writing these notes, I come under Captain Usov again, I shall be able to say:

'I have done everything that was in my power. And here I am—back where I started.'

PART ONE

The Beginning

MY NAME is Anatoly Marchenko and I was born in the small
Siberian town of Barabinsk. My father, Tikhon Akimovich
Marchenko, worked his whole life as a fireman on the railway.
My mother was a station cleaner. Both of them were totally
illiterate and my mother's letters always had to be written by
somebody else.

After eight years of schooling I quit school and went as a
Komsomol volunteer to Novosibirsk to work on the hydro-
electric power station there. This was the beginning of my
independence. I was made a shift foreman with the drilling
gang, travelled around to all the new power station sites in
Siberia and worked in mines and on geological surveys. My
last job was on the Karaganda power station.

It was there that I first fell foul of the law. We young
workers lived in a hostel and went dancing at the club. In the
same settlement lived some Chechens who had been exiled
from the Caucasus. They were terribly embittered: after all,
they'd been transported from their homes to this strange
Siberia, among a strange and alien people. Between their
young people and us constant brawls and punch-ups kept
breaking out and sometimes there was a knife fight as well.
One day there was a huge brawl in our hostel. When it had all

died away of its own accord the police arrived, picked up everyone left in the hostel—the majority of those involved had already run away or gone into hiding—arrested them and put them on trial. I was one of the ones arrested, and they took us away from the settlement, where everyone knew what had happened. They sentenced us all in a single day, with no attempt at finding out who was guilty and who innocent. Thus it was that I found my way to the terrible camps of Karaganda.

After that the circumstances of my life turned out in such a way that I decided to escape abroad. I simply could see no other way out for me. I made my run together with a young fellow called Anatoly Budrovsky. We tried to cross the border into Iran, but were discovered and captured about fifty yards from the border.

That was on October 29, 1960. For five months I was kept under investigation at the special investigation prison of the Ashkhabad KGB. All that time I was kept in solitary confinement, with no parcels or packages and without a single line from my family. Every day I was interrogated by KGB investigator Sarafyan (and later Shchukin): why did I want to run away? The KGB had entered a charge of high treason against me and therefore the investigator was not very pleased with my answers. What he was after was to get the necessary evidence from me, wearing me down by interrogations, threatening that the investigation would go on until I had told them what was required of me, promising me that in return for 'worthwhile' evidence and an admission of guilt, I would have my twice daily prison rations supplemented. Although he didn't get what he was after and got no material whatsoever to support the charges, either from me or from any of the forty witnesses, nevertheless I was tried for treason.

On March 2–3, 1961, our case came before The Supreme Court of the Soviet Socialist Republic of Turkmenia. It was a closed court: not a single person was present in that huge chamber, except for the court officials, two guards armed with tommy guns at our backs and the guard commander at the main entrance. For two days they asked me the same questions as they had been putting during the investigation and I gave them the same answers, rejecting the charge. My fellow escapee, Anatoly Budrovsky, had evidently not been able to stand up to the interrogations and solitary confinement and had yielded under pressure from the investigator. He gave evidence against me, thus shielding and saving himself. The evidence of forty other people was in my favor. I asked why the court paid no attention to this and was told: 'The court itself decides what evidence to believe.'

Although I refused any defence, my lawyer attended the court and pleaded my case. He said that the court had no grounds for convicting me of high treason: no trust could be placed in the evidence of Budrovsky in that he was an interested party and was being tried in the same case. The court ought to take account of the evidence of the other witnesses. Marchenko could be convicted for illegally attempting to cross the border, but not for treason.

I refused to take up my right of having the last word: I did not consider myself guilty of treason and had nothing to add to my evidence.

On March 3 the court pronounced its sentence: Budrovsky got two years in the camps (this was even less than the maximum in such cases, which was three years) for illegally attempting to cross the border, while I was given six for high treason—this too being considerably less than the permitted maximum penalty—the firing squad.

I was then twenty-three.

Once more I was taken back to prison, to my cell. To tell the truth, the length of my sentence made no impression on me. It was only later that each year of imprisonment stretched out into days and hours and it seemed that six years would never come to an end. Much later I also found out that the label of 'traitor to the Homeland' had crippled me not for six years but for life. At the time, however, I had only one sensation, and that was that an injustice had been committed, a legalized illegality, and that I was powerless; all I could do was to gather and store my outrage and despair inside me, storing it up until it exploded like an overheated boiler.

I recalled the empty rows of seats in the chamber, the indifferent voices of the judge and prosecutor, the court secretary chewing on a roll the whole time, the silent statues of the guards. Why hadn't they let anyone into the court, not even my mother? Why had no witnesses been called? Why wasn't I given a copy of the sentence? What did they mean: 'You can't have a copy of the sentence, it's secret'? A few minutes later a blue paper was pushed through the little trapdoor for food: 'Sign this to say that you've been informed of your sentence'. I signed it and that was that. The sentence was final, with no right of appeal.

I went on hunger strike. I wrote a statement protesting against the trial and sentence, pushed it through the food trap and refused to accept any food. For several days I took nothing into my mouth but cold water. Nobody paid any attention. The warders, after listening to my refusal, would calmly remove my portion of food and soup bowl and bring them back again in the evening. Again I would refuse. Three days later the warders entered my cell with a doctor and commenced the operation known as 'forced artificial feeding'. My hands were twisted behind my back and handcuffed, then they stuffed a spreader into my mouth, stuck a hose down my gullet and began pouring the feeding mixture—something greasy and sweet—in through a funnel at the top. The warders said: 'Call off your hunger strike. You won't gain anything by it and in any case we won't let you lose weight.' The same procedure was repeated on the following day.

I called off my hunger strike. And I never did get a reply to my protest.

Several days later a warder came to fetch me. He led me via a staircase and various corridors to the first floor and directed me through a door lined with black oilcloth. A little nameplate said: 'Prison Governor'. In the office inside sat the prison governor at his desk, beneath a large portrait of Dzerzhinsky;* on the couch were two men familiar to me from the investigation of my case, the legal inspector of prisons and the head of the investigation department. The fourth man was a stranger. One glance at him and I shuddered, so unnatural and repulsive was his appearance: a tiny little egg-shaped body, miniscule legs that barely reached to the floor and the thinnest scraggy little neck crowned by an enormous flattened globe—his head. The slits of his eyes, the barely discernible little nose and the thin smiling mouth were sunk in a sea of taut, yellow, gleaming dough. How could that neck hold such a load?

They told me that this was the Deputy Public Prosecutor of the Turkmen Republic, and invited me to sit down. The conversation was conducted in an informal and familiar tone. They asked me how I felt and whether I had ended my hunger strike. Thanking them for their touching delicacy and interest I informed them that it was ended and asked in turn: 'Can you tell me, please, when and where I will be sent?'

* Founder of the Soviet secret police, called the Cheka, then GPU, in his time.

'You are going to a Komsomol* site. You'll be a Komsomol worker,' answered the monster, absolutely wreathed in smiles as he enjoyed his little joke.

I felt unbearably revolted. On me, who had been sentenced by them for treason to my country, it somehow grated to hear them utter these words here, in this office, and to see their cynical sneers. They all knew perfectly well what it meant. And I knew too.

Back in my cell I thought of the various sites I had worked on. Outside every one there had been a camp, barbed wire, control towers, guards and 'Komsomol workers in reefer-jackets'.† I recalled how as a nineteen-year-old youth I had been sent on a two-month assignment to Bukhtarma power station. The quarters where we free workers lived were at Serebryanka, some way away from the site, and the camp was there too. Both we and the camp convicts were taken to each shift and back again by train. The 'free' train consisted of five or six ancient four-wheeled wagons. It used to stop about 50 yards from the guardhouse and then we would show our passes to the soldier on guard duty and walk through the entrance passage. After this they would open up the gates and the endless train with the cons on board would roll straight inside the site perimeter. This one was not like ours with its hopeless little four-wheelers, but consisted of big, strong, eight-wheeled cars into which the cons were packed like sardines. On every brake platform sat a pair of tommy gunners and the rear of the train was brought up by an open platform full of soldiers. The soldiers would open the doors, drive out the cons, herd them away from the cars and line them up five deep. Then began the count by fives: the first

* The Komsomol is the Soviet youth organization.
† Reefer-jacket is the ironic term used for the flimsy cotton-quilted jackets issued to prisoners.

five, the second, the third, the fifteenth, the fifty-second, the hundred and fifth ... counting and recounting. Suddenly there would be a mistake and they'd start counting all over again. Shouts, curses and yet another recount. After a thorough check the cons would go to their work places. Then, when the shift was over, the same thing would take place in reverse order. I had worked side by side with them, these 'Komsomol workers in reefer-jackets'. I used to get my pay, go to dances on my days off and never think a thing of it. Only one incident had embedded itself in my memory.

One day at the beginning of August one of the watch towers had suddenly started firing in the direction of the river Irtysh. Everybody downed tools and ran to the river bank, crowding up against the fence, with the free workers and cons all mixed up together. They tried to drive us away, of course, but we stayed put and gaped. A swimmer was already more than halfway across the river, closer to the opposite bank. We could see clearly that he was having difficulty in swimming and that he was trying to go as fast as possible. It was a con. It seemed he had bided his time till the dredger stopped working and then had crawled through the pipe and plunged into the Irtysh some way out from the shore. They hadn't noticed him at first and by the time they had opened fire, he was already a long way off. The guard launch had already set off in pursuit and now was about to catch up with the fugitive; it was only about a dozen yards behind, but the officer with the pistol in his hand was for some reason holding his fire. 'Well, if he shoots and kills him and the con goes to the bottom, how's he going to prove afterwards that he hasn't escaped?' explained the cons in the crowd. 'He's got to have either a living man or a body to show them.'

Meanwhile the fugitive reached the far shore, stood up and staggered a few steps. But the launch's bow had already struck the stones and the officer leapt out and found himself within two paces of the con. I saw him raise his pistol and shoot him in the legs. The con collapsed. Some tommy gunners ran up and as they stood there and in full view of the crowd on the opposite bank the officer fired several times into the prostrate prisoner. The crowd gasped and somebody swore obscenely.

The body was dragged over the stones like a sack and tossed into the launch. The launch set off downriver in the direction of the camp.

Now I couldn't help but think of Bukhtarma and this incident, and also other sites. No matter where they sent me now I would always be a 'Komsomol worker', I would be soaked and frozen during the checks, I would live behind barbed wire, I would be guarded by armed guards with sheepdogs; and if I couldn't bear it and tried to escape, I would be shot down just like that fellow in the Irtysh.

Convoys

THE FOLLOWING day I was sent away. They gave me back my clothes, which had been taken away when I was arrested, with the sole exception of my boots—these had been cut up into little pieces in their search for the 'plan of a Soviet factory'. I was ordered to get dressed and was then led out of the prison. A black maria stood right up against the door. I was thrust into a 'box' in the back and locked in. The van moved off. My cage had no windows, so that I couldn't see out but could only feel the van's motion. Suddenly the van slowed, turned and began to back up. So I was being transferred to a train. Then hurry, hurry again out of the van, between two solid ranks of soldiers and straight into the train. The prison coaches (they are still called 'Stolypins'*) are the same as normal passenger coaches: a narrow corridor runs the full length of one side, with the separate cabins or compartments on the other side. The connecting doors, though, are not solid but barred. There are no windows whatever. One side of the coach is completely blank, while the windows facing the corridor are filled with bars. None of this

* Named after P. A. Stolypin (1863–1911), Tsarist minister of the interior who savagely repressed uprisings and was assassinated by a revolutionary.

can be seen from outside however—they are covered with blinds—so that to look at it's a coach just like any other coach, and no one would guess that it's carrying convicts. It's true, of course, that all the windows are blocked up and shuttered, nobody looks out and waves to friends on the platform. It's as though all the gloomy and unsociable passengers have gathered together into this one coach.

Each compartment has three shelves on either side, one above the other. Between the middle ones a board can be fixed to form a single solid bunk. This means that generally there is sleeping room for seven—eight if you crowd up tight—but usually they cram twelve to fifteen people into each compartment or cage, and sometimes even more. And their luggage as well. And everything is stoppered up tight, so that there is no chance of any fresh air getting in, except perhaps during a halt, when they open the door to take somebody out or shove an extra one in.

The corridor is patrolled by soldiers armed with pistols. If a soldier happens to be a decent sort he will open one of the corridor windows in passing and for a short while a draught of fresh air will blow through the bars of the door. But some of the escorts won't give you any air no matter how much you beg them. And then the cons choke in their cages like fish thrown up on the beach.

From Ashkhabad to Tashkent I travelled like a prince, with a whole cage to myself! The other cages were packed tight. When I asked my neighbors through the wall how many they were, they replied 'seventeen'. It turned out that the explanation of the comfort offered to me was not any special regard for politicals but a fear of bringing them into contact with ordinary criminals—in case they corrupted them during the journey. As a result, I did not suffer from overcrowding like the others. In every other respect, however, my ride was just as unpleasant as everybody else's.

In Ashkhabad prison I was supplied with victuals for my next journey: a loaf of black bread, one and a half ounces of sugar and a salted herring. No matter how far it is to the next transit point, that is all you get; they don't feed you in the prison coaches. But worse than hunger is the thirst that tortures prisoners on the move. Morning and evening they give you each a mug of hot water and as for cold water, it depends on what soldier you get. If he's a good one he'll bring you two or three kettles, but if he can't be bothered to fetch and carry for you, then you can sit there till you die of thirst.

Towards evening I decided to have some supper. I unwrapped my Ashkhabad ration, tore off half the herring with my fingers and ate it with some bread. Then I asked the soldier for some water, but he refused. 'You can wait till the rest get it.' I waited. About twenty minutes later they started giving out the hot water. A soldier with a kettle walked down the corridor, pouring hot water into the mugs held out through the bars. He came to my cage.

'Where's your mug?'

As it happened, I had no mug, I had lost it during my investigation. So I asked:

'Maybe you could lend me yours. . . .'

'What bloody next! Give him my mug! Maybe you'd like my prick as well?'

And he went further. I started to dip my bread in the sugar and eat it dry. Yet I had a terrible thirst. I hadn't drunk anything for ages, my mouth was all dried up, and on top of it all I had just eaten salted herring. For some reason they always give prisoners salted herrings when they travel—on purpose probably. And later, no matter where or when I travelled, I was always given salted herring. Old cons also told me that they always got salted herrings and nothing to drink.

My neighbors in the next cage, hearing that I had nothing to drink and nothing to drink from, started asking the soldier to pass me one of their mugs of hot water. He swore black and blue, but nevertheless passed it to me. I drank the water down, together with my sugar.

'Keep the mug yourself,' they shouted, 'it will come in handy!' And so it did. It stayed with me wherever I went for the next six years—to Mordovia, to Vladimir prison and back to Mordovia again.

Then came fresh torments. I asked the soldier to let me go to the toilet. He replied:

'You'll have to wait.'

Well, of course I would have to wait, what else could I do?

There is one toilet in each prison coach: one seat and one wash basin. They take you there one by one. First they unlock the barred door of your cage, stand you in the corridor opposite the door with your face to the wall and your hands behind your back, then they lock the door behind you and lead you at the double down the corridor. While you do your business the door of the toilet is left wide open and the soldier stands and watches you. All the time he hurries you up: get a move on, get a move on! When you've finished you don't even get time to do your trousers up, but, still at the double and with your hands behind your back, are rushed back to your cage again. The coach is packed full, so that by the time you take everyone that way it's time to start again. But the soldiers are too tired, they don't want to: why should they have to chase up and down the corridor all day with these damned layabouts? And so they shout: 'You have to wait!' and don't take you, no matter how you plead with them, even if you were to break into tears. You have to wait until everyone is taken, and then until it's your turn.

It's the worst kind of torture you can imagine, both with the drinking and the toilet. And a very old invention, so they say. And it's still practised and will probably go on being practised so long as convicts are transported around Russia.

All the way to Tashkent I slept like a log, was tortured by thirst and was also hungry. And I really enjoyed hearing the voices behind the wall: all day long it was one continual sound of cursing and blinding, either at the soldiers, or else at each other or more distant neighbors in the other cages. The stream of obscenities was music to my ears—for five months I hadn't heard a human voice, except for the KGB investigators and the people in court.

The following day the train arrived in Tashkent. One by one we were taken out of the train, driven through a narrow corridor formed by two ranks of soldiers and crammed into a series of vans.

As I went up the steps the cons inside were already yelling that there was no more room. But the escort roared obscenely at them, then grabbed hold of me and shoved me in, right on top of the others. After me, several more were crammed in in the same way. The 'black maria', consisting of a closed van, was divided inside by a barred grille with a gate. On one side of the grille were us cons, on the other—two escorts. On the escorts' side were also two or three 'boxes'—iron lockers for single prisoners; you had to tie yourself up in a knot in order to get into them at all. But it was even worse in the communal section. Low benches ran right round the walls, with a space in the middle. There was room for about ten men (both sitting and standing), but no more. Into this space about thirty of us had been crammed. The first ones sat down on the benches, tight up against one another. The next ones sat on their knees. And the rest had to stand. This in itself would have been all right, but think what standing meant! The roof was so low that you could only stand by stooping, with your head and shoulders pressed up against the iron top. And there were so many men crammed in that you literally couldn't budge, let alone change position. In you went, and whatever position you ended up in you had to keep till you arrived. Your back, shoulders and neck turned numb and your whole body started to ache from the unnatural position. But even if you were to lift your feet off the floor, you wouldn't fall, you would still be propped up by the bodies around you.

The last one couldn't get in at all, and then the two soldiers put their hands against him, leaned their full weight behind the load and squeezed him into the mass of bodies, afterwards forcing the gate slowly shut. Somehow they got it closed and then locked it. Our van was ready. But the others still had to be crammed, and so we were forced to wait. The soldiers closed the outer door, sat down and lit cigarettes. Now there was absolutely nothing outside to tell you what sort of van this was or what was going on inside. A closed body with no windows, except for one tiny window over the rear door, where the escorts sat, and even this had a small green curtain drawn over it.

The men began to gasp for air. Somebody started cursing: 'When the fucking hell do we get started?'

'When you've done your time you can ride about in a limousine,' came the sarcastic reply of one of the soldiers, 'but this is a black maria, not a limousine.'

The con couldn't even talk properly, but only croaked:

'What's a fucking fancy boy like you doing worrying about limousines? You've never even been near an ordinary car. Been fucking starving all your life, and now when they put a gun in your hands you take the piss out of us.'

'Go on, go on! We'll see at the end how talkative you are in handcuffs.'

Then some others joined in:

'That's the only way you can do anything, with handcuffs!'

'Fucking fascists! Sticking us in their "gas vans"*!'

'It's the tommy guns that give the orders! Take those away and they'd be kissing our pricks—that's what they're used to!'

We heard an officer come up to the van. The cons fell silent, trying to listen to what he said. Our two soldiers called him 'lieutenant', but we couldn't hear anything that was said, except 'let them wait'. Then the cons started yelling again:

'Boss! Let's go!'

'Making fools of us!'

'Fascists with red notebooks!'

The men here had nothing to lose, they had been driven to despair by all these torments, and so they shouted the first thing that came into their heads. A criminal con, incidentally, can get himself charged on a political count, tried again and given an additional sentence of up to seven years for anti-Soviet agitation. But in these conditions nobody thought of anything like that or looked ahead in any way. Who had thought them up, these 'gas vans' (black marias), the salted herrings and all the rest? Just give him to us, that clever inventor!

The van trembled as the engine started. We set off. We were shaken and thrown about by the journey, but there was no room to fall down. Not even a dead man would have fallen there, but would have remained standing there upright, supported on all sides. How long it took I don't remember. All ideas of time got jumbled in those conditions and a minute seemed an age.

* A reference to the mobile gas extermination trucks used by the Nazis for mass executions.

When the van slowed and made several turns, we realized we were nearly there. Hurry up! Oh to get out of there, straighten up and take a deep breath. But then when the van halted, nobody even bothered to let us out. We no longer had the strength either to beg or swear. At last one of the soldiers started to open up. First he let the separate prisoners out of the boxes, and they were so doubled up when they emerged that they couldn't straighten up at first. Then he opened the door of our grille:

'Get out!'

This turned out to be not so simple. The men had got so compressed and entangled on the way that no one was able to disentangle himself or extricate himself from the general mass. By the time the first had managed to extricate himself he was forced literally to undress, leaving his padded jacket behind in the back of the van. And when almost everybody had left the van, someone brought his jacket out and gave it to him.

Having got out at last I, like the rest of them, was unable to straighten up, nor to walk a step. My whole body was a mass of aches and pains.

We had arrived at the Tashkent transit prison. Over the entrance was a huge slogan printed in white on red calico: 'Under the conditions of Socialism every man who leaves the path of labor is able to return to useful activity.' To begin with we were stuck in a quarantine cell—a gloomy, cavernous chamber with a double tier of bunks round the walls and a tiny barred window. Then they fed us the usual prison supper and took us to the bath house.

Attached to the bath house was a barber's shop. It came as a great surprise to realize that somewhere on earth there existed such clean rooms with white curtains on the windows. And con-barbers in white coats. And mirrors on the wall.

What miracle was this? It turned out that this barber's shop served the entire prison administration, from the warders right up to the top brass. And here I too was cropped.

In general, all prisoners are cropped close as soon as they are arrested, but this rule doesn't apply in KGB prisons. There they leave your hair on. But this lasts only as far as the first transit point. To the envy of my cell mates, I was still equipped with my usual hairstyle. They were amazed and I explained it to them:

'You and I have different sponsors—yours is the MVD (Ministry of the Interior), while mine is the KGB (Commissariat for State Security).'

Noticing my hair in the bath house, one of the warders grabbed me by the sleeve and led me to the barber's shop. In a trice I was shorn, and now I looked exactly like all the other cons.

The bath house in the Tashkent transit prison was hell upon earth, especially after the neat and clean barber's shop with its mirrors. In the changing room there were two benches—and they herded a hundred of us in there. Underfoot squelched a messy porridge of crumbling, disintegrating plaster, mud from the street and water. When you had undressed you handed in your underwear to be fumigated and then had to stand there stark naked and wait, until everybody else was ready. But some had no room, some took their time, and some had to be taken for haircuts. Meanwhile it was freezing cold in the changing room and the skins of those of us who were naked turned blue and were covered in goose pimples. Everyone was yelling and cursing, not only the warders but also those who were holding up the rest. Only when everyone was ready did a warder unlock the door of the washroom. Everyone was issued a microscopic piece of soap; but a fat chance there was of soaping yourself! Not everyone had had time even to get some water, when: 'All out! Don't make a meal of it, you're not home now!' Somehow or other we rinsed ourselves and went out. When we were out, of course, our underwear still hadn't come back from the fumigator, so once again we had to wait there naked and wet in the freezing cold.

Finally they brought back the enormous hoops on which each of us had hung his underwear before the bath. It was supposed to have been baked so as to destroy the fleas, but it hadn't even had time to get heated up and was only warm. Just so long as the formalities were observed and could be ticked off: the prisoners have been washed and their clothes processed. But then, how could they possibly manage to do everything properly when so many people were herded through day after day?

I got back my underwear and started to dress. And though I can say, I think, that I'm not the sensitive type, still it turned me over to think of pulling my trousers over feet that had been standing in that filth. If I wiped them with my towel, what would I have to wipe my face the following day? I fished my only undershirt out of my things, wiped my feet with it, then spread it out on the floor and stood on it. Somehow I managed to dress. Around me, pushing and shoving and bumping into one another, the rest of the cons also got dressed, each one shifting for himself as best he could. And curses, obscenities, the warders shouting: 'Hurry, hurry!'

We were taken back to the same cell as before. We sorted ourselves out somehow or other, but nobody settled for long—soon we would be split up for the next stage of our journeys. In the meantime we amused ourselves as best we could. A game of cards started in the lower bunks, while on the top tier a number of masters of the trade worked at making a new pack. Someone had already been beaten up.

Some people had found neighbors or countrymen and were deep in conversation.

After a couple of hours the duty officer came in with a pair of warders, called out twenty-five people on his list and led them away. Later a second party was led away. Then a third. I turned out to be in the fourth.

We were taken to a detention cell, which was exactly like the quarantine cell we had just left. The same grime and suffocating closeness; hardly any light from a tiny window and a light bulb burning around the clock. The bunks had initials cut into them. On the walls there were various inscriptions, most of them bawdy, but there were also messages and information: 'Ivan and Musa of Bokhara have gone to number 114. Greetings to all Bokharans!'

There were about eighty of us in the cell altogether. Some would be there only a day or two, others would have to wait up to a month for their convoy to leave. And all this time on bare planks, without bedding; all this time without exercise—instead of exercise you had half an hour's toilet break twice a day. In one corner of the cell was an enormous, rusty slop-tank, just one for all eighty of us, and the whole cell reeked of its stench.

Supper was brought. They handed out badly washed, sticky spoons that stuck to our hands and started to pour out the skilly. A line was formed at the food trap by those still waiting to be served, swearing among themselves and blindly cursing the cookhands. Then, when they got theirs and were carrying their bowls back from the trap, they cursed the skilly as well: 'Gnat's piss, dish water.' There wasn't enough for all of us (including me), somebody had made a mix-up with the lists, and about forty minutes passed before they sorted it out. What we got then was some sort of slop water that had gone completely cold already. There was nowhere to sit for meals. Some settled down on their bunks, others drank their skilly standing up, over the side or 'over the gunwhales', as we used to say. Then somebody would bump into somebody else—which was easy enough to do in such a crush—the skilly was spilled (they would never give you any more in such cases) and there'd be uproar and a fight. Another man might climb up to one of the top bunks to have his supper and spill some; the broth would splash through the cracks between the boards on to those below, and again there'd be an uproar and fighting. And so on every day.

I spent about twelve days in this cell. I got to know it well and found myself a comfortable spot on the upper tier. I got to know one or two people. The occupants were always changing, since some were always being taken away on convoys and new ones came to fill their places. The arrival of new men in the cell was always an event—there weren't any other events in any case. Everybody would stop whatever he was doing to examine the newcomers and call out to old friends. And although I had no expectation of meeting any friends here, nevertheless I too, like all the rest, used to hang down from my bunk to stare at them.

And then one day, when a new bunch was brought in, who should I see but Budrovsky—Anatoly Budrovsky, my codefendant, who had ditched me in order to save his own skin! Having seen him, I leaned back in my bunk and watched from the safety of darkness, so that he wouldn't see me. As he entered the cell, Budrovsky swept a quick glance over the bunks and cons all around and walked past me. The door was then closed behind the newcomers and locked. At that point I climbed down and sat on one of the lower bunks, gazing straight at Budrovsky. His kisser was plump and well-fed. At last he caught sight of me and his expression changed in an instant. He huddled at the far end of the cell and watched me closely, without approaching. He was afraid, of course, that I would tell the others about him double-crossing me, for then they would beat him up to within an inch of his life, or maybe even kill him. The cell was full of criminal cons and their rule was simple: once you sell a comrade down the river you pay for it!

The time came for our toilet break. Budrovsky stayed where he was and refused to go. I reassured him:

'Come on, don't be scared. I won't tell anyone, and besides I want to talk to you.'

We went out together. And at this point my co-defendant burst into tears:

'Tolik, forgive me. I couldn't help it, I was scared. The investigator told me you had given the necessary testimony and that if I didn't confirm it, that meant I was worse than you. Then, come what may, it would have meant death for both of us. . . .'

'And did they show you "my" testimony?'

'No, Tolik, but it made no difference, I couldn't help it. The investigator insisted and threatened to have me shot— you know, for high treason.'

'What did they want you to do?'

'To say that you had hostile intentions, that you intended to hand over . . .'

'You damned fool, what could I possibly hand over! And so you thought you'd save yourself and leave me to face the firing squad?'

'No Tolik, not the death sentence, but only six years. It would have been all the same to you if it had been more, you're older than I am, and we agreed that you'd take most of the blame on yourself. Tolik, forgive me!'

'What's the point of talking to you!'

We returned to the cell. When the hot water was brought I

took out my provisions—the remains of my day's ration, a pinch of sugar. Budrovsky came up to me with his. He undid a parcel and I gasped: inside were sweets and cakes!

'Where did you get them from?'

'Ashkhabad, the prison.'

'Yes, but how come? Whose money?'

'The investigator had some transferred to me. He said they had a special fund for people on remand and twice a month had about seven to eight rubles transferred to me at the prison shop. And the cigarettes were free. I didn't realize it at first and used to use the money to buy them with.'

'I don't seem to have had a single copeck transferred to me.'

'No, Tolik, he said it was for people who behaved themselves.'

'Oh, I see, it was for the cigarettes and the seven rubles at the shop!'

'Tolik, forgive me! Here, take some!'

It made me sick to look at him and his yellow, well-fed tearstained face.

A few days later Budrovsky was sent with a convoy to Vakhi, to work on some power station. And I remained behind.

One cell-mate of mine, a man who knew the ropes, Volodya, explained to me that I was being held here wrongly, that since I was a political I couldn't be kept in the same cell as criminals. Evidently they had got mixed up in all the confusion and had failed to make the distinction. But I kept quiet about it—I was afraid of ending up alone again. After five months of solitary I was enjoying being here with other men. Then, when I had enough of this filthy, gloomy cell, I asked the duty officer during inspection one day how much longer they were going to keep me hanging around in there.

'Just as long as we have to, so you just wait.'

'But I'm not supposed to be in here.'

'What do you mean? What are you in for? What was the charge?'

'You just look up my case and you'll find out.'

The officer shot out of the cell and a few minutes later came back with another one.

'Marchenko, pick up your things, quick. How did you get into this cell?'

'Well, I certainly didn't pick it.'

I was transferred to an empty cell and two days later sent on by convoy to Alma-Ata.

Now my life of luxury came to an end, I no longer had a cage to myself. From Tashkent they had so many prisoners and exiles to send that there was no question of obeying rules. All the cages of the prison coaches were packed as tight as they would go. Eight men sat below, four on the middle tier and two lay up in the galley. Up there it was hellishly hot and stuffy and they were soaked, with the sweat absolutely pouring off them. However, everybody down below was soaked as well. And they had been known to pack even more in sometimes, regardless of the torture it caused.

From Tashkent they were sending into exile the 'parasites'.

One of the cages had women in it—they had a fraction more room than we did, they were only thirteen (instead of fourteen). But one of them had a baby that was still breast feeding. Throughout the whole coach we could hear the baby crying, the woman asking the soldier for something and the soldier roughly refusing. The woman began to weep and her neighbors to shout and swear at the soldier. At that moment the officer in charge of the coach came into the corridor, a captain:

'Stop this caterwauling! Is it handcuffs you're after?'

Sobbing, the woman explained what was the matter. The baby had messed itself and she only had one change for it— could she go to the toilet to wash it out?

'Nothing will happen to it, you can wait!'

'But I've got nothing to change the baby into, what shall I do?'

'You should have asked me that before you had it,' replied the captain and walked away.

When the women started to be let out for their toilet break, the child's mother was the first to go. Somehow she managed to wash the baby's things out in the wash basin and leave them there. The next woman rinsed them as much as she had time for and again left them there. And the next and the next. By the time all the women had been led out, the things were well washed and the last one brought them back with her. Then they dried them inside the cage.

It is fortunate that people remained human, even behind bars.

The whole way there were endless checks and inspections. Before you go into the prison coach you are searched—they even poke and prod at the piece of bread you've just been issued with in prison. Then a complete check: surname, name, patronymic, date of birth, charge, sentence, completion date . . . Finally they check you against your photograph. 'Okay, you can go. Next . . .' When you leave the coach again, another check. At the transit prison another search, another check, more questions about your case: surname, name, patronymic, date of birth, charge, sentence . . . When you're called out for the next stage of the journey—yet another search, another check, questions about your case, and so on every day and several times a day.

How far would I have to go? And where? At least as far as Novosibirsk via Alma-Ata and Semipalatinsk. But then where—to the Urals? The far north? Siberia? There are 'Komsomol'* sites everywhere . . .

In Alma-Ata, after we had been let out of the 'gas vans', we were lined up in fives according to the regulations and counted and checked by name before being taken to the prison block. At the tail end of the column were the women who had been in our coach. Before they had even had time to recover from the ride the criminal cons started to chat them up. The warders and officers yelled at the cons and drove them away from the women with threats: it was forbidden even to talk at all, let alone with women. 'Get lost, officer, and your cooler with you,' one of the cons would say. 'Let me at least look at a dame and then you can stick me inside. I haven't seen a dame for five years, except for postcards of those fucking Komsomol girls of yours.'

While we were being led through the yard to the prison block, one of the cons started to filter back towards the rear of the column, to where the women were. A warder noticed this, halted the column, pulled the offender out and dragged him up to the front again.

'You fancy boy, you queer!' screeched the con. 'I hope a prick grows out of your forehead!'

The warder began to stutter something about having to protect the women from types like him. Then the women started:

'Look who's sticking up for us!'

'A rope's too good for you people!'

The commotion brought some other warders running. The resisting con had his arms twisted behind his back and was handcuffed. At the same time he yelled:

'If you feel sorry for these dames, then bring me your own!

* Ironical reference meaning prison camps. The Komsomol is the official Soviet youth movement.

Or turn round and let me get at that fat arse you've put on with all that free grub!'

They began beating up the troublemaker and the column buzzed with indignant cries. Then they pulled one more out of the column at random, put handcuffs on him too and started to hack him in the legs with their boots. The pair of them were then dragged off and the column continued to the prison block.

The transit prison in Alma-Ata differed from Tashkent only in the abundance of its bugs. There were so many of them that the cell walls were completely red. It was the same in Semipalatinsk, although here they had iron double cots instead of bunks with wooden boards. In no transit prison do they give you any mattresses or pillows, you have to flop there from arrival to departure just on the bare boards or metal mesh. And the trains have bare boards too, on top of which there's no room to stand or lie down, not to speak of the salted herring, nothing to drink and the refusal to let you go to the toilet.

Novosibirsk transit prison was full of rats. They were running about the floor underfoot, running between the men sleeping there and even crawling over them. It was there that I met a group of prisoners in the corridor who didn't stand like the rest of us, but were slumped against the wall. There were about eight of them and they had horribly gaunt faces. We were in the same cell together. I found out that these were religious believers. They had refused to participate in the elections and so had been arrested, tried in closed court and sentenced to exile as 'parasites'. From the very day of their arrest the whole lot had proclaimed a hunger strike and kept it up throughout their remand and trial. They had been fed artificially, just as I had been at Ashkhabad. After the trial they still didn't end their hunger strike and so were despatched, half-starving, to Siberia. At every transit prison they had the feeding mixture forcibly poured down their throats before being posted further. 'We are suffering for our faith,' they said.

From Novosibirsk I was sent to Taishet, where there used to be enormous camps for politicals. But when I arrived there turned out to be not a single one left. Three days earlier the last special convoy had left for Mordovia. Nature abhors a vacuum, however, and the Taishet camps immediately began to fill with criminal cons. They were brought here from all over the Union—the land had to be cleared and the bottom prepared for the future reservoir of the Bratsk Power Station. Who else would come here to 'labor with Komsomol enthusiasm', if not the cons?

In the transit prison at Taishet I found myself for the first time in a cell with other politicals—a few men had somehow got left behind, for various reasons there hadn't been time to despatch them with all the rest. Up till now I had kept wondering to myself what sort of men they would be, what they were in for, how they behaved and what they thought about.

There weren't many of us in the cell. Two older men, both with twenty-five-year terms, one a Volga German—an old man with a bushy gray beard whose name I don't remember—and the other erect and jaunty, with an obviously military bearing. He had indeed been a soldier, first as a captain in the Red Army and then as a commander in General Vlasov's army on the side of the Whites. His name was Ivanov. Ivanov was a year older than the German and invariably addressed him as 'young fellow'. There was also one other with twenty-five years, Ivan Tretyakov, a very nice fellow. In addition there was also Sasha, a vociferous character who had been a front-line officer in the Soviet army throughout the war and had been many times wounded. And of us younger men there were three: myself, a student from Leningrad and a young fellow who was cracked. We got along well in the cell, without quarrelling, and the old men watched over us, teaching us the ropes about how to make the best of camp life—they themselves were old hands at the game, for each of them had ten to fifteen years behind him of the most terrible camps in existence.

At the end of April some fellow from Afghanistan was tossed into our cell. He hardly spoke a word of Russian and we had difficulty in finding out what had happened to him. It turned out that several years ago he had walked across the frontier into the Soviet Union. Life was hard back home in Afghanistan, working as a shepherd for some rich landowner. He was at once clapped into jail, of course, but after a time they satisfied themselves that he was neither a spy nor a saboteur and allowed him to live in the Soviet Union, which was precisely what he wanted. He was sent to a kolkhoz (collective farm) to work as a shepherd again. But the Afghan didn't care for the kolkhoz and started asking to go back home, but here came the crunch—they wouldn't let him. Well, he didn't stop long to think about it and set off to return by the way he had come. He was caught, tried and sentenced to three years for attempting to cross the border illegally. His three years were now up and he was due in a few days to be released. The Afghan used to walk up and down the cell, striking himself on the head and saying: 'Fool, what fool!'

'Where will you go now? Back to the kolkhoz?'

'No, no!' the Afghan shook his head furiously. He didn't want the kolkhoz any more. 'Go Afghanistan.'

'But they won't let you go! And if they catch you you'll get ten years—this time for high treason.'

'Go Afghanistan,' insisted the Afghan. 'Kolkhoz no.' Just before his release they gave him a new quilted coat and a pair of black, camp trousers. He was so infuriated that he pushed both the trousers and coat into the sloptank and left in the rags and tatters he was standing up in. What happened after that I don't know. 'I've never met him since in any of the prisons I've known' as they sing in the song.

On May 4 we were all put on the train and sent away. More convoys. Back to Novosibirsk once more and then westwards: Sverdlovsk, Kazan, Ruzayevka.

En route our ranks were added to by new companions and at one transit prison we picked up a number of Ukrainian 'nationalists'. They were also in for twenty-five years. One of them I remember particularly well, Mikhail Soroka, an extremely calm, goodhearted and strongminded man. Then there was a fellow from Poland. His father had been one of the Polish officers shot in Katyn Forest.* His mother had been arrested and also perished. He himself had been placed in an orphanage, where he stayed till he was sixteen, and when he got his own passport he was entered as a Russian. He kept insisting that he be allowed to go to Poland, but they said he was 'Russian' and wouldn't let him go. He also wrote to the Ministry of Foreign Affairs and the Polish embassy—and ended up in the camps.

In Kazan our 'grandfather', Ivanov, was summoned to the orderly room. He had just completed fifteen years and they informed him that upon arrival at the other end he would have to go to court again. The point was that the twenty-five year sentence was being done away with and men who had

* In spring 1940, 15,000 Polish officers and men from Soviet POW camps were shot by the Soviet secret police. See *Death in the Forest* by J. K. Zawodny, University of Notre Dame Press, 1962.

earlier been given the full term were now having their sentences reduced to the new maximum of fifteen.

I was overjoyed for Ivanov and for others serving twenty-five-year terms:

'Now you've got hardly any time to go. By the time we arrive you'll be able to walk straight out! And I'll be there to see you out of the camp too,' I added to the old Volga German.

'No, Tolya, I shan't see freedom again,' he replied. 'I shall be behind barbed wire till I die.'

Mordovia

AT THE end of May we arrived in Potma. After five months in the remand prison, after the so-called trial, after the convoys and transit prisons, I had made my way at last to the celebrated camps of Mordovia.

The whole south-west corner of Mordovia is criss-crossed with barbed wire and fences of a special kind of construction, strewn with watch towers and lit up at night by the bright beams of coupled searchlights. Here the whole place is littered with signs saying 'Halt! Forbidden Zone' in Russian and Mordovian.

Here, you will come across more military escorts and armed guards than Mordovians—and a superabundance of officers. Here there are more dogs per head of population than there are dogs per head of sheep in the Caucasus. Here statistics in general have been turned on their head, including the proportion of men to women and the national composition of the adult population. Russians, Ukrainians, Latvians, Estonians and 'individual representatives' of other nationalities have been living behind barbed wire here for so many years that they've exceeded all requirements for a certificate of permanent settlement. The fathers and elder brothers of today's prisoners have sunk for ever into the soil of Mordovia,

either as skeletons or as a miscellaneous scattering of bones
mixed up with sand. The children of today's prisoners come
'for an outing' from every corner of this colossal, multina-
tional land of ours. And now I too had arrived here, after all
my preliminary ordeals, to give yet one more tiny tilt to the
crazy statistics of Mordovia.

From the Potma transit prison I was directed to camp
number ten. Like any novice I took a long, cautious look at
my new companions and surroundings and simultaneously
lost no time in getting myself settled in. You might well ask
what sort of settling in is required of a con, what sort of
belongings, chattels and furniture does he think he has?
However, a novice in camp is up to his ears in jobs. First he
has to find himself a place in a hut and get himself a cot,
straw mattress, pillow, blanket and bedding and regulation
overalls for work, and meanwhile sign for everything and get
it back to his place. They pointed out to me our company
'steward' (also a con). He took me off to look for a cot,
questioning me on the way about this and that—where did I
come from, what was I in for, what sentence had I got. When
I told him six years he grinned ironically: 'Child's play!'
Many others would also grin later when they heard that I had
only five years and a bit to go.

Behind one corner of the hut, where the steward had led
me, a number of rusty iron cot frames were lying about on
the ground. We picked out one of the better ones and I
dragged it back to the hut. Inside, the whole hut was
crammed full with 'sleeping places': the cots stood one on top
of the other in two tiers and pushed tight together in fours. A
place was found for me in the upper tier. I fixed my frame to
the lower bunk and the two of us went off to search for a
wooden panel (four narrow boards nailed together and placed

in the frame of the bunk instead of a wire mesh). After scouring the entire zone we at last found a suitable one.

The lockers in the hut were allocated on a basis of one to four people. The steward showed me my half shelf, but I hadn't anything to put on it yet—not even my own spoon.

By the time I had finished these preparations it was time for dinner. The cons were already making their way over to the big canteen hut and I followed them. The inside of the canteen hut was crowded with long tables consisting of rough boards with red paint slapped over them, and were flanked by benches of a similar nature. The canteen was packed solid. Some of the men, having found themselves a place, were eating their skilly at the tables. Others ate standing up, wherever they could find a place. Long lines stretched away from the serving hatches. I stood at the back of the line for the first hatch. But how was I going to eat without a spoon? Having noticed my indecision, one of the lads from our company came over and handed me his spoon—he had already finished. The line advanced quickly. I hadn't had time to blink before the server plucked a bent aluminum bowl from the high pile in front of him, splashed a ladle-full of cabbage soup into it and thrust it into my hand. I moved away and looked around me—all the places were taken, there was nowhere to 'settle'. Then I saw a con standing by the window and just finishing up, he was licking his spoon already. I managed to arrive there just as he finished and stepped back, and quickly slipped into his place: standing my bowl on the window-sill, I started to drink the slopwater that somebody had dignified as cabbage soup. Then, leaving my cap and spoon on the sill, I went to stand in the line for dessert. Just as nimbly as the first, the server at the second hatch whisked the bowl from my hand, banged a ladle into it and shot it back on to the tin-plated sill of the hatch. On my way back to my place I glanced into it: a watery wheat gruel was spread over the bottom—about three spoonfuls. It didn't take me long to deal with that. I licked my spoon thoroughly all over—'polished' it, as the cons used to say—and left the canteen.

I was in luck. The stores turned out to be unexpectedly open outside of official hours and I was able to get my camp equipment immediately after dinner. They issued me with a mattress, blanket, pillow—all so ancient that they looked as if they must have been around in my grandfather's time—gray, washed out, unbleached calico sheets, a pillow case, two gingham towels, and an aluminum mug and spoon. I could also have got my overalls at the same time, but for these I was in no hurry—I would have five and some odd years in which to get sick and tired of them.

For today my equipment and arrangements were complete and I could afford to look around. But it turned out that I had an important appointment awaiting me that day: the steward came and said that the company officer had ordered me to see him.

After knocking on a door with 'Company Officer' written up on a plaque, I went inside. It was a small office, extremely clean and tidy. The company officer was sitting behind a desk and rummaging in one of the drawers. On one wall hung a portrait of Lenin, with a tear-off calendar just below it and a duty roster for the internal order section. On the opposite wall, exactly opposite Lenin's picture and eye to eye with it, was a portrait of Khrushchev, together with a large map of the Soviet Union. A large cupboard and rows of chairs along the walls completed the furnishings. Hearing me enter, the officer closed the drawer, locked it and raised his head:

'Take off your headgear! While talking to representatives

of the camp administration a prisoner is obliged to remove his headgear—got it?'

I took off my cap.

'A newcomer, eh? Arrived today. Sit down.'

I sat down and the company officer started to leaf through my file and ask me questions: surname, name, patronymic, charge, sentence—the usual formal information about a prisoner. Finishing this, he tilted his chair back and rapped out curtly:

'All right, tell me about it.'

I was astonished—what was I supposed to tell him? Then the officer explained that he wanted me to tell him about my crime. I refused:

'I'm not under investigation and I'm not on trial. This is my jail and I don't want to discuss such things with my jailers.'

The company officer wasn't very pleased with my statement, he frowned but kept quiet. Then, curtly and coldly, he read out to me the duties of a prisoner and the rules of internal discipline: 'The prisoner is obliged . . . obliged . . . obliged. . . To appear for work in the official prison clothing. . . To go to political training sessions. . . .'

I asked him who conducted the political training sessions. It turned out that he did himself, once a week on Tuesdays. Then he explained the punishments that awaited me if I failed to turn up at these sessions, and also for other infringements of the rules. I could be deprived—at his discretion and command—of visits from relatives, shop privileges, gift parcels, letters—in short any or all of the few privileges to which I had a right in the camp. Besides this, I could also be sent to the punishment block . . . And so on—a list of punishments that was even longer than my duties. Everything was taken into account, every single movement regulated.

'Go to the stores and get your regulation clothing,' concluded the company officer. 'Tomorrow you'll start work. You've been put into the farm gang. You may go now.'

I went out. Back in the hut I was surrounded by the other cons in our company.

'Well, how was it? Did you make the acquaintance of Captain Vasyayev? How did you like him? And he you? Alas, alas, you're soon to be parted—he gets his pension soon . . .'

Somebody said irritably:

'They're tough bastards. Look how many of 'em hang on with pensions—public money for nothing. And all earned by breaking our backs, instead of doing any work themselves.'

They asked me what gang I was in and said the farm gang worked outside the camp and went under armed escort.

'And don't try wearing your own clothes to work. They'll have you straight out of the guardhouse and into the cooler for a fortnight!'

Then they asked me about my trial: had it been open or closed? Had I been allowed to see my sentence? And after every answer, heads nodded understandingly. Well, of course, almost everybody here had been sentenced in closed court; and the majority, just like me, hadn't been shown a copy of the sentence, but had signed to say it had been read to them, as if they were all illiterate. There were, it is true, a few dozen men in the camp who had been sentenced in open courts— these were policemen, wartime collaborators, war criminals, men with bloody crimes on their record, crimes against humanity. These they tried openly and they described the trials over the radio in clubs and parks and wrote about them in the newspapers. 'And the charges against them are the same as against you and me, so the people think that all the people in the camps are the same sort of traitors and renegades . . .'

They started asking me about life outside: what was it like now, how did people live, were things getting better—you couldn't tell from the newspapers—was there sugar and butter in the shops?

Then somebody took pity on me:

'Let the lad go, he's late for the stores and tomorrow he has to start work.'

The cons reluctantly dispersed and I went to the stores to get my clothing: cotton trousers and tunic, forage cap, wadded coat, two sets of underwear, foot rags and felt boots. How long would I have to work to pay all this off! By the time I'd settled these debts my ankle boots would be worn out . . .

For supper they gave us some sort of watery soup and a tiny piece of boiled cod. The soup was so thin that there was no point in using a spoon on it, and following the example of the other cons I drank it straight from the bowl. After supper, more hungry than satisfied, I went for a stroll round the camp before lights out. There would be plenty of time to get to know the other people later, when I had had time to size them up.

It was a warm evening in spring, the grass looked green. Dusk was creeping up slowly. The cons wandered about here and there. On one bench beside a table they were playing dominoes, while elsewhere a game of chess was in progress. Many cons had settled down in the open air with a book or magazine. Animated conversations and arguments could be heard here and there. As I walked I passed other strollers going in the opposite direction in ones and twos. The majority were young or middle-aged, but I also noticed that there were a number of old men here, some of them completely senile. Then I was passed by a young fellow of about twenty-five to twenty-eight, who was tapping the ground with a stick, poking it out in front of him and moving it from side to side. As he drew level with me I saw that in place of eyes he had two little blue scars, from which tears were oozing in a constant trickle.

'Where are you off to, Sanya?' somebody called to him.

'I'm going to the medical post, my stomach's giving me pains,' replied the blind man. For a long time I stood watching him go and then I headed in the same direction. The medical post hut was quite close to the guardhouse. I walked all around it. In one wing lived the invalid prisoners and on a bench in front of the hut I saw a whole assembly of cripples: blind men, legless men, armless men, paralytics. I hastened to move away.

'Hey there, countryman! You're fresh here aren't you, just in from the outside?' It was a passing con who spoke, short, about forty to look at and going noticeably bald.

I replied: 'Still wet behind the ears—six months remand in solitary.'

We introduced ourselves and later became quite close friends. It turned out that he really was a countryman of mine and what's more my namesake: he was called Anatoly Pavlovich Burov.

Later that evening, but before it was yet dark, lights suddenly flared up all round the camp—these were the lamps and searchlights stationed round the perimeter. I went back to my hut in order to make my bed before lights out, after that it would be impossible to see. When I had finished I went out again, I didn't feel like sitting still.

I had walked as far as a red brick building when I was overtaken by the signal for lights out. Ten o'clock. Ten ringing blows on a rail resounded across the camp. When the last stroke had died away I clearly heard the same signal being repeated in the distance. And then still further strokes, barely

audible. And I imagined these chimes continuing right round
the country, from camp to camp, and the blows on the rails
being answered by the clock chimes on Spassky Tower in the
Kremlin. . . .

However, it is forbidden to wander about the camp after
lights out. It was time to go 'home'. The corridor of our hut
was still crowded with cons. Wearing just their underwear,
they were having one last smoke before bed or continuing
arguments that had been started during the day. Four cons
were hurrying to finish letters. Suddenly somebody shouted
from the doorway: 'Guards!' and everyone rushed for their
beds, tossing their home made fags away as they went. The
letter writers jumped up from the table, grabbed their paper
and pens and scuttled to their places. And I too hurried to
my cot. I undressed by the light of the blue lamp over the
door and then turned several circles with my togs in my
hand, wondering where to put them. Then I suddenly
guessed, thrust them under the foot of my mattress and
climbed into my top bunk. The other cons were still convers-
ing in low voices, but gradually the noise was dying down.
My neighbor, an old man of sixty or seventy, asked in a
whisper:

'Well, my lad, how do you like your new home?'

'Not bad . . . It's paradise after those prison trains and
transit prisons.'

I didn't exactly hear, but rather felt the old man laughing:
my cot, which was hard up against his, began to tremble.
After a moment he explained:

'Man's worse than a hog. Wear him out with a few transit
prisons first, then stick him into a camp and he's even grateful. He knows where he is. Well, you'll see what sort of a
paradise it is. Time to sleep now, good night to you.'

The old man turned away from me and fell silent. But I

didn't feel like sleeping and for a long time I didn't go to sleep, I was thinking. No, I wasn't going back over the camp, my new acquaintances, the conversation with the company officer. At last I was in a camp—and it was time to think of escaping. I had long since decided that I wasn't going to squat behind barbed wire, no matter how much of a bed of roses it might turn out to be. I simply couldn't reconcile myself to the idea of imprisonment. I would run away, even at the risk of my life. It didn't even occur to me to pretend that it was worse here than I had expected, or that it wasn't too bad, that I could manage. I would run away. All I had to do was think carefully about how to do it. And who with. Surely I could find a pal? At that point I began to recall all the people I had happened to meet that day. I didn't know a thing about any of them. But maybe one of them was even then thinking about the same thing as I was . . .

I fell asleep towards morning. I was woken again by a swaying motion, my cot was bucking and shaking like a boat—the old man next to me was climbing down from his cot, and our neighbors below had already made their beds. All four cots—two above and two below—were fast secured by ropes to aid stability, and it only needed one of us four to stir for all the rest to be set trembling and swaying. Seeing that I was awake the old man said:

'Well, my lad, what did you see in your dreams in your new home?'

'The public prosecutor, of course, or maybe the judge,' answered my neighbor below. 'Well, am I right?'

'No, you're wrong. I'm not looking at any dreams in my new home, so as not to worry afterwards whether the omens are good or bad.'

'What do you mean? How do you manage not to look if you're dreaming?'

'Well, as soon as a dream starts to show itself I screw my eyes up nice and tight. Try it yourself and you'll see.'

The young man protested:

'I don't agree, I like dreams. They're interesting; and besides I keep dreaming about life outside. At least in dreams there's a chance to live.'

'Ah, just you stay in as long as we have, my lad, and you'll forget even how to dream about it. All you'll see will be those same old warders' gobs,' remarked an elderly Ukrainian with a bushy moustache. 'Not that I wish you a stretch like mine, of course. It was just a manner of speaking.'

The old men all agreed that none of them thought about the world outside any more, even in their dreams.

Together with the rest I washed myself, swiftly gulped the morning 'soup' and returned to the hut to wait for roll call. My neighbors sat down to drink tea. They call it 'tea', but in fact it's hot water slightly tinted with ersatz coffee. It is 'brewed' in huge cauldrons sufficient for the whole camp and the duty orderlies carry it round the huts in barrels. I had nothing to eat with the tea except my bread ration. My neighbors invited me to join them and treated me to sugar and margarine. In those days, in 1961, food parcels were still allowed in the camps and you could buy food in the camp shop up to ten rubles' worth per month, and not only with the money you earned, for you could also be sent it by your family. All these blessings, it is true, could be banned for the slightest trifle, but nevertheless, in those days many men had their own food.

While we were sipping our tea the time for roll call came around—half past seven. Cons started to gather slowly in front of the guardhouse. Then the work supervisor came out with one of the warders. The supervisor would call out a gang and the cons in that gang would leave the crowd and move closer to the gate. The warder then took a sheaf of cards out of a box—there was a separate compartment in the box for each gang—and began to call out the names. There was a card filled out for each individual (this was only for roll calls; in the orderly room there was a whole file for each man) bearing his name, charge, sentence and photograph. When your name was called out you had to walk over to the gate, past the warder (who would look you up and down from top to toe to see if it was you, whether you were properly dressed and had your hair properly cut) and into the buffer zone, which was separated from the living zone by a barbed wire fence. While the names were being called out the latecomers would come running up, still chewing a last mouthful or buttoning their uniform tunics. They could be punished for arriving late. And the cards of those who didn't answer to their names at all and didn't go out to work were put back in the box by the warder. After the roll call they would receive separate attention, and not from the warder this time but from the company officers.

In the buffer zone we would be searched, after which the gate was opened and the whole gang would go outside the zone. On the side where we were there was yet another buffer zone, where we went through another inspection and roll call and where we were placed under the supervision of armed escorts with dogs (the warders are not allowed to have weapons inside the camps—a precaution that is taken in case the cons should disarm them and take the weapons over for themselves). We were ordered to form a column of fives, counted five at a time, warned that in cases of disobedience the soldiers had orders to shoot and then: 'Quick march!'

Our gang was working in the fields. They led us to our place of work and posted little red flags to mark the forbidden limit; beyond this the guards would shoot without warning, for that already constituted an attempt at escape. The patch where we were was as flat as a pancake and there were seven guards to watch your every step—no, you couldn't escape from there, it was hopeless!

We were planting out young cabbage and tomato plants and sowing potatoes and carrots: ordinary peasant tasks, only enforced with a big stick. The peasant works with one eye on the harvest, but we were purposely not sent to gather them in, except perhaps to dig spuds—you can't eat spuds raw.

And the norm was such that you worked all day bent double and still could only just manage to fulfil it. And those who didn't and worked poorly had their parcels docked, were stopped from going to the camp shops and put on starvation rations as a punishment—these were all measures of a rehabilitatory nature, designed to instil love of labor into the cons.

I worked extremely hard—after all deductions from my monthly earnings I had exactly 48 copecks left in my personal account. Not even enough for the shop! And from the second month I had nothing left at all.

I wouldn't have given a tinker's cuss for this drudgery, whether it meant the cooler, a special regime camp or God knows what. But I had resolved come what may to escape, and for that I had to look around and get to know the other cons a bit better. Maybe, somewhere among them, I would find some helpers.

Burov

ONE OF the men working in my gang was Anatoly Burov, the
same one who had called out 'countryman' to me on my first
day. In spite of his appearance, he turned out to be not forty
but barely gone thirty.

He had still been quite small, about two or three years old,
when his family were proclaimed 'kulaks'* and dispossessed.
All he remembered was how he and the other children, together with his mother and father and blind grandmother, had
been driven out into the winter snow in what they stood up
in. Somehow they got by till spring, in somebody or other's
cowshed, and then in spring all the dispossessed families were
rounded up, loaded on to a steamer and transported down the
river Ob. They were put ashore on the deserted bank, hundreds of miles from the nearest habitation, and left to fend
for themselves as best they could. And the steamer sailed
away again.

At first they dug pits for themselves, then they began to
fell trees, build homes and clear the land of undergrowth.

* Kulak ('fist') was the term used by the Soviet authorities during
the collectivization of agriculture in the 'thirties for peasants who refused
to join the collective farms. The policy of 'liquidating the kulaks as
a class' resulted in the disappearance of five million peasant house-
holds.

50

With tremendous difficulty they adapted themselves to this new spot and got some sort of small farms going. Sometimes about five or six of the men would get together and go off secretly 'to the mainland', take jobs to earn extra money and bring back cattle, tools and utensils. About three to four years later the steamer returned with officials on board. There was no landing stage at the village, so they rowed over by boat, walked from house to house and inspected the farms and ploughed fields. They were amazed! There were supposed to be only graves. Just look at these damned kulaks! Exploiters, and even here they manage to survive! The powers that be boarded their boat again, rowed off, the steamer left and in two months returned together with another and larger one. A multitude of armed soldiers disembarked and proceeded once more to dispossess the kulaks: everyone was thrown out of his home, being allowed to take not even a pot or a pan along with him, herded on to the steamer and transported further. What could happen to them—even in a swamp they wouldn't peg out; and if they did, serve them right, and the mosquitoes could eat the corpses. Kulaks and all their breed—they didn't deserve any pity!

It was harder to adapt to this new place, they lived at starvation level. A few of them quietly made their way to 'the mainland'. Burov's father died and the family started to go to pieces. Just then the war broke out and things became very bad. At the end of the war it was time for Anatoly to go and he was called to the army. He was about to be sent to the front, but before arriving he was redirected to Omsk for tank training. Burov, however, didn't want to serve either at the rear or at the front and he ran away from the tank training school. He was caught, charged with desertion and sentenced to five years. Then he found out that he was being sent to

Norilsk to do forced labor—from there no one returns. And once you were there escaping was out of the question, like trying to get off the moon. And so Burov came to an agreement with three other cons—they resolved to escape from jail while there was still time, before they were sent away. Better to perish here from a bullet than to die a lingering death in Norilsk.

One evening when they were being taken to the toilet, they attacked their warders. They had reckoned on being able to tie them up, gag them and get away—the four of them would easily manage two warders. But at the very last moment, one of the four got cold feet, and three were not enough to deal with the other two properly, especially without making a noise. While two of the cons tied up their warder, the third grappled with the other warder singlehanded. The latter struggled free and made a run for it. The whole plan was collapsing. The con picked up the heavy lid of the sloptank and let the warder have it on the back of the head. And killed him! Well, it was all up now. They rang for the sentry, killed him too, took his pistol and managed to get out of the jail. They went into hiding and then made their way to Mongolia, travelling at night and sleeping during the day. But when they reached Mongolia and entered a Mongolian village, they were arrested and of course handed over to the Soviet authorities. Their sentence they knew in advance: for killing a warder and a sentry all three were condemned to death.

For seven months Burov and the other two languished in the condemned cell, expecting every day to be taken out and shot. After seven months the first one was called out. With his things. That meant to be shot. Later they led the second one away as well. Burov waited alone for several days. At last his turn also came. He was led down a corridor and at the far end of the corridor was ordered to halt and face the wall. He waited for the end to come. He was so unnerved that it didn't even occur to him that they would hardly shoot him, right there in the corridor. They ordered him to turn and face the warders and he saw an officer in front of him holding some sort of document. Burov was sure that they were going to read the sentence to him again before proceeding to carry it out. The meaning of the words did not get through to him. They repeated them once more: '. . . the death penalty to be commuted to twenty years' hard labor.' But only when they led him to the bath house did he believe it—condemned men are not given a bath first.

Soon Burov was sent away to the river Amur, to the camps outside Komsomolsk. There he met prisoners who had been inside since the 'thirties, who had built this town and now were building roads and factories around it. The town was named Komsomolsk in honor of the Komsomol volunteers, but there had never been any to speak of. It had been built by cons, and all around it were camps, camps, camps. . . .

Burov ran away from the camp. This time he lasted three days outside. He was picked up in town by the police. Another trial, another term to be added to his twenty years' hard labor. And this time it was Norilsk. By 1961 he already had sixteen years of camps and prisons under his belt. From Norilsk he was transferred to some camp in Siberia, then to another and a third. When he had been in Tobolsk prison in 1959, some warders had beaten him and three other cons unconscious. In doing so they had broken Burov's arm. Then, to get rid of him, they had packed him off to Mordovia.

I liked Burov—he was a dare-devil. We became good friends and began to plan our escape.

Richardas's Story

BUROV AND I started sizing up the people around us. Who would join us in our bid to escape? First we would cautiously sound them out in conversation, get to know them better, and only then would we ask straight out: 'Will you risk escaping with us?' In this way we got quite a group together: Anatoly Ozerov, Anatoly Burov, myself and several others whose names I don't wish to give. We decided to dig a tunnel—no other way out of a camp exists. We decided that we three Anatolys would undertake a reconnaissance to find out where it was best to dig and then we would tell the others.

We all knew perfectly well what risks we were taking. We knew that if political prisoners are caught trying to escape only a miracle can ensure their survival. The usual procedure is first to beat them up, maim them and set the dogs on them, and only then to have them shot.

One of the prisoners here in camp number ten was a Lithuanian, Richardas K. He had once taken part in an escape bid and he told me how they had been caught. Three of them, all Lithuanians, had somehow managed to elude their escorts while at work in the fields and had only been noticed when near a wood. They came under fire, but it was already too late. Then the tommy gunners were called up from division headquarters; they put a cordon round the wood and soldiers with dogs began to hunt the fugitives. It was not long before the dogs found the scent and soon Richardas and his comrades heard the chase almost at their backs. They realized that come what may they could not avoid it, but still they tried to hide in the hope that the guards with the dogs would plunge straight past them. The other two shinned up an oak tree and hid in the foliage, while Richardas buried himself in fallen leaves (the time was autumn) beneath a bush. The scene that followed happened literally before his very eyes.

He had not even had time to camouflage himself properly with the leaves when two soldiers appeared with dogs. The dogs circled the oak trees and clawed at the bark with their front paws. A further six tommy gunners ran up together with an officer holding a pistol. The young men in the tree were discovered at once. The officer shouted: 'So you wanted freedom, you mother-fuckers? Come on, get down!'

The lowest branch was about six feet off the ground. Richardas saw one of his companions put his feet on the branch, then crouch down and ease his stomach on to the branch so that he was hanging across it, with his hands on the branch and his legs in the air, ready to jump down. At that moment he heard the sound of several bursts from a tommy gun and the young man fell to the ground like a sack. But he was still alive, he writhed and squirmed with pain. The officer fired another shot into him and ordered the dogs to be unleashed. The man on the ground, meanwhile, was unable even to defend himself. When the dogs had been dragged off, he remained lying motionless on the ground. The officer ordered him to be picked up and carried away. They dug the toes of their boots into him, but he did not rise. Then the officer said: 'Why spoil your boots on him? What do you think your weapons are for?' The soldiers started stabbing the wounded man with their bayonets and jeering: 'Come on, come on, stand up, don't try to pretend!' The wounded man labored to get to his feet. His bullet-riddled arms flapped like empty sleeves. His tattered clothes had slipped off down to his waist. He was completely smothered in blood. Prodding him along with their bayonets, they led him to the next tree. The officer called out: 'Guard halt!' The fugitive collapsed at the foot of the tree. Two soldiers and a dog remained to keep watch on him while the rest turned their attention to the second youth. He too was ordered to climb down from the tree. Having decided, evidently, to be more clever, he did not go as far as the lower branches, but plummetted on to the ground at the very feet of the soldiers. No one had time to fire. As he lay there on the ground the officer bounded over to him and fired several shots into his legs. Then he received the same treatment as the first: he was kicked unconscious, savaged by the dogs and then stabbed by bayonets. Finally the officer ordered the beating to stop, went over to the youth and said: 'All right, free and independent Lithuania, tell me, where's the third?' The youth was silent. The officer swung his boot into him and repeated the question. Richardas heard his comrade croak: 'I'd call you a fascist, but you're worse than that.' The officer was outraged: 'I fought against the fascists myself! In the front line. And with fascists like you as well. How many of us did you shoot back home in Lithuania?'

Again they threw themselves on the wounded youth and started to beat him. Then the officer ordered him to crawl on his hands and knees to the tree where the first man lay: 'If you don't want to walk you can crawl!'

And the wounded youth, with his legs broken, started to crawl, egged on by bayonets like the first. The officer walked along beside him and jeered: 'Free Lithuania! Go on, crawl, you'll get your independence!' Richardas told me that this youth was a student from Vilnius and had got seven years for distributing pamphlets.

When the two fugitives were together they were beaten and bayonetted again, this time to death. Finally there were no more groans or cries. The officer assured himself that they were dead and sent to the settlement for a cart. He evidently counted on dealing with the third one by the time the cart arrived. Richardas, however, took quite some time to find. Whether it was the dogs who were tired, or perhaps the smell of decomposing leaves that threw them off the scent, they were quite unable to find him. Soldiers ran about the wood, almost stepping on him and the officer stood no more than two yards away from his bush. Richardas said that on several occasions he was ready to leap up and run for it. And it was only when Richardas could already hear the sound of cart wheels grinding along the road that the officer came up to the pile of leaves, prodded them with his toe and instantly yelled: 'Here he is, the bastard! Get up!' At that moment the cart came along. 'Where are the escaped prisoners, comrade major?' Richardas stood up. The major was aiming his pistol straight at him. Instinctively Richardas jerked round at the very instant the shot rang out, then felt a searing pain in his chest and shoulder and fell to the ground. He did not lose consciousness, but lay there motionless, trying not to stir or groan. Other men gathered around and somebody asked 'Maybe he's still alive, comrade major?' And the major replied: 'Alive my foot! I shot him point blank in the chest.' He could not have noticed how Richardas had turned away.

Richardas was thrown into the bottom of the cart—even then he managed not to groan—and the two corpses were piled on top of him. The cart moved off towards the camp.

Richardas heard someone approach the cart and heard the major say: 'Killed while trying to escape.' It was obvious from the tone of voice that both the questioner and the major were fully aware of what that meant. Then the cart came to a halt—they must have reached the guardhouse. Somebody ordered the corpses to be unloaded and left there but when they laid hold of Richardas he groaned. 'Look he's still alive,' they said. He opened his eyes. It was still light, not even the lamps on the fence had been lit. That same major detached himself from a group of officers and came towards him, dragging his pistol out as he advanced. Richardas thought: 'Now I've had it.' But the chief officer followed him and grasped his arm: 'It's too late, stop! Everyone's looking.' It was true. Lots of people had crowded round the guardhouse, both soldiers and civilians; they had all come running to see the fugitives brought in.

Richardas was tipped out of the cart. Someone in the administration gave instructions to the soldiers. They came up to him and asked if he could walk on his own. He said he could. They led him to the guardhouse and once inside the warders immediately ushered him into the cells.

There he was left alone for the first few days. Nobody came to see him, although he had asked to be bandaged. Only on the fourth or fifth day had a con orderly come and bandaged his wound. And the following day a woman doctor came and examined him and said he should be taken to hospital. He had a fever and his arm was in great pain. In the hospital they cut off his arm at the shoulder—it was too late to heal it. Then he was tried, his sentence was extended and he was sent to Vladimir prison. That was three years before I got there and many still remembered this incident.

But a trial's only a trial and escaping prisoners are intentionally killed while being caught so as to put off the rest from trying. And the injured and beaten are purposely not healed. Seeing someone like Richardas without an arm, many men think twice about whether it's worth the risk. But a trial, a prison sentence—that would stop nobody under the conditions that exist in our prison camps.

But even without Richardas's story I well remembered the incident at the Bukhtarma power station. There the officer had fired practically point blank at an unarmed fugitive. I had seen that myself. And I and all the others knew that if we were caught the odds were against us remaining alive. But nonetheless we decided to take the risk.

Excavations

The first thing the three of us did was to investigate the ground. In our camp they had dug trenches under the huts, and these trenches always had water in them. Perhaps, though, it wasn't the same all over the camp? We got hold of a strip of iron (there were no shovels inside the camp, nor any other sort of tool) and one night after lights out, round about eleven o'clock, slipped out of the hut one by one as if going to the toilet. Then we crawled under the front steps and found ourselves beneath the hut. All the huts in the camp were raised on high foundations and every week the warders checked with hooks and pointed metal rods to see if there were any tunnels. Burov and I crawled farther back and started digging, while Ozerov kept watch. We removed the top layer of stones and chips and then came to sand, which was easy to dig. But two feet down we came to water. It was useless to go any further. We filled in the hole and sprinkled rubbish over the top again so that the warders wouldn't notice anything when they checked, and crawled back to Ozerov. We showed him by signs that nothing had come of it—water! Now we had to hurry back to our places. At two o'clock they made an inspection of all the huts, the warders would come in, switch on the light and check the number of sleepers. If somebody was missing from his bunk at that time it aroused suspicion that a con was preparing to escape. For this you got strictly punished—a spell in the cooler or perhaps even prison. But we were in time. Everything had passed off successfully.

The following night we investigated the remaining huts, even the ones that were a long way from the perimeter. Everywhere it was the same: water. Not a single place for a tunnel could we find in the living zone. Then we decided to try the work zone as well.

The work zone in camp ten was small, consisting of a bakery, a garage for three vehicles, a sawing shed, a small machine shop and a shed where rabbits were reared. And there, next to the rabbit shed, a new machine shop was being built. The work area was right next to our living zone and was separated from it only by two strands of barbed wire, moreover this fence had no lighting of its own. Only the sentries in the watchtowers would aim their searchlights at it from time to time. So it was possible to get in there all right. But when? The second shift used to work there until one a.m., and at two a.m. the huts were inspected. There was nothing for it, we would have to work between two o'clock and dawn, although it was very dangerous. And what if somebody in our hut was not sleeping? What would he think if he saw one of the cons dressing and leaving the hut fully dressed and staying away not for ten minutes but for several hours? Every hut had its stool pigeons. Go outside at night and there were warders and watchmen prowling round, trusties with special armbands from the internal order section. And then there were three of us, not just one, although it was sufficient for only one to be noticed.

In spite of all these dangers we were somehow lucky, they didn't catch us once. We had decided in advance where we were going to dig. The bakery was out of the question, it was working all round the clock. The garage workshop had a concrete floor. We settled on the machine shop—it was closer to the perimeter fence, so that if the ground turned out to be dry we wouldn't have far to dig.

We made an arrangement to meet by the rabbit hut after the night inspection was over. We managed to make our way safely into the work zone, avoiding the night watchman, and creep up to the machine shop. The door was padlocked, but we easily opened it with a nail. Ozerov again stayed on guard while Burov and I went into the workshop. The lights were switched off but it was easy to see: the perimeter lights shone in through the window. The workshop itself was no good, it had a raised wooden floor. We went round the various store-rooms and found one that seemed suitable: the floor consisted of bricks laid straight on top of sand, with no cement. Just take the bricks out anywhere and dig. What's more the store-room was littered with wooden blocks, so that after digging we had only to strew them about again and nothing would be noticed. If only the ground was dry, what a marvellous place it would be! Only four to five yards from the inner fence, then twenty-two yards between the two fences that flanked the main wall, then a few yards more from the far fence to freedom—thirty to thirty-five yards would do it. That was nothing, that could easily be dug. And the hole in the store-room could be covered with a wooden platform—there was enough material lying around—sand could be sprinkled on top, the bricks laid back in place, camouflaged, and left till the next night's work.

Burov and I let our dreams have their head. But now it was time to leave, soon it would be getting light. We agreed to start digging the next time. We chose a suitable night, crept into the workshop, then into the store-room, and started to dig. Another failure! Just as in the living zone, water came into the hole at a depth of two feet. This one too had to be filled in and stamped down and the place of our reconnaissance camouflaged with bricks and components.

All we had had till now was one failure after another, with the one possible exception that at least we hadn't been caught. Obviously we had to think up another plan. Maybe we would have to give up the idea of a tunnel altogether, although not all the places had been checked yet. Until we could think of something better, however, we would have to go on looking for a place without water. We couldn't possibly give up the whole idea of escaping and we still couldn't believe that the whole camp was standing on water.

Meanwhile our strength was giving out. It was no joke going without sleep so many nights and spending them digging, and then going out to work again during the day. On camp rations at that. And Burov an invalid with his broken arm. Then I was transferred to the construction gang, which was even tougher than working in the fields. And in June I fell ill.

The Cooler

I HAD CAUGHT a chill in the Karaganda camps already and had received no treatment. Since then I had suffered from a chronic inflammation of both ears, which from time to time would become acute. This time it was also my ears that caused the trouble. My head was splitting in two, I had shooting pains in my ears, it was difficult to fall asleep at night and painful to open my mouth at meals. On top of that I had fits of nausea and dizziness.

I went to the camp medical post, although the old hands warned me that it was useless, that the ear specialist came once a year and summoned everyone who had complained of ear trouble during the past year to come to him at the same time. There were quite a few. 'What's wrong?' 'My ears.' Without further ado the specialist would note it down in his notebook and write out a prescription for hydrogen peroxide. No further inquiries and no proper examination, and there was no chance of being excused from work—it was out of the question. Only if you turned out to have a high temperature would they consider excusing you from work for a few days.

I appealed to the doctor several times and each time heard only insulting assertions that since I didn't have a temperature I must be well and therefore was simply trying to dodge work. And at the end of June, for failing to fulfil my norm, I was given seven days in the PC or punishment cell, in other words the cooler. I found nothing surprising in this: given that I was failing to fulfil my daily norm, the cooler was inevitable. At first they call you up in front of your company officer to listen to a sermon about every con having to redeem his sin in the eyes of the people by honest labor.

'Why didn't you fulfil your norm?' asks the officer when his homily is finished. This when he can see that the man in front of him can barely stand up. 'Sick? How can you be when you've got no temperature! It's very bad to pretend, to dissimulate, to try and dodge your work.' And just to make the point clear he gives you several days in the cooler.

Now what did the punishment cell look like in 1961? First there was an ordinary camp barrack block, divided into cells. The cells were various: some were for solitary, others for two people, five or even twenty, and if necessary they would pack up to thirty or even forty in them. It was situated in a special regime camp about a quarter of a mile from camp ten. A tiny exercise yard had been specially fenced off; it was pitted and trampled hard and in it, even in summer, there was not a single blade of grass—the least shoot of green would be swallowed at once by the starving cons in the cooler.

The cells themselves were equipped with bare bunks consisting of thick planks—no mattresses or bedding were allowed. The bunks were short, you had to sleep bent double; when I tried to straighten out, my legs hung over the end. In the centre of the bunk, running crosswise and holding the planks together, was a thick iron bar. Now what if this bar had been placed underneath the planks? Or set in a groove, if it had to be on top, so that it didn't stick out? But no, this iron bar, two inches wide and almost an inch thick, was left sticking up in the very middle of the bunk, so that no matter how you lay it was bound to cut into your body, which had no protection from it.

The window was covered with stout iron bars and the door had a peephole. In one corner stood the prisoner's inseparable companion, the sloptank—a rusty vessel holding about twelve gallons, with a lid linked to it by a stout chain. Attached to one side of the tank was a long iron rod threaded at the other end. This was passed through a special aperture in the wall and on the other side, in the corridor, the warder would screw a big nut on to it. In this way the sloptank was fixed immovably to the wall. During toilet break the nut would be unscrewed so that the cons could carry the tank out and empty it. This procedure took place daily in the morning. The rest of the time the sloptank stood in its appointed place, filling the cell with an unspeakable stench. . . .

At six a.m. came a knocking at all doors: 'Wake up! Wake up for toilet break!' They started taking us to get washed. At last it was our cell's turn. However, it was washing only in name. You had hardly had time to wet your hands when you were already being prodded from behind: 'Hurry, hurry, you can get all the washing you want after you've been released!' Less than a minute is the regulation time for a con to wash in, and whoever fails to get washed has to rinse his face over the sloptank in the cell.

And so, back in our cell once more, we waited for breakfast—alas nothing but a name: a mug of hot water and a ration of bread—fourteen ounces for the whole day. For dinner they gave us a bowl of thin cabbage soup consisting of almost pure water, in which some leaves of stinking pickled cabbage had been boiled—though little enough even of that found its way into the bowl. I don't think even cattle would have touched this soup of ours, but in the cooler the con not only drinks it straight from the side of the bowl, but even wipes the bowl with his bread and eagerly looks forward to supper. For supper we got a morsel of boiled cod the size of a matchbox, stale and slimy. Not a grain of sugar or fat is allowed to prisoners in the cooler.

I hate to think what we prisoners were driven to by starvation in the cooler. Return to camp was awaited with even greater eagerness than the end of your sentence. Even the normal camp hunger rations seemed an unimaginable feast in the cooler. I hate to think how I starved in there. And it is even more horrible to realize that now, even as I write this, my comrades are still being starved in punishment cells. . . .

The time drags agonizingly between breakfast and dinner and between dinner and supper. No books, no newspapers, no letters, no chess. Inspection twice a day and after dinner a half-hour walk in the bare exercise yard behind barbed wire—that's the extent of your entertainment. During inspections the warders take their time: the prisoners in each cell are counted and recounted and then checked with the number on the board. Then a meticulous examination of the cell is carried out. With big wooden mallets the warders sound out the walls, bunks, floor and window bars to see whether any tunnels are being dug or any bars have been sawn through and whether the prisoners are planning to escape. They also check for any inscriptions on the walls. During the whole of this time the prisoners all have to stand with their caps off (I will explain later why this is done).

During the thirty-minute exercise period you can also go to the latrines. If there are twenty of you in a cell, however, it is difficult to manage in time. There are two latrines, a line forms and again you are chivvied: 'Hurry, hurry, our time's nearly up, what are you sitting around for!' If you don't manage it, there's always the sloptank back in the cell, and they never let you out to go to the latrines again, not even if you're an old man or ill. Inside, during the day, the cell is stifling and stinks to high heaven. At night, even in summer, it is cold—the cell block is built of stone and the floor is cement: they are specially built that way so as to be as cold and damp as possible. There is no bedding and nothing to cover yourself with, except for your reefer jacket. This, like all your other warm clothes, is taken away when you are searched before being stuck in the cooler, but they give it back to you at night.

There is not the slightest chance of taking a morsel of food with you to the cooler, or even half a puff's worth of cigarette butt or paper or the lead of a pencil—everything is taken away when you are searched. You yourself and the underwear, trousers and jacket that you are forced to take off are all poked and prodded through and through.

From ten o'clock at night till six in the morning you lie huddled on your bare boards, with the iron bar digging into your side and a cold damp draught from the floor blowing through the cracks between them. And you long to fall asleep, so that sleeping, at least, you can forget the day's torments and the fact that tomorrow will be just the same. But no, it won't work. And you can't get up and run about the cell, the warder will see you through the peephole. So you languish there, tossing and turning from side to side until it is almost light again; and no sooner do you doze off than: 'Get up! Get up! Toilet break!'

Incarceration in the punishment cell is supposed to be limited to not more than fifteen days, but the officers can easily get round this rule. They let you out to go back to camp one evening and the next morning condemn you to another fifteen days. What for? A reason can always be found. You stood in your cell so as to block the peephole; picked up a cigarette butt during your exercise period (that one of your camp friends had tossed over the fence to you); answered a warder rudely . . . Yes, you can get a further fifteen days for absolutely nothing at all. Because if you really rebel and allow yourself to be provoked into making a protest, you get not simply fifteen days in the cooler but a new trial by decree.

In Kargal I was once kept in the cooler for forty-eight days, being let out each time only so that a new directive could be read to me ordering my 'confinement to a punishment cell'. The writer, Yuli Daniel, was once given two successive spells in the cooler at Dubrovlag camp eleven for 'swearing at a sentry'—this happened in 1966.

Some men can't bear the inhuman conditions and the hunger and end up by mutilating themselves: they hope they will be taken to hospital and will escape, if only for a week, the bare boards and stinking cell, and will be given more human nourishment. While I was in the cooler, two of the cons acted as follows: they broke the handles off their spoons and swallowed them; then, after stamping on the bowls of the spoons to flatten them, they swallowed these too. But even this wasn't enough—they broke the pane of glass in the windows and by the time the warders had managed to unlock the door each had succeeded in swallowing several pieces of glass. They were taken away and I never saw them again; I merely heard that they were operated on in the hospital at camp number three.

When a con slits his veins or swallows barbed wire, or sprinkles ground glass in his eyes, his cell-mates don't usually intervene. Every man is free to dispose of himself and his life as best he can and in whatever way he wishes, every man has the right to put an end to his sufferings if he is unable to bear them any longer.

There is also usually one cell in the punishment block that

is filled with people on hunger strike. One day, as a mark of protest, a con decides to go on hunger strike, so he writes out an official complaint (to the camp governor, the Central Committee, Khrushchev—it is all the same who to, it has absolutely no significance; it's simply that a hunger strike 'doesn't count' without an official complaint, even if you starve to death anyway) and refuses to take any more food. For the first few days no one takes a blind bit of notice. Then, after several days—sometimes as many as ten or twelve—they transfer you to a special cell set aside for such people, and start to feed you artificially, through a pipe. It is useless to resist, for whatever you do they twist your arms behind your back and handcuff you. This procedure is carried out in the camps even more brutally than in the remand prison—by the time you've been 'force-fed' once or twice you are often minus your teeth. And what you are given is not the feeding mixture that I got at Ashkhabad, but the same old camp skilly, only even thinner, so that the pipe doesn't get blocked. Furthermore the skilly you get in the cells is lukewarm, but in artificial feeding they try to make it as hot as possible, for they know that this is a sure way of ruining your stomach.

Very few men are able to sustain a hunger strike for long and get their own way, although I have heard of cases where prisoners kept it up for two to three months. The main thing is, though, that it's completely useless. In every instance the answer to the protest is exactly the same as to all other complaints, the only difference being that the governor himself comes to see the hunger striker, insofar as the enfeebled con is unable to walk:

'Your protest is unjustified, call off your hunger strike. Whatever you do, we won't let you die. Death would save you from your punishment and your term isn't up yet. When you go free from here you are welcome to die. You have made

a complaint, you are complaining about us to the higher
authorities. Well, you can write away—it's your right. But all
the same it is we who will be examining your complaint. . . .'

And this was the sanatorium I had been sent to on account
of my illness. I served my seven days and came out, as they
say, holding on to the walls—they had worn me to a shadow.
Nevertheless, despite my weakness, I still had to go out to
work the next day in order not to earn myself another spell in
the cooler.

The Last Attempt

WHILE I was doing my seven days, Burov and Ozerov fell
into despair and lost all hope of digging a tunnel. It wasn't
that I was the leading light in the affair, but simply that two
people tend to lose hope quicker than three. One of them,
say, suddenly begins to doubt that there is anywhere at all to
dig when there is water everywhere, and then the other involuntarily falls in with him. And there is no third to say: 'So
what, brothers, we can't wait around with our arms folded,
let's find another way to escape while we're all still alive. . . .'

In short, after I was let out of the cooler and had had time
to get my strength back a bit, we again started to make plans
for our escape. We decided to have one more go at digging in
the work zone—this time in the half-built workshop hut. Our
decision was reinforced this time by the special advantages of
this new place for a tunnel: the walls, already up to roof
height, would screen us from the sentries and security guards,
the piles of fresh earth around the hut would help us in
disguising the traces of our tunnel, and finally, we could
easily get in through the window opening, so that there would
be no messing around with locks. . . . I find it hard to decide
now, but I have a feeling that if we had been forced to think
up a new plan, and then another and another, we would

always have found advantages in every new variant, so intolerable was the thought of having to stay there much longer.

We agreed among ourselves to make our way the following night to the uncompleted hut to see how far down the water was there. A film show had been announced for the night in question. In summer films were shown in the open air in front of the canteen. They began after supper, when it was already getting dark, and went on late till well after the usual time for lights out. So that twice a month in summer the cons were able to wander round the place till late at night breathing in the fresh night air, for hardly anybody watched the films; bit by bit, after the newsreel, they would slip away in ones and twos, trying, of course, not to get noticed by the warders. And it was for just such an ideal evening that we made our plan: we would go to the film show, sitting in different places, and then after the newsreel skedaddle to the work zone. We also talked, of course, about the kind of risks threatening us in this new spot. It was near one of the watch towers—we would have to be very careful making our way there and to work without making a sound. We decided that Burov would act as look-out for the night watchmen, while Ozerov and I would do the digging. Burov, who had been working during the day in the rabbit shed next to 'our' hut, explained that the construction gang always left their hand-barrows overnight—which was excellent, they would come in handy—but that their tools, as usual, were always taken back and handed in. Still, there was all sorts of lumber lying about, we would do our best to dig with sticks and pieces of wood.

On the agreed evening I was strolling about the living zone, waiting for the show to begin, when suddenly I heard the voice of our company commander, Captain Vasyayev—or rather not his voice but his yell:

'I see you're asking for more PC, parasite!' he was roaring at some unfortunate, who, like myself, had only just come out of the cooler. 'You're falling short of the norm again! Do you think the state's going to feed you for nothing? We've got too many of you damned layabouts here!'

'I didn't ask to come here and get my grub free,' replied the con. 'I used to work in a factory—the pay was rotten but still I used to keep myself and my family, so how does that make me a parasite?'

A knot of cons had gathered round to listen to this argument, obviously sympathizing with their comrade, and at this the captain lost his temper even more.

'I don't know what you earned there, but here you get your rations for nothing,' he went on, continuing his task of education.

The con also lost his temper and couldn't keep quiet, although he knew what he would get for it:

'It's not for the likes of you to count what I earned, captain. I was paid for my work at least, but why should somebody like you get paid twice as much as a worker? For standing over us hard workers with a stick?'

'I'm serving my country!'

'Serving your country? Proud of it, are you? That's in here, but I bet when you go on holiday you don't tell the others where you serve? You're too damned ashamed to come out in the open and admit to people what you get your fat salary for!'

While this was going on the captain caught sight of a couple of warders at the back of the crowd of cons.

'Get him!' he pointed to his opponent, 'And take him to the guardroom!' And he went off to write the order for another fifteen days.

This time the argument had ended relatively luckily for the

con: more often than not such lippy prisoners are sent for trial again on a charge of 'anti-Soviet propaganda' and the whole affair ends with another sentence added on, or else 'special regime' or prison.

'He would have to go and get into a row with him!' said the cons quietly as they dispersed. 'Found a right one to try and teach lessons to. You can't make no impression on 'em!'

'So it's better to keep quiet, is it? Keep quiet, no matter what they say or what they do to you,' exploded somebody, probably one of the younger ones—fortunately it was too dark now to see who it was. Captain Vasyayev had already gone away, but even among us cons there could easily be stool pigeons: they'd only have to squeal and then this young fellow would get exactly the same treatment as the man in the quarrel.

Escape, come what may, no matter what the risk, only escape. We're not humans in this place, we can't even defend ourselves from insults. . . .

It was dark. Going over to the canteen, where the screen was already in place, I peered into the crowd. Burov and Ozerov were both there. They also exchanged glances with me and each other and then the three of us immediately looked away again. Even a silent exchange of glances could seem suspicious to one or other of the stool pigeons, all of whom couldn't wait to curry favour with the bosses.

After the newsreels, just as we had reckoned, we were able to melt away unnoticed. Three rows of barbed wire and the low little wall separating the living and work zones—all were negotiated successfully: it was dark here, the searchlights were trained only on the outer fence. By the rabbit shed we had to move about in absolute silence: the night watchmen were very much on the alert to guard the rabbits against hungry prisoners.

At last we were in our half-built hut and could breathe more easily, for the walls blocked us from view. We looked around. Here was the wall that was nearest the main fence, this was where we would dig. If only the ground would turn out to be suitable, with no water! Then we would disguise the hole with boards—there were plenty about—sprinkle earth over the top and continue the trench on later nights. Silently, without even whispering to one another, we took up our places: Burov crawled out of the hut to keep an eye on the watchmen, while Ozerov and I started digging. Ozerov turned out to have a strip of iron, the same piece he had had when we crawled under our own hut: he had managed to keep it hidden till now. The work got under way. As we were digging a beam of bright light would slide over the hut from time to time—the sentry in the watch tower was shining his searchlight back and forth over the work zone—and inside the hut it would turn as light as day. Down we would crouch on the ground. The beam slid over us and past, and then we would dig again, trying not to bang or clink anything. When we had dug down to a depth of about twenty inches the sand grew damp; another foot and the bottom of the hole filled with water. Failure again! We had still not realized that our whole plan had folded when Burov came crawling back into the hut:

'A watchman just walked past the window here.'

Had he heard us digging? He could even have seen us if he had looked through the window.

'Which way did he go?'

'Over there,' Burov pointed in the opposite direction to the guardhouse.

If he had heard anything and wanted to tell the guards, he would have to pass us again on his way to the guardhouse. We decided to start filling in the hole as quickly as possible until the watchman passed us on his way to the guardhouse, and only then to run for it. For if they discovered traces of our work, they would turn the whole zone upside down and search for those who were planning to escape. And even if they didn't catch up with us, nevertheless the sentries would be on their guard and would start keeping a close watch on every single con—where he went, what he had in his hand, who he exchanged whispers with. . . . We would have to give up our escape plans indefinitely, perhaps even forever. No, that was something we had to avoid at all costs. If a tunnel was out of the question, then we would put our minds to it and think up some other means of escape.

Hurry, hurry, fill up the hole! Burov crawled outside again to keep an eye on the watchman: as soon as he headed for the guardhouse we would abandon our work and make a dash for the fence. Maybe in the living zone we would be able to lose ourselves among the rest of the cons. If they caught us they wouldn't exactly kill us—the warders weren't allowed weapons inside the perimeter—but we'd be beaten half to death and maybe even crippled for life.

Ozerov and I started hurling soil into the hole without even bothering to keep quiet. Several minutes later Burov appeared again:

'The warders are coming!' Then we realized that the watchman, who had heard us, instead of going to the guardhouse had gone to the other watchmen and they had informed the guard.

We sprang out of the hut. All around was bathed in bright light: the sentry was training his searchlight directly on the hut and on us. Blinded by the brilliant light, we made a dash in the direction of the living zone. I hardly remember how I came to be in the rabbit shed, I jumped on to a low wall by the barbed wire fence and saw a line of warders already stationed along its entire length. I jumped down again, back into the rabbit shed, and crawled under the hutches. Somewhere nearby were my companions: I had seen Burov at my side several seconds ago.

Warders ran into the shed, each one armed with a lantern and a sharpened thick stick.

'Surround them and make sure no one gets away!' I heard the voice of Major Ageyev who was directing the hunt.

The warders started poking under the hutches with their sharp sticks. The first to be found was Ozerov.

'Come out!' they ordered.

But when he attempted to crawl out they prodded him so cruelly with the sticks that he retreated even farther under the hutches. Nevertheless they succeeded in driving him out and I saw and heard several warders start pounding him with their boots and jabbing him with their stakes. Meanwhile the others went on with the search. Burov and I were discovered practically simultaneously, we were under neighboring hutches. And we received the same treatment as Ozerov. I don't know how long the beating went on for. Probably not long, for no bones were broken.

The noise and the shouts brought the other prisoners running and they crowded up to the barbed wire fence on the living zone side. Some other warders attempted to disperse them, but they resisted, and from the crowd came shouts of 'Murderers!' and 'Hangmen!' Then the sentries in the watch towers fired several bursts from their tommy guns over the cons' heads, but that didn't help either. Major Ageyev ran up to the wire:

'Aren't your sentences long enough? We'll soon see to that! There's plenty of room in prison still—and in the special camps. Get back!'

But the crowd didn't get back. The three of us were picked

up and prodded away from the fence in the direction of the guardhouse in the work zone. As they drove us along they continued to beat us. From behind we were jabbed continually with the sharp sticks. Now and again one of the warders would take a run at us and hack us in the legs with his steel shod boots. Or the boots would be aimed higher—a running jump would land them on our ribs or somewhere else in that region—it didn't matter where, so long as it hurt as much as possible. I bent my head low as I walked and hunched myself up as best I could, with my hands clasped over the back of my head: these were to protect my head from blows, while my elbows covered my ribs. My arms were numb and indeed my whole body had long since ceased to feel any pain from the blows.

In the guardhouse the beating continued. Then Major Ageyev conducted a brief interrogation.

'Who else wanted to escape with you?'

Each of us replied that there was nobody apart from the three of us. After the interrogation we were due to be taken from the guardhouse to the cooler, and the cooler, as I have already mentioned, was in the other zone. And so the three of us had only one thought in our heads: would they handcuff us or not? If they didn't, it meant they had decided to shoot us en route. They would shoot us in the back and then report us as 'killed while trying to escape from their guards on their way to the punishment block'. How many times had it happened before.

We automatically answered Ageyev's questions and waited to see what would happen—handcuffs or an immediate command to leave.

At last some more warders came in—carrying handcuffs. We exchanged glances and I was aware that Burov and Ozerov were thinking the same as me.

One pair of handcuffs fastened me to Burov on one side and another to Ozerov on the other. The major himself secured me and Burov, while the sergeant major put on the other pair. The major was out to do his best and hammered the handcuffs tight with the butt of his pistol. My wrist was twisted so tightly that I almost whimpered. Burov's face was distorted with pain.

'Tighter, tighter, make 'em remember it for the rest of their lives,' the major commanded the sergeant and Ozerov grimaced and groaned.

We were pushed through several narrow doors and led across the railway track to the next camp. I was still afraid they'd shoot us on the way for here, outside the zones, our escorts were armed with tommy guns and Major Ageyev had his pistol in his hand. But no, even this reign of lawlessness evidently had its own laws: a con in handcuffs may not be shot. All the major did was hammer us under the ribs with his pistol butt.

Leaving their weapons at the guardhouse entrance the major and our escorts took us to the guardroom. Here they stood us up against the wall and started to beat us again. We for our part, imprisoned in the handcuffs, couldn't even cover our faces to ward off the blows. Then they threw us on to the floor and started kicking and trampling on us.

'That'll teach the fucking bastards,' chanted Ageyev. 'Make sure they remember and tell the others what it means to escape.'

Finally they removed the handcuffs, dragged us down a corridor and threw us into a cell.

For three to four days we lay there without getting up. The door would open and the cookhand would call us to come and get our rations or dinner, and we were unable to stand. Then the cookhand would call a warder who, merely glancing at us from the doorway, without stepping inside, would order the cell to be locked again. Only after about three days did we begin to get up for dinner and our bread ration. One morning they read out a decree awarding us each fifteen days in the cooler. That was from the administration. Then we would be put on trial and would be sentenced to two or three years in prison according to the legal code. Thus, when our fifteen days in the cooler were over, we would stay in that same cell waiting for trial, only now under normal conditions: camp meals, bedding on the bunks, books, exercise once a day and permission to smoke. That's why unsuccessful fugitives were given a fortnight in the cooler to start off with—it was the tradition already—so that they didn't get too much enjoyment out of all this luxury.

Our cell was a small one, for three people, but on the other hand it was in a busy spot. Situated at one corner of the hut, it had a barred window overlooking two exercise yards and facing the latrines, and you could also see the guardhouse from it. So that during the last few days of cooler, when we had recovered enough to walk about our cell, all we did was crowd to the window all day, gaping at the cons exercising (and they at us) and at the new arrivals being led from the guardhouse to the huts. Sometimes we also managed to get a few words in unnoticed with the cons in the exercise yard.

These cons were on special regime. The camp too was called a 'special'. 'Done special' the cons used to say.

Special Regime

DURING MY first spell in the cooler I hadn't really got to know either the camp or the men in it, except for my cellmates. But now, during my second stay in the cooler and subsequently on remand, awaiting trial, I and my companions not only got a closer look at the special regime but also got to know a few of the cons doing special. In some of the camps I stayed in later, and also at the prisoners' hospital, I met many cons who had at some time done special, so that I know very well what it amounts to.

The living zone of a special regime camp is equipped with cell blocks about eighty yards long and twenty-five to thirty yards wide. A long corridor runs down the middle of the block from end to end, while a transverse corridor divides it in half. Both corridors terminate at each end in doors that are equipped with a variety of locks and bolts. The long corridor has rows of doors on either side that lead into the cells, these being the same as you find in the punishment block: plank bunks, bars on the windows, a sloptank in one corner and doors equipped with shuttered peepholes (the shutters are on the outside, of course, so that only the warders can move them—otherwise the cons might look out into the corridor). The cells are divided from the corridor by double doors: on the corridor side there is a massive iron-lined door double-locked with a conventional lock and a padlock; the door on the inside, which is also kept permanently locked, consists of a grille formed by heavy iron bars set into a heavy frame, as in a cage for wild beasts. Set into the barred door is a food trap, which is also kept locked and is opened only when food is being served. The barred door is opened only to let cons in and out, for they are driven out to work, in the words of Captain Vasyayev, so as to pay for the bread they eat.

The appearance of the living zone in a special regime camp is completely different from that of an ordinary or strict regime camp: the zone is completely deserted. After work everyone is kept under lock and key until morning, until the parade for work again. The whole of your free time is spent in the cells, with the warders padding noiselessly up and down the corridors in their felt knee-boots, eavesdropping and peering through the peepholes. . . . But who are the people held on special regime, behind thick bars and behind locked and bolted doors, behind rows and rows of barbed wire and behind a high wall? What fearsome, bestial bandits are these?

Officially, special regime, like prison, is reserved for particularly dangerous and hardened offenders, and also for cons who have committed an offence in camp. That is the rule for ordinary, everyday criminals: first normal regime, then intensified, then strict regime and finally special regime or prison. Politicals begin their camp career at once on strict regime— we are all 'particularly dangerous' from the very beginning, so that for us the path to special regime or prison is significantly shorter.

You can also get special regime as part of your court sentence—for a second political offence. The most common course, however, is for cons to come here from strict regime camps—either for escaping (if, of course, they're not shot on being caught), or attempting an escape, or else for refusing to work, failing to fulfil the norm, 'resisting a guard or a warder'. . . . To become a bandit or a vicious hooligan in camp is easier than falling off a chair: all you have to do is preserve an elementary sense of your own dignity and one way or another you are certain to end up as 'a vicious wrecker of discipline', while developments after that depend entirely on the whim of admin—will they limit themselves to administrative measures of correction or have you tried in court again?

Here is an example. I have already pointed out that in the cooler they don't give you a chance to have a decent wash; and there isn't the remotest chance of being allowed to clean your teeth—do it back in the cell, if you please, over that stinking sloptank. The very desire of a con even to do such a thing provokes righteous indignation and anger on the part of the warder: what, a common criminal, and he's talking of cleaning his teeth! But they don't even let you have an ordinary wash. No sooner have you wet your hands in the basin than: 'Enough! Back to your cell!' And if you don't step back on the instant they grab hold of you and pull you away. At this point, God forbid that you should resist even instinctively or ward off the hand that is dragging you away from the basin. The warders will then drag you into the guardroom and start insulting you, mocking you, prodding you. They only want one thing—that the con should bear all this in silence, submit, so that it is clear for all to see: the con knows his place. And if you dare to answer an insult or a blow—there's your 'vicious hooliganism' for you, 'resistance to the representatives of law and order', followed by a report to the prison authorities, a new trial and sentence by decree, which can be anything up to and including the death penalty. At the very least your term will be extended and you'll be put on special regime.

Somewhat later, in the Potma transit prison, I met several cons from camp ten who had been sent to special regime camps or to prison for 'organizing a political party' in the camp. Chinghiz Dzhafarov said something, a stool pigeon squealed to the fuzz (a KGB detective in this case): and they started to round people up—not only those who took part in the conversation, but also anybody who happened to be around and might have heard it.

In practice any con that the authorities take a dislike to is liable to end up on special regime or in prison—if he's too difficult, say, or independently minded, or popular with the other cons. Everybody has more than enough of such crimes in his book as failure to fulfil the norm or breaking the camp rules. And sometimes it's simply a matter of chance, the result of sheer bad luck. After I had been taken out of camp ten, for instance, it was decided for various internal reasons to transform it from a political into an ordinary criminal camp. But what to do with the political prisoners? Some of them were distributed to other political camps, but the majority were sent to a special regime camp—it was the closest to hand. And on my way back to the camps in 1963, as I passed through the familiar territory, I saw that several new cell blocks with barred windows had been added to the special regime camp. Inside were my comrades from camp ten.

Iron bars, bolts, extra guards, confinement to cells outside of working hours—all this, of course, is only part of the corrective measures applied to these particularly dangerous offenders. Here the work is also heavier than in the other camps.

First you build a brick factory, for instance, and then you have to work in it. A brick factory even in normal conditions is no bed of roses, and in the camps it is even worse. The main machine is the celebrated OSO—two handles and one wheel plus handbarrows, and that's the extent of the mechanization. Working in the damp and the cold, the cons get soaked and freezing; then comes the long, long roll-call. One cell at a time they are taken from the work zone to the living zone. Before passing through they are thoroughly searched, one by one, while the rest are forced to wait all this time in the rain, the snow or the frost, stamping their feet to keep warm. Finally they are back in their cells with not the slightest chance to warm themselves or change their boots or clothing: all they have is what they stand up in, both for work and for indoors in the cell after work—filthy, damp and sweaty. Somehow or other the con tries to dry out his clothes overnight with the warmth of his own body; before he's finished, however, it is already morning, time to get up, parade for work, and again it's hurry-hurry, don't stand around, if you don't fulfil your norm you go on punishment rations. And the norms are such, of course, that it is impossible to fulfil them, so that any con can at any time be punished for falling short of them.

The main punishment and the strongest corrective measure in the camps, easy to carry out and well tried in practice, is starvation. On special regime this measure is particularly sensitive: parcels and packages are in general forbidden. All you can get from the camp shop is toothpaste, toothbrushes and soap; in order to buy tobacco you have to write a special application to admin and then it's up to them to decide. No food from outside is ever allowed in, all you get is rations. And everyone knows what camp rations are like: you won't quite kick the bucket, but you won't be in a hurry to shit either—you've got nothing to shit with. And even then, if you don't fulfil your norm, admin can put you on punishment rations—the same as in the cooler.

And so men sentenced to special regime camps live for years in these terrible, inhuman, indescribable conditions. It isn't too difficult, it seems, to reduce a man to the condition of a beast, to force him to forget his own human dignity, to forget honor and morality. On top of this the cells are apportioned in such a way that there are never less than two stool pigeons to each cell—to report on their comrades and each other. But what can a stool pigeon gain on special regime? First, he doesn't get put on punishment rations; secondly, he may not have his visits cut out. Here a con is permitted one visit a year lasting up to three hours—this is usually reduced to half an hour, and more often than not is not allowed at all. The main thing, though, is that admin can make representations to the judiciary for a prisoner to be transferred from special regime back to strict regime before his time is up, for 'starting on the road to rehabilitation'. Not before half his term is served, true, but still it's a hope! Somehow to break out of this hell six months or a year ahead of schedule, this is the lure that leads men to become informers and provocateurs and to sell their comrades.

I have already mentioned self-mutilation in the cooler and such cases are even more frequent on special regime. Men gouge their eyes out, throw ground glass in them, or hang themselves. At night sometimes they slit their veins under the blankets; and if their neighbor doesn't wake up soaked in blood, yet one more martyr is freed of his burden.

One day three cons agreed to put an end to themselves in the usual way, that is with the help of the sentries. At about three in the afternoon they took three planks from the brick factory and placed them against the wall. The sentry in the watch tower shouted:

'Stand back or I'll fire!'

'By all means, and deliver us from this happy life,' replied one of the cons and started climbing. Having reached the top, he got entangled in the barbed wire there. At this moment there was a burst of tommy gun fire from the tower and he slumped across the wire and hung there. Then the second man climbed up and calmly awaited his turn. A short burst of fire and he fell to the ground at the foot of the fence. The third man followed and he too fell beside the first.

I was told later that one of them had remained alive, he had been seen in the hospital at camp three. So at least he had escaped from special regime for a time. The other two, of course, had escaped for ever, shot dead on the spot. In general this suicide was just like many others, differing only in that it was a group affair. Individual instances are common, and not only in special regime camps.

A sentry who picks off such an 'escaper' in this way gets rewarded with extra leave to show admin's gratitude. But the attitude of the other soldiers to the marksman doesn't always coincide with admin's. Once, in camp seven in the autumn of 1963, a sentry shot a routine suicide case, a fellow who was ill, when he was on the wall. He got his leave all right, but he was black and blue when he set off for home: that night the other soldiers had organized a little farewell party for him, though under a different pretext, of course.

On the whole, many soldiers are ashamed of this type of service and don't even tell their families that they are guarding prisoners. Sometimes it happens that when you get talking to one, and he's sure you won't give him away, he'll say quite openly what he thinks of the camps and his duties:

'In a year I'll be free again and this fucking military service can go to hell.'

The way he talks it is clear that his three years are as much a prison sentence to him as the con's years inside. So you say to him:

'But if they order you to, you'll shoot me too, and if you're up in the watch tower you'll fire on a con just the same, even when you know he's not escaping but simply doing it in desperation . . .'

'Of course,' he agreed. 'If they order me I'll fire and I'll shoot to kill. What else can I do when it's an order?'

'Yes, what can we do?' says another.

'I don't like the idea of being put inside myself,' replies a third.

Many soldiers perform their duties out of fear, and not because they're conscientious. And when Burov, Ozerov and I were beaten up, the soldiers did it more for show than in earnest. The warders, though, are a different kettle of fish. It's true they're not conscientious and work only for the money, but they try to suck up to admin, try to last out till they're pensioned off and try not to get thrown out beforehand; then they also like to be praised and they hope, perhaps, for promotion to senior warder. Moreover their absolute power over the cons corrupts them (and the higher administration too for that matter).

Nonetheless in a large camp, where there are very many cons, the warders sometimes try to ingratiate themselves with the prisoners. Now and again they will turn a blind eye to the fact that you have brought away a packet of cigarettes from a meeting with relatives, or for a bribe will pass you a pick-me-up (a bit of extra food). Some of them speculate in tea and vodka, especially in the criminal camps. They exploit the cons and their families and at the same time want to be popular and pass for decent fellows among the cons. After all they have to stay in the camps for days at a time, and you never know what to expect from men who have been bitterly antagonized and driven to despair.

The authorities justifiably place no trust either in the soldiers who serve as guards or in the warders. Both groups are infiltrated with stool pigeons. Strict watch is kept to see that the soldiers don't talk to the cons, especially political cons. As guards for the Mordovian camps they try to bring in soldiers from the national minorities or from distant republics (though never from the Baltic republics!), in other words those who don't know much Russian.

Here, in the special regime camp, I also saw something I had only heard about before, but hadn't been able to confirm: inscriptions tattooed not only on men's arms and body, but also on the face—on the cheeks and forehead. Usually they are criminal cons, of whom there are quite a few nowadays in the political camps.

Criminal cons often, so to speak, 'volunteer' to be transferred to political camps. There is a persistent legend going around the criminal camps that conditions for politicals are not too bad, that they are fed better, the work is easier, they are treated more humanely, the guards don't beat you up and so on. At the root of this legend lies the rumor of an actually existing Mordovian camp for foreigners who have been sentenced for espionage: conditions there are indeed almost like a holiday camp—unlimited parcels, as much food as you can eat, no work norms demanded: if you feel like it—work; if not, you can play volleyball in the zone. Returning home after his time is up the foreigner can find nothing bad to say about our camps and prisons. And among our own people, of course, the newspapers create an impression that every one of our political prisoners is bound to be a spy and a foreign intelligence agent, and so the rumor goes about the camps that politicals live in a kind of paradise. In actual fact conditions in the political camps are far worse than in the criminal ones. But there is also a grain of truth in the legend. Politicals are no longer sent to do logging and lumbering, they are guarded more carefully now, for logging means working almost without guards, and then it also means having axes and saws. Furthermore politicals have different attitudes among themselves: they don't kill one another or slit one another's throats, and in general they respect their comrades and do their best to help them out in time of trouble. And this means that the guards in such camps hesitate to beat the prisoners up in public.

And so a criminal resolves to commit a state crime in order to get into a political camp, even if it means getting an extra sentence. He writes a denunciation of Khrushchev or the party—usually half the words are obscenities. Or else he puts some rags together to make an 'American flag', drawing as many stars on it as he can manage (he hasn't a clue how many there are, all he knows is that it's a lot). Then he has to get caught. He hands out copies of his denunciation to the other cons, somebody is bound to inform admin. Or else he sticks it on a wall in the work zone for everybody to see. The flag is hung up in a prominent position or perhaps he parades with it at roll call. Thus a new state criminal is prepared.

In the political camp he starves even worse than in the criminal one. On one occasion or another he gets a spell in the cooler and on the way there gets beaten up in the guardroom by the warders. He starts to write official complaints, but is soon convinced that this is useless. Meanwhile he has a long term ahead of him; and he has brought his own forms of protest with him from the underworld, together with its customs and point of view. And this is where the tattoos come in.

Once I saw two former criminal cons, then politicals, who were nicknamed Mussa and Mazai. On their foreheads and cheeks they had tattoos: 'Communists = butchers' and 'Communists drink the blood of the people'. Later I met many more cons with such sayings tattooed on their faces. The most common of all, tattooed in big letters across the forehead, was: 'Khrushchev's slave' or 'Slave of the CPSU' (Communist Party of the Soviet Union).

Here in the special regime camp, in our hut, there was a fellow called Nikolai Shcherbakov. When I caught sight of him in the exercise yard through the window I almost collapsed; there wasn't a single clear spot on his whole face. On one cheek he had 'Lenin was a butcher' and on the other it continued: 'Millions are suffering because of him'. Under his eyes was: 'Khrushchev, Brezhnev, Voroshilov are butchers.' On his pale, skinny neck a hand had been tattooed in black ink. It was gripping his throat and on the back of the hand were the letters CPSU, while the middle finger, ending on his adam's apple, was labelled KGB.

Shcherbakov was in another corner cell similar to ours, only at the other end of the hut. At first I only saw him through the window when their cell was taken out for exercise. Later, though, we three were transferred to another cell and we often exercised simultaneously in adjoining yards. In secret conversation, unnoticed by the warders, we got to know one another. I became convinced that he was normal and not cracked, as I had thought at first. He was far from stupid, he used to read quite a lot and he knew all the news in the newspapers. Together with him in one cell were Mazai and the homosexual, Misha, both with tattooed faces!

In late September 1961, when our cell was taken out for exercise, Nikolai asked us in sign language whether anyone had a razor blade. In such cases it is not done to ask what for—if somebody asks, it means they need it, and if you've got one you hand it over, with no questions asked. I had three blades at that time which I still had from camp ten, before landing in the cooler, and I had hidden them in the peak of my cap as a necessary precaution; in spite of all the searches they had never been found. I went into the latrines, ripped open the seam under the peak with my teeth and took out one blade. Back in the yard, when the warder's attention was distracted, I stuck it into a crack on one of the wooden fence posts to which the barbed wire was secured. Nikolai watched me from his window. The blade stayed there in the crack all day long. Many other cons saw it—the boys used to scour every corner of the exercise yard while outside, every pebble, every crack, in the hope of finding something useful. But once a blade has been placed somewhere, that means it already has an owner waiting to pick it up; in such a case nobody will touch it. Furthermore Nikolai spent the whole day at the window, keeping watch on the blade just in case. While exercising the following day he picked out the blade and took it back to his cell.

Later that evening a rumor passed from cell to cell: 'Shcherbakov has cut off his ear'. And later we learned the details. He had already tattooed the ear: 'A gift to the 22nd Congress of the CPSU'. Evidently he had done it beforehand, otherwise all the blood would have run out while it was being tattooed. Then, having amputated it, he started knocking on the door and when the warder had unlocked the outer door, Shcherbakov threw his ear through the bars to him and said: 'Here's a present for the 22nd Congress.'

This incident is well known to all cons in Mordovia.

The next day we saw Shcherbakov at the window of his cell. His head was bandaged and in the place where his right ear should have been the bandage was soaked with blood, and blood was on his face, neck and hands. A couple of days later he was taken off to hospital, but what happened to him after that I do not know.

And that is the reason why cons always have to be without their caps during inspection and to uncover their foreheads, so that they can be checked for tattoos. Men with tattoos are first sent to the cooler and then put in separate cells, so as not to corrupt the others. Wherever they go after that they are always accompanied by a special section in their files, listing the location and texts of their tattoos; and during inspections the tattoos are checked against these lists to see whether any new ones have been added.

Shcherbakov's cell-mates, by the way, were all hauled in for helping him—for taking part in anti-Soviet propaganda.

But how do cons in the cooler and in prison contrive to tattoo themselves? How do they get the needles and ink? I have often seen it done, both in special regime camps, in transit camps and in Vladimir prison. They take a nail out of their boots or pick up a scrap of wire in the exercise yard, sharpen it on a stone—and there's your needle. Then to make the ink they set fire to a piece of black rubber sole from their boots and mix the ash with urine.

But it wasn't the technique so much as the very idea of such activity that astonished me. What did these unfortunates want? Why and to what end did they deform themselves for life? For to do that meant to brand yourself forever, to brand your whole life, it meant you felt yourself to be, in the words of the song, 'an eternal convict', if you disfigured your face in such a way. Or, say, cut off an ear. Why? But sometimes, in moments of helpless despair, I too caught myself thinking: my God, if only I could do something—hurl a piece of my body into the faces of my torturers! Why? At such moments the question doesn't arise.

In time I grew used to those faces and bodies smothered with decorations and inscriptions, and was able to laugh at the newcomers when they almost collapsed at the sight of them, just as I had done on arrival: 'Just you wait awhile and you'll see worse than that!'

We stayed in the special regime cell for three months. First we spent a fortnight in the cooler. Then, in accordance with the regulations, the pre-trial investigation began. On the six-

teenth day we began to be called out one by one for interrogation in the governor's office. The three interrogators were
an officer from admin, Major Danilchenko and the governor
of camp ten. Ozerov was the first to be called. Major Danilchenko asked him:

'Who else wanted to escape with you?'

Ozerov, just as Burov and I did later, replied that there
was no one else, only the three of us. That was all, and then
they started to lecture him. Ozerov said that we had been
beaten up both inside the camp, and in the guardhouse, and
on the way to the cooler, while we were handcuffed, and then
again in the cooler guardroom:

'Major Ageyev was present during the beating. He himself
battered us with a thick stick and beat us with his revolver.'

'That's a slander!' shouted the officer. 'Who will believe
you? You don't show any traces of beating!'

'It was sixteen days ago. We demanded a doctor at the
time, but nobody came to see us, not even the warders.'

After Ozerov they summoned Burov and the same sort of
conversation took place. Only when they informed Burov that
the bit about being beaten up was a slander, he replied:

'Well, all right, I shall probably never get out of here and
will die as a con. But those two are both young still, they'll
sit out their six to eight years inside and then go free. You
might at least preserve appearances, because when they get
out they might tell someone what Soviet prison camps are
really like.'

'If they do they'll only find themselves back in here again,
do you think they don't realize that? Thousands of others go
free all the time, without those two, and they keep their
mouths shut. And anybody they do talk to makes a note of it
and tries not to come here himself.'

When I was called I didn't bother to ruin my nerves with

senseless conversations. The interrogation came to a swift conclusion.

'Yes, we were beaten up, me, Ozerov and Burov.'

'Why did you keep quiet about it? Your fellow conspirators made official protests.'

'You would also call my protest a slander, although you know just as well as we do that it's the truth. You, for instance,' I turned to Danilchenko, 'were just the same as Ageyev before you became a governor, and you used to do the same things. . . .'

'Take him away!' broke in Danilchenko.

The warder standing behind me pushed his fist into my side and led me back to the cell.

There were no more interrogations and we 'rested' in our cell for about three months, until the trial. This was indeed a break: we weren't driven out to work, they gave us normal camp rations and books, we were allowed to smoke and our exercise period was extended to one hour a day. At first we were held in that same corner cell for three, but shortly before the trial began we were transferred to a larger cell with about twenty men in it. The rest of our cell-mates were also waiting to go on trial, some for refusing to work, some for consistently failing to fulfil their norms, and others for their religious beliefs. In the neighboring cell there were another twenty men awaiting trial.

At the end of September (a few days after the Shcherbakov affair) the court arrived at our camp, consisting of a judge, a prosecutor and two people's assessors. The court was held in the office where we had been questioned. One after another the cons were led away, first from the adjoining cell and then from ours. Returning literally after only a few minutes, each one announced: two or three years of prison, at Vladimir. The time came for Burov to be led away and brought back again:

two years in Vladimir. I was next. The warder ushered me into the office and remained standing behind me. Apart from the members of the court the office also had its own 'public'— a crowd of officers and staff from the camp administration. The judge, a substantial man wearing a well cut suit, was sitting at a table covered with some red material, with the two people's assessors sitting on either side of him. I wasn't thinking either of the trial or my fate (it was a foregone conclusion), but watched the two assessors.

They looked completely alien and lost in this office among the men in military uniform and the impeccably turned out judge. One of them was an elderly man wearing a threadbare cotton jacket and a dark-gray shirt that showed signs of repeated washing. He didn't know what to do with his calloused, almost completely black hands, poor fellow, sometimes placing them on the table in front of him and then shyly removing them to his knees. The second assessor was a woman with a wrinkled face, a scarf tied in a knot beneath her chin and workworn hands. She had an even more pitiful, downtrodden and hunted look about her than her partner. I felt extremely sorry for them, they were looking about them so apprehensively, and then they didn't understand their role in the court and their subordinate positions. Nobody paid the least attention to them for the duration of the trial, as though they were voiceless puppets; nobody asked if they had any questions and the decisions were reached without any reference to them.

When the judge started to ask me the usual procedural questions, I at once announced that I refused to take part in this farce or to play the game called 'people's court'. This announcement caused no surprise at all. My company officer, Captain Vasyayev, read out my character assessment: Marchenko is a vicious parasite, a vicious malingerer and a

vicious disrupter of camp regulations; he has not responded
to corrective training, he has absented himself from political
instruction sessions, he has refused to take part . . . failed to
repent . . . been a bad influence. . . . After that came a brief
but pointed speech by the prosecutor; without going into
detail, he said:

'Three years in jail is what I think.'

Not bothering, even for the sake of appearance, to whisper
to his two assessors, the judge at once informed me that three
years of my camp term would be substituted by a prison
sentence.

I was led away and the next one called. Back in the cell
they asked:

'How many, two or three?'

All three of us—Burov, Ozerov and I—got the same treatment, so that 'none of us would be offended' as our cell-mates
put it.

In the days remaining before our dispatch the more experienced of our companions, who had already been inside Vladimir or had heard about it, told us what awaited us. It
added up to little that was good of course. Everyone agreed
that prison was even worse than doing special—and special
was what we saw all around us. And we felt even worse when
we remembered the convoys, prison coaches and transit jails
that lay ahead of us.

Soon after the trial they brought our things from camp ten
and five days afterwards the first party was dispatched. We
three landed up in the second party, which left the special
regime camp for Potma at the beginning of October. Then
came two days in Potma transit jail, prison coach, two days
in Ruzayevka transit jail, prison coach, transit jail in Gorky.
And the same transit jails and prison coaches as everywhere
else.

In Ruzayevka one prisoner in our party fell ill and was unable to get up at inspection time. The duty officer and warders started to heap obscene curses on his head and forced him to stand. The men in the cell began to mutter, and demanded that this mockery be ended and a doctor called. The result was the usual one: they grabbed hold of a number of men at random, dragged them outside and proceeded to beat them up.

From Ruzayevka transit jail we were taken to the station during the day. The black marias stopped on the far side of the railway tracks, opposite the station, for the jail was out of town. We were taken out of the vans, lined up in fives and herded across the tracks—beneath a footbridge—to the station. On all sides the column was surrounded by armed guards and dogs and the guards kept yelling at us: 'Stop talking! March, march, quickly, stop dragging your feet!' A large number of people had gathered on the footbridge and their numbers were constantly being added to. They called down to us:

'Hey, lads, where have you come from? And where are you going?'

Packets of cigarettes and money wrapped in paper rained down on the column from the bridge. And at this point some character in civvies appeared from somewhere, asked for the officer in charge of the convoy and at once started to bawl him out:

'What the hell's all this in aid of? You've been told before not to parade prisoners in front of the whole town!'

The officer tried to excuse himself:

'Well, they won't give us any night trains, we've asked and asked for them. We ourselves don't like it either. Just listen to what they're saying about us on the bridge.'

'I should think so! You've got enough audience here to fill

a theatre. And then the police have to disperse them, I suppose!'

I remembered how often I had read that always in Russia, throughout her history, the common folk had taken pity on convicts, had given them bread and in the villages brought them milk to drink. Dostoyevsky writes that on holidays their jail used to be snowed under with all sorts of holiday fare: fancy bread, cakes, meat.

Nowadays they just herd you from place to place and you're not even allowed to look.

PART TWO

I'll tell such truth about you
That lies will be eclipsed...
   Griboyedov,
   ('Woe From Wit', 1824)

Vladimir

THE PASSENGER train to which our prison coach had been coupled arrived in Vladimir at three in the morning. The black marias had already been backed up to the platform and we were rammed into them like sprats in a barrel; then we were rushed through the deserted nocturnal streets of this ancient Russian city. . . .

I remembered reading how Herzen,* before his departure abroad, used to stand on the balcony of his house here in Vladimir and watch the convicts, all in chains, being driven along the famous 'Vladimir road'—'from Russia to the wastes of Siberia.' I remembered Levitan's† 'Vladimir Road'—I had once seen a postcard with a reproduction of it. Probably that well-beaten road, trodden down by the feet of convicts, no longer existed. Nor did the chains. Nobody would see us and no one remember us, except for our jailers. And there was no contemporary Levitan or Herzen to tell the world about our prison convoys in the year 1961.

While I was thinking this the van came to a halt. We had arrived. 'Get out!' The door opened and I stepped straight

* Alexander Herzen (1812–1870), writer, philosopher and publicist, lived in exile (chiefly London) from 1847.
† I. I. Levitan (1860–1900), Russian landscape painter.

out of the van and into the door of a building to which we had been backed up. I was led down some corridors and into a large hall which was already full of prisoners who had arrived in the night—some of whom I knew and most I didn't. There were also criminal cons there—all the way from Gorky to Vladimir we had kept stopping to pick them up. We were kept apart, though, and here too we were split up into different cells; I saw them only while in the hall, and then not for long before they were taken away.

We were thrust into 'boxes'—tiny chambers set into the stone wall, one man to each. From there we were summoned one at a time, together with our things. There were the usual questions: surname, name, patronymic, charge, sentence . . . Then a meticulous search. They made us take off all our clothes, inspected us carefully from head to feet, even separated our toes to look between them, pinched the soles of our feet and peered into our back passages. Every single thread of our personal belongings was squeezed and poked and then they took away everything but what we stood up in. We were allowed to take with us two pairs of cotton socks, two hand-kerchiefs, a tooth brush and tooth powder. And that was all. Not even a change of underpants, not even woollen socks, nothing. All the things taken away from us were listed on receipt forms and in place of the con's pitifully meagre pos-sessions—which were nonetheless extremely dear to him (the handkerchiefs may have been keepsakes, a present from his wife or mother; warm socks were needed for the winter ahead, they would come in just right for the cold floors of those stone cells)—in exchange for the things taken away each man received a piece of paper. The only food we were able to take was our convoy rations—twenty five ounces of bread (black only) and one salted herring. Thus whoever had managed to save something or other from the camp—ten days' worth of uneaten sugar, say, the remains of some food parcel or something bought at the camp shop—was forced to part with it here.

After being questioned and searched we were taken into the prison yard. Separate from all the other blocks, behind the hospital block and barricaded off from the rest of the prison by a high wall, was the special block for political prisoners. Not even the prison warders were allowed in there without special permission. We were being led past the hospital block when suddenly we heard a cry: 'Help, the Communists are taking it out on me!'—evidently they had mental patients too. The warders at once started to chivvy us: 'Hurry, hurry, there's no need to gawp all over the place.'

We were halted by the last door in the block. The warder unlocked the door, let us in and then locked the door behind us again. From the vestibule in which we found ourselves a staircase led to the upper stories, at the top of which was another locked door. The warder unlocked it and let us into the corridor on the first floor. The door behind us was again at once locked and bolted and we were put into the various cells. The cells were empty and we were being put into them temporarily until we had been given baths and assigned to permanent cells. And it was here we experienced our first prison reveille. A very loud bell was sounded, or rather it wasn't a bell but some booming mechanical hooter, and at once the corridors filled with warders banging their keys on the doors and shouting: 'Get up! Get up!' And to dawdlers: 'Is it the cooler you want?' Five minutes later keys rattled in the lock of our door and we were taken out for the toilet break. Then we got breakfast: eighteen ounces of black bread for the whole day, about seven or eight rusty sprats all runny like melting jelly, and a bowl of soup without a single trace of fat or meal in it or a morsel of cabbage or potato, but consisting of lukewarm cloudy wash that we drank straight over the sides. After such a soup the bowls didn't even need washing.

At about nine o'clock we were taken for a bath. The main point of this exercise was not to get washed but to have our heads cropped. Stark naked and covered in goose pimples (although it was called a bath house it was pretty cold inside) we submitted one by one to the tender attentions of the barber (one of the criminal cons). They shave not only your head but also all beards and moustaches—such embellishments are not permitted in jail. Seeing this, one old Ukrainian with luxuriant moustaches almost burst into tears: 'I'm sixty-five years old and—'

He refused point-blank to submit. Immediately a number of warders seized him by the arms and legs and dragged him away. (I met him a year later in that same prison—moustacheless, of course. He told me that they had dragged him into some dark sort of cage, then manacled him and gave him a thorough beating before taking him back in handcuffs to have his moustache shaven off. He got ten days in the cooler for 'rebellion'.)

I also had a moustache, while many of the religious prisoners had both beards and moustaches. We all faced the same fate as the elderly Ukrainian. My turn came after his. I sat down on the bench and the barber set about my head. After running his clippers over it several times he made a move towards my moustache. I said I didn't want it cut off; even in my file all the photographs showed me with a moustache. The barber went over to one of the warders: 'Here's another one that refuses.' Two warders (Vanya and Sanya) grabbed hold of me, twisted my arms behind my back and threw me on the ground, then the two of them held me down while a third twisted my head back by the ears and the barber in a jiffy relieved me of my moustache. The same thing happened to two of the religious believers while the rest no longer objected. We weren't sent to the cooler; the first had been sent as a warning to the rest of us and that satisfied them for the present, or perhaps there was no more room.

After the barber we were all let into the washroom: several benches, a couple of dozen basins and one hot and one cold tap. Lines formed immediately in front of the taps. Hardly had the last ones had time to get any water when the warders set about pushing us out again: 'Enough, that's good enough!' And to underline their point they turned off the hot water. Willy-nilly we were forced to return to the changing room, where we dried ourselves on some sort of gray rags of towels that had been issued to us. We were not allowed to dress, however. Everything that we had been wearing before had to be handed in to the store and in exchange we were issued with prison clothing. I can't possibly convey how sick I felt putting on that regulation underwear for the first time—God knows how many prisoners had been in it before me. Long underpants and shirt, regulation cotton trousers and tunic, canvas boots with miniscule tattered foot-rags, a regulation convict's cap, a padded or 'reefer' jacket, everything worn and worn again, everything patched and patched again. The underwear was so threadbare that you were almost frightened to put it on—before you knew where you were it might crumble to bits in your fingers. Our own things had to be tied up in bundles and whoever had bags or suitcases put the things inside, then a tag with your name on was hung on each bundle and in exchange you received yet another receipt.

After our bath we were locked up in our original cells on the first floor and then called out one by one. At last it was my turn. A warder took me to some sort of store-room. There I was ordered to strip down to the buff once more. While one of the warders examined my gear—the outfit I had just that minute received in that same jail—several of the others searched me as I stood there stark naked. I was ordered to stretch my arms out in front of me and perform a series of knee-bends; and they felt me all over in each different position. Then I was allowed to get dressed and sign out some bedding: a mattress that was so hard and heavy it seemed to be filled with bricks; a gray mattress cover that did duty as a sheet; a lumpy pillow on the same lines as the mattress; a flannel blanket that barely held together. Also they gave me an aluminum bowl, mug and spoon. Then I was taken with all my belongings along the prison corridor to cell no. 54, where we halted. The warder unlocked the door and I found myself inside, in the cell in which I might be spending the next three years of my life.

Prison Cell, Prison Regime

IT WAS a cell for five. When I was let in there were already three men inside, all newcomers from the same convoy as myself. Hardly had I time to look round when the keys rattled in the lock again, the door opened and into the cell, weighed down with a mattress and all the rest, walked Ozerov. That meant we were now complete.

We began to examine our surroundings. The cell was cramped, about five yards long by three yards wide, in other words about fifteen square yards or three square yards apiece. Directly opposite the door, high up in the wall, was a tiny window filled with cloudy, opaque glass reinforced with wire mesh (unbreakable). Nothing could be seen through such glass, of course, and so little light got through even in the daytime that an electric light bulb was kept on in the cell right round the clock. The window, of course, was barred, and in addition was protected outside by a shield or 'muzzle' (not all the prison windows have muzzles, only cells for prisoners on strict regime; there is also normal regime and these cells have no muzzles over the window). In the older blocks dating from before the revolution the windows had been four times as big—they had been bricked up later, for the new masonry still showed up clearly in the old walls.

Two iron cots stood against each of the blank walls and a fifth stood under the window. The cots consisted of an iron lattice and were attached to the wall in such a way that they could be lifted and hung on the wall with their legs folded flat. Against the right-hand wall, by the window, was an iron box bound in iron and fixed immovably to the wall—the 'sideboard'; it was divided inside into several compartments in which we kept our soup bowls, spoons, mugs and bread. Attached to the floor in the middle of the cell was a small table with iron legs, with a pair of small benches flanking it, also with iron legs and also attached to the floor. One other item of the furnishings remains to be mentioned—the inevitable sloptank by the door: without this object prison wouldn't be prison. Oh, and then there was the door, of course, an ordinary prison door with a peephole and a food trap, iron-bound and always locked from outside. The peephole was made of glass with a shutter on the corridor side; and the food trap was also kept locked and bolted. The entire furnishings of the cell—tables, benches, 'sideboard', door—were painted in dark red.

Cells on normal regime are also equipped with a radio—usually an ancient speaker hanging over the door. It is on from six in the morning until ten o'clock at night, being switched most of the time to the internal prison station. This offers the cons information on infringements of the rules—committed, of course, by 'individual' prisoners and quite untypical—and then they read out various orders and decrees on how the culprits are to be punished. Quite often the prison doctors give lectures on 'How to Avoid Tuberculosis', 'How to Prevent Stomach and Bowel Diseases', 'On the Dangers of Alcoholism', or 'How to Guard Against Venereal Diseases'. The advice is well-known: observe personal hygiene, eat clean food, avoid chance relationships, don't mix too closely with invalids, and so on. Both the healthy and those with T.B. sit and listen to these broadcasts with great good humor: how do you divide up a sloptank between cons, how do you get to breathe air that isn't infected with dampness? The other advice (wash vegetables in running water, chew your food thoroughly, observe a proper diet) might even come in handy in later life, say in five, ten, fifteen years time . . . Cons on strict regime, however, are deprived even of this entertainment.

These were the sort of cells that stretched down both sides of the corridors, though there were also cells for three— 'triple-headers'. One side of the cell block faced inwards, towards the exercise yards and the other blocks. On the other it faced the cemetery (which was also divided from us, like the rest of the outside world, by a stone wall, a ploughed strip and barbed wire). It's true you still couldn't see anything out of the prison windows but occasionally on the cemetery side you caught the sounds of a funeral march being played—the sole living evidence that beyond the prison walls life was still following its normal course: aha, somebody's number was up. Our cell was on the cemetery side. The cell block was pierced on the inner or courtyard side by three entrances, one in the middle and one at each end. We were always led in through one of the end doors; inside there was a landing on each floor and a locked door leading to the corridor. A staircase also led from the middle entrance to the upper stories. Here the stair landings divided the long corridors exactly into half: a barred gate, locked on the landing side, led into each half of the corridor. Inside each half-corridor and locked in, as in a cage, were warders who padded up and down in soft, felt knee-boots and spent their time peering through the peepholes, one after another. According to regulations the warders upstairs were not supposed to have keys to the barred gates—during

111

working hours they too were locked in—but at Vladimir, as everywhere else, this regulation was disobeyed. All keys to all the floors were kept by the chief duty warder, who sat downstairs in the guardroom (and there was also a duty officer in charge of the whole block).

I have already mentioned that our block was divided from the others by a high wall. On one side of the wall was a series of tiny exercise yards for political prisoners; on the other were blocks for civil prisoners, criminals, the hospital and the bath-house. A part of the buildings had been constructed before the revolution. When we were taken to the bath we tried to make out the date—it was something like 1903 or 1905.

One difference between the pre-revolutionary buildings and the Soviet ones, as I have said before, was in the size of the windows. Another was something you couldn't see: it was much colder in the newer blocks. The cells were damp and made you shiver even in summer, while in winter, even wearing a reefer jacket, it was impossible to get warm. Thrusting their hands into their jacket sleeves and with the collars well turned up, the cons would stamp about the cell and bang their feet together, while those who didn't have room to walk about would sit hunched up on the benches with their knees thrust up to their stomach and their noses tucked into their jackets. Everybody's prison cap, meanwhile, would be pulled right down to the eyebrows: if you leant your head to the right you could warm your right ear, but the left would almost drop off. In the old, pre-revolutionary blocks, although they were also built of stone, it was much warmer and drier.

The politicals' block, alas, was a new one.

The entire prison was enclosed by a ten-foot high stone wall, on both sides of which, as in the camps, were barbed wire fences consisting of several rows; between them was a ploughed and raked strip of land designed to show footprints. The watch towers were manned by sentries with tommy guns and at night the whole barrier was illuminated by powerful searchlights. It says in books that in former times men simply used to escape from prison. Now there are no prison escapes, particularly from political prisons. The cell is locked, the floor is locked, then comes the inner fence, the ploughed strip and the wall. And even if you stumbled across a sympathetic warder, he still couldn't help you. The security and supervision system is so worked out that the warders control each other—one has the keys to the cell, the other the keys to the floor. And you won't get away with sawing through the bars and hanging a rope-ladder out of the window either: every day there's an inspection, everything is minutely examined, pinched, tapped. In short there's no getting away from it, they make a first-class job of prison.

The daily schedule of prisoners in jail is the same as on special regime in the camps, the only difference being that you aren't sent out to work. At six a.m. it's reveille, followed by toilet break, inspection, breakfast, dinner (with exercise either before or after dinner), supper, inspection, lights out at ten o'clock. From reveille to lights out it is forbidden to lie on your bunk: if you do you earn yourself one to two weeks in the cooler. Sit, walk, stand, doze off standing up or sitting down, but don't on any account lie down. It is also forbidden to go near the window. That is to say, you can go up to it to open the ventilation flap or close it, but if they notice you craning up to it and attempting even with half an eye to look out at the free world outside, the cooler's a dead cert. Singing, talking loudly or making any sort of noise in the cell is also forbidden and for violations the whole cell is punished.

So what is there to do during those sixteen hours out of the twenty four? Just read or write. You can buy exercise books in the prison shop; you are allowed two school-type books, twelve pages in each, per month. What you write is checked by the warders—if anything looks suspicious the notebook is taken away. They also let you have chess and dominoes. Books and newspapers can be had from the prison library, two books per person every ten days. After a certain time, however, with sixteen hours a day available, even reading loses its charm for the man with a permanently empty stomach. What's more, if a warder sees the prisoners reading in the cell he switches off the light. He has a right to, of course. After all, it's broad daylight outside and the fact that it's dark in the cell is of no concern.

One prisoner in each cell has to be on duty—the duty goes by turns. It is his responsibility to sweep and scrub the cell, to carry out and wash the sloptank during the toilet break, report to the prison officers during inspection or non-regulation visits on how many prisoners there are in the cell and whether there have been any incidents or not. And woe betide the prisoner who makes a bad job of his duties!

I have already said that there are two regimes for prisoners in jail: normal and strict. When I came to Vladimir the system was as follows. Prisoners coming to jail for the first time were held on strict regime for the first two months; those who had been in jail before got six months (thus Burov, for example, faced six months of strict regime, while Ozerov and I were due for two). Prisoners were then put on normal regime and strict regime was reserved for punishment. Since 1964 these obligatory two or six months have been abolished and now the matter is entirely at the discretion of the prison administration. Normally all prisoners are now kept permanently on strict regime, being transferred to normal regime only for periods of six to eight weeks at a time and even then only after a special prison commission (with the invariable assistance of a doctor) has decided that retention on strict regime will endanger a prisoner's life. So they keep a man on normal regime for a while and when he perks up again they send him back to strict.

And so it goes on for years and years—there are men in Vladimir prison with sentences of ten, fifteen, twenty-five years. The difference between these regimes might seem infinitesimal to someone who hasn't experienced them on his own back, but for a prisoner it is enormous. On normal regime there's a radio, on strict regime not; on normal regime you get an hour's exercise a day, on strict regime half an hour, with nothing at all on Sundays; on normal regime you're allowed one visit a year lasting thirty minutes. . . .

Hunger

THE MOST basic difference of all, however, is in the food you get. Here is what a prisoner on normal prison regime receives: 18 ozs. of black bread per day; $\frac{1}{2}$ oz. of sugar—he usually gets five days' worth at a go: $2\frac{1}{2}$ ozs. For breakfast he gets 7–8 stale sprats, a bowl of 'soup' ($12\frac{1}{2}$ ozs.) such as we had the first day after our arrival and a mug of hot water—this you can drink as 'tea' with sugar. Dinner consists of two courses, the first being $12\frac{1}{2}$ ozs. of cabbage soup (water with leaves of rotten cabbage in it, sometimes you get a tiny fragment of potato), the second $3\frac{1}{2}$-5 ozs. of watery gruel, usually made with wheat but very occasionally with oats. For supper you get $3\frac{1}{2}$-5 ozs. of mashed potato—so watery and so little that when you peer into the bowl you see the tiny blob of your supper spread out like a miniscule pancake, with the aluminum bottom showing through. On very rare occasions, instead of mashed potato you get a so-called 'vinaigrette' for supper: the same old rotten pickled cabbage with the occasional piece of rotten pickled tomato. But even this pig swill was considered a delicacy by the prisoners. They say that on normal regime it is stipulated that a few grains of fat should be included in the food. Maybe it's true, but I must say that I have never been able to notice it in any of the soup or gruel that came to me.

On strict regime the rations are even more meagre: no sugar and no fat is permitted, not even a single grain. You get 14 ozs. of black bread, only sprats and hot water for breakfast, just cabbage soup for dinner (no second course) and the same supper as on normal regime.

Also included in the rations is a packet of cheap tobacco (1¾ oz.) every six days. What's more the prisoner on normal regime can also take advantage of the prison shop—until November 15, 1961, he was allowed to spend up to three rubles a month, but since that time the allowance has been reduced to two rubles and fifty copecks. And once a year he is allowed to receive one parcel weighing not more than 10 lbs.—ten pounds of food!

The prison 'shop', however, deserves a word of explanation. It refers to a process that takes place once a fortnight. Several days beforehand the prisoners start trying to guess which particular day it will be. One day at dinner time the warder puts a list of products available through the food trap, together with blank forms for each prisoner. After dinner he collects the completed forms, showing who wants to buy what, and he may bring the things the same evening or else on the following morning. Everyone looks forward to this moment. Or rather almost everyone: one man, perhaps, has been deprived of shop privileges, another has no money because he's got no one to send him any. A friend might ask his family to send something to a comrade—two and a half rubles a month wouldn't break anybody—but the trouble is that all letters are censored and that's the sort of request they won't let through. And so some are impatient while others await with sadness the day when orders may be made.

My Testimony

The question is: what to buy and how to dispose of this princely sum of one ruble and twenty-five copecks? I have the right to buy up to four pounds of bread (only black since 1961), up to 7 ozs. of margarine, up to 7 ozs. of sausages, up to 7 ozs. of cheese (you are not allowed to buy butter and sugar). But the permitted sum is not enough to buy what I have a right to, the more so since they only have the more expensive sorts of sausage and cheese—at $1\frac{1}{2}$ to $1\frac{3}{4}$ rubles a pound. And besides, I need soap, tooth powder, socks, envelopes, so that I shall have to take even less margarine, sausage and cheese than I am allowed (nobody refuses the bread, however; it's cheap and you can fill yourself up with it at least once in a fortnight). For those who smoke, though, it's far worse, since practically all your money goes on smokes. In prison they smoke a lot, a packet of shag lasts for barely two days; but from the shop you can't buy tobacco—only cigarettes: 'Byelomor' at 22 copecks a packet, or 'Sever' at 14 copecks. A packet a day is only just enough, which means that on top of the shag you'd need another twenty packets a month. Two and a half rubles don't go very far. . . .

At last they bring the things you've ordered. Men who have been starved for two weeks hurl themselves upon them and eat the lot within the first two or three hours: four pounds of bread with margarine, sausage and cheese—everything they've bought. Far from everyone has the strength of mind to stretch the pleasure out over two or three days. And then back to starvation rations again for another two weeks, at the end of which you again stuff your stomach with four pounds of bread at a single go. (I also decided to stuff myself full one day. I ate my loaf of bread straight off and then at once felt extremely unwell, I got heartburn and felt dizzy, but I still had no sense of being full and my eyes were still greedy for more.)

Prisoners in jail soon begin to fall prey to stomach disorders—catarrh, colitis, ulcers. The sedentary life gives rise to hemorrhoids and heart disease. And all this together leads to nervous complaints. In prison you won't find a single healthy man, except perhaps for newcomers—and they don't last long. At any rate those with whom fate and prison authorities threw me together between 1961 and 1963 included not one healthy man.

No, it is impossible to convey the essence of it, this torture by starvation. He who has never experienced it will find it difficult to comprehend.

... It is almost morning. Long before reveille not one of the five of us is sleeping. We are all waiting for reveille and then—bread. The moment the hooter sounds we are up. The more impatient among us start to pace about the cell: two steps forward and two steps back. Not everyone can walk about, there's not enough room, therefore the rest are sitting. Sitting and waiting. Toilet break is over. The food trap is open and the cookhand peeps in—he is checking the numbers against his list. The entire cell is already lined up at the food trap: hurry, hurry! One prisoner takes his ration quickly and moves away, another lingers by the food trap as long as possible, trying to size up the rations and choose the biggest bit and jealously comparing his own piece with that of his neighbor—as if that fraction of an ounce could save him from hunger! The next one carries his bread off to the 'sideboard' and puts it into his compartment. Another carefully and neatly breaks his bread into three—for breakfast, dinner and supper. At the same time he meticulously gathers all the crumbs and puts them into his mouth. Yet another can't resist and swallows the whole of his ration on the spot, right beside the food trap, before breakfast. And how he watches for the rest of that day as his more patient comrades eat their breakfast, dinner and supper with their bread!

But then how does it feel to be tortured by hunger all day, knowing that in your compartment lies the bread you have saved for dinner and supper! You think about that bread all day and night up to supper time, so long as there's a morsel left. What a magnet it is! How you long to take it out and eat it! Sometimes you can't endure it, you go over to the box, break off a tiny fragment of the crust and place it on your tongue or in the back of your cheek, where you start to suck on it, trying to stretch it out as long as possible, and you suck on it like a child with a sweet, only this morsel of bread is far, far tastier. But then the crust comes to an end, and how you long to go back to that bread again!

So it goes, day after day. You go to bed and you think: let the night go quickly so we can have some more bread again. You get up, wait for your bread and skilly, and before you've finished drinking it you are already thinking: let it be dinner time. Then you hurry the evening along: let it be supper time. Wiping a crust (if you've got one left) over the last traces of the mashed potato in the bottom of your bowl you are already dreaming: let it be lights out, morning, ration time . . . The con's chronometer and the con's diary in prison is simple: bread—breakfast—dinner—supper, and again bread—breakfast—dinner—supper, day after day, month after month, year after year.

Prisoners in a cell need great discipline and great moral strength in order to preserve themselves in such inhuman conditions, in order to preserve their human dignity and human relations with one another. After you've sat in the same cell for several months, everything about your neighbor begins to irritate you: how he stands, how he sits, how he walks, how he eats, how he sleeps. And you in turn are irritating him. Even with outwardly peaceable relations, everybody's nerves are stretched to the limit and you hold on only because you can't allow yourself to go to pieces and pour out your spite on your neighbor. But think of the situation in cells with civil and criminal prisoners, which are full of men unused to controlling themselves! Scandals, hysterics, fights—and it always ends up, of course, with the cooler for the lot of them, both the innocent and the guilty. But you get scandals and fights in politicals' cells too: it takes all sorts (and then there are plenty who become 'politicals' by accident), everyone's nerves are shot to pieces, and the circumstances are such as to drive even the calmest and most stable of men to extremes. There is no way of getting away from them, except perhaps in the cooler.

In winter the most frequent cause of quarrels is the ventilation flap. The point is that one is permitted to open the ventilator at any time (between six in the morning and ten at night) in order to air the cell, but at the same time there is no chance to clear the stench of the sloptank and of all those stale, badly washed human bodies and the tobacco smoke— you can cut the smell with a knife. And so one of the five cell-mates prefers to freeze so long as he can breathe fresh air. The others, though, are not in a condition to stand the cold— they are emaciated, even without the vent open their teeth are chattering. There are old men among them, and sick men in a cold sweat from their illnesses. And here you have grounds for a quarrel, an uproar—and the pros and cons of the argument are bound to be settled by the cooler.

Even more common are quarrels over food. Just think of it, one part of the prisoners in a cell are on normal regime, while the rest will be on 'strict quota of nourishment'. This is another form of punishment—normal living conditions combined with reduced rations. Then one man will have shop privileges, another will be without; one is allowed food parcels, the other isn't. It makes things difficult for both of them. How can those who are allowed no parcels or shop privileges prevent themselves from staring hungrily at their comrade with a parcel? Or the man with a loaf of bread just bought from the camp shop? Or even the man with a five-day sugar ration—two and a half ounces? And what about the man who has a bit more than his neighbors—what is he to do? Should the hungry man share with the one who's still hungrier? Ignore him and eat his own food, knowing all the while that it gives his comrade hunger spasms just to look at him?

Not every prisoner has the strength to share his parcel or his shop food with his cell-mates. But in my opinion, to eat and look upon those starving, pain-filled eyes is even harder and more intolerable. That's why some prisoners, when they do get a parcel, eat the food on the sly, so the others won't see them—at night, say, under the blanket. Everyone who is free, of course, will condemn such a man—how can you refuse to share with a comrade? But I'm not so sure that he who condemns that prisoner, after going through six months of strict regime, wouldn't hoard his sugar under the pillow and fish out one lump at a time in the night—secretly, so that the others wouldn't hear and be jealous. And how many men who not only have never taken anything from their neighbor but have never even coveted anything of his, now become thieves and steal their neighbor's food from the 'sideboard'. Hunger proves an insuperable ordeal. When he reaches this ultimate degree of degradation a man is prepared for anything. Admin usually knows who these scum are and use them for their own ends—if only to introduce discord into a 'quiet' cell. It is enough to bring in just one of these and then it begins: one man notices some bread missing, another misses some of his sugar—who has taken it? They all start to look at one another with suspicion—and that is exactly what admin wants. Now they have a pretext for handing out punishments right and left, and in any case men lose their self-control and become easy bait, if necessary, for calling out for a 'mischief' or a 'violation'.

Ivan Mordvin

OUR CELL no. 54 was a peaceful one, we tried not to make life any more miserable for one another than it already was. By December 1961 there were only four of us left (the fifth had been transferred elsewhere): Tolya Ozerov, Nikolai Korolev— the 'terrorist', Nikolai Shorokhov—I think he'd got himself re-classified as a 'political' after being in a criminal camp, and me. One day in the middle of December they moved a fifth man into our cell: Ivan Mordvin. I don't remember either his surname or what he was in for, everybody called him simply Ivan Mordvin—Ivan the Mordovian.

No sooner had he arrived than he started to tell us, keeping nothing back, why and how he had been transferred to our cell. It turned out that beforehand he had been next door. One of his cell-mates was Oleg Danilkin, a 'religious believer' (I later shared a cell with him myself for several months), and one day Oleg received a parcel from his sister in Moscow. Inside were the regulation ten pounds of food. He treated all his cell-mates, including Ivan Mordvin, to the contents, but put aside one 18 ozs. packet of sugar for later: some sort of religious holiday was approaching and he wanted to save the sugar until then, when he intended to celebrate the holiday by treating the whole cell to tea with sugar. The sugar was left not in his compartment but on top of the iron box. Ivan could not control himself—there was the sugar in front of him, all he had to do was stretch out his hand. In the day-time, of course, in full view of everybody, there was no chance of taking it. But at night you could get up to relieve yourself at the sloptank and there was the sugar right next to you. Ivan couldn't resist the temptation: he took it once, then again, and after that it entered his system. Night after night he would get up as if to relieve himself, listened—and if all was quiet and everyone sleeping, would slip over to the packet and take some; then, after waiting a while to be sure, he would get up and take some more. The fact that the sugar was disappearing was unknown to the others; there lay the packet and it stayed there, and its owner didn't bother to check the contents—why torture himself for nothing?

And so Ivan Mordvin went on stealing the sugar until someone caught him right by the 'sideboard'. Ivan bellowed loud enough for the whole block to hear, as though his throat were being cut—he explained to us that he did this on pur-pose so that the warders could come as quickly as possible, before they beat him up. The warders did in fact get there before a fight broke out and after establishing what the mat-ter was, took him out together with his things (i.e. for good) and put him for the time being in one of the 'triple-headers', which was empty at this time. Afterwards he was taken to see the officer in charge of the block. Ivan made a clean breast of everything, telling him all about the stealing and why he had kicked up such a rumpus. In return he was given no punishment and was transferred into our cell.

Ivan told us all this without the least trace of shame and even as though proud of himself, as if to say: look how clever I am, look how crafty I am—I managed to steal the stuff and I got away scot free.

I don't know whether he really didn't realize the vileness of his behavior and expected us to applaud him, or whether he hoped to win our trust by the frankness of his confession. In the event, of course, he won neither our trust nor applause. We all despised him equally and avoided talking to him. But soon our cell too was subjected to a similar incident.

At that particular time we had all just completed two months on strict regime and had just reverted to normal regime. The muzzle had been removed from the window and our exercise period lengthened again. Now we were waiting for our permitted parcels. The first to receive one, from his mother, was Nikolai Korolev: five pounds of sugar—in five packets—plus some food and a home-made cake: his mother had baked it herself. Nikolai shared his parcel with everyone—each of us got one packet of sugar. And he also shared the cake round, leaving a slightly bigger bit for himself. After all, it didn't represent only food to him but also his mother's care—Nikolai deeply loved his mother and was doing time because of her. We all realized this perfectly well. Ivan Mordvin ate his share up at once, including the whole pound of sugar. The rest of us, without discussing the matter, all decided to stretch our food for as long as possible. I, for instance, decided to take four lumps of sugar a day and no more—two in the morning and two in the evening—so as to drink not just hot water but sweet tea (in general I've got a sweet tooth and two lumps per mug is too little for me; here I had to economize, however, and not indulge myself).

The following evening, just before lights out, Nikolai collected all the food left from his parcel, put it into his pillow-case and stowed it under his head for the night. We all exchanged glances in silence. Both I and the others, I think, felt awkward and somehow ashamed, as if each of us suspected the others of some sort of underhand behavior. I

couldn't go to sleep all night or obtain any peace of mind.
After all, nobody had forced Nikolai to share out his parcel,
so why should he have to hide his precious things away from
us now, as if he feared for them and didn't trust us? Only in
the small hours did I grow exhausted and doze off. But I
hadn't had time to fall asleep properly before reveille sounded
and I had to get up again in order to steer clear of the cooler
and avoid being put back on special regime. We all got up,
tidied our cots and settled down to wait for toilet break and
breakfast. Ivan was pacing up and down the cell impatiently,
Ozerov and Shorokhov sat on their made-up bunks with their
arms clasped round their knees and reefer jackets over their
heads—this was the best way to snatch forty winks, keeping
yourself warm and dozing until the warder shouted at you.
Evidently they had also spent a bad night. Korolev was reading some book or other with large print. I also picked up a
book and looked at it, but it was impossible to read, so
uncomfortable was the atmosphere in the cell. Nor could I
look at anyone—it would be too shaming and painful.

The warders were running along the corridor, rattling their
keys and looking into the peepholes: 'No more sleep, no more
sleep, is it the cooler you want?' This was addressed to
Ozerov and Shorokhov, but more for form's sake than anything else; they were dozing sitting up and not lying down. At
last there came a bang on the door: 'Toilet break!' We stood
up and took off our padded or reefer jackets—no matter how
cold it was it was forbidden to wear your outer clothing for
toilet break. Today Shorokhov was on duty and it was his job
to carry out the sloptank. But the sloptank was heavy and
then after two months of starvation on strict regime he didn't
have the strength any more. Usually two men carry the sloptank, one always helps the man on duty. This time we two
carried it out, Shorokhov and I. While we were doing our

stuff they came banging on the door, as usual, and the warders shouted: 'Come on, come on, don't hang around, you're not the only ones here, have you forgotten where you are?'—and more in the same vein.

By the time we were making our way along the corridor the servers were already bustling about at the far end and the old man who heated the water (a prisoner) was distributing his hot water. No sooner had the door been locked behind us than the food trap was opened: 'Give us your kettle for the hot water!' We handed out the empty kettle and received it back full again together with our rations. Hot water is awaited in winter with even greater impatience than the skilly: it's hot and at least warms you for half an hour, while the skilly's the same water, only luke-warm. We started to drink our tea—with sugar, for everyone now (except Ivan Mordvin) had a pound of sugar from Korolev's parcel. I took two lumps from my packet and sat warming myself with my tea. At the same time I didn't look up at a soul, I still couldn't recover my composure after yesterday's events.

I didn't see how Shorokhov went to get his sugar and how he arrived at Ivan's side. I came to only when Shorokhov let Ivan have it full in the face. Ivan leapt up and they started to grapple. Shorokhov turned out to be the stronger (although he looked punier than Ivan), or perhaps the madder: he split Ivan's lips, knocked out some of his teeth and bloodied his whole face. The rest of us, having jumped up from our places, stood around in silence while the fight took its course, without interfering. We still couldn't make out who was attacking whom or for what. And one shouldn't imagine this scene as being like some ordinary street brawl. Prisoners who have done a good stretch in prison, and on strict regime what's more, haven't the strength to punch an opponent properly, nor to stay on their feet after a gentle push. They fasten their fingers on to each other's faces and are afraid even to break away—in case they fall down. And so they just stand there, swaying from weakness, and endeavor with their fingers to tear at each other's faces. . . . It is a pitiful, degrading picture!

We came to our senses only when the door opened and the warders came bursting into the cell. The fight was immediately stopped. When the warders left again they said that both Shorokhov and Ivan would be punished.

Later, after the skilly, Shorokhov explained to us what had happened. It turned out that when he went to get his sugar, more than half of the packet had disappeared since the day before. He had immediately thought of Ivan—he couldn't possibly have suspected one of us—and Ivan didn't deny it but merely sat there silently on his cot. After that Korolev said that on the first night after his parcel arrived he had lost half the food and half the sugar out of it—that was why on the second night he had decided to hide everything under his pillow, so as not to lose the rest. Ozerov said that he too had found several lumps of sugar missing.

I also wanted to have a look at my packet, but I put it off till the evening—for some reason I felt too embarrassed to check it right away. In the evening, when I took out some lumps for tea, I secretly counted the top layer—seven lumps were missing. (This was extremely easy to do: a con keeps track of every single lump of sugar, he remembers how many he ate yesterday, the day before and even a week ago, and also how many layers there are in a packet, how many rows in a layer, how many lumps in a row—all this is carefully calculated in advance and just as carefully apportioned.) And so I was short of seven lumps. I thought back once more to how many lumps I had taken the day before yesterday, how many yesterday and how many today—still there were seven short. That was too many for me to have made a mistake—two, say, or three, that was possible, but not seven. But then how come I hadn't noticed it before? Of course, I used to get my sugar without taking the whole packet out and it had never occurred to me to count. Nevertheless I told no one that I too was short—perhaps I was too embarrassed. But I was mortally offended. Why, that meant practically two whole days' worth of sugar . . .

That same day the block officer called out both Shorokhov and Ivan Mordvin. Ivan got off with a reprimand, while Shorokhov was put on strict regime rations but left in the cell with us.

Hunger Strike

SEVERAL DAYS after these events Ozerov was removed from our cell, for no particular reason, and replaced by a young fellow from next door, Andrei Novozhitsky. Andrei was in for high treason. He had been serving in a tank unit in East Germany, had crossed over to West Germany and after about a year there, feeling homesick for his native land, had decided to go back. They didn't dissuade him in the West but warned him that once back in Russia he would be sent to a camp. He didn't believe them, putting it down to bourgeois propaganda. So he came back and was sent straight to a camp (he had been sentenced in absentia to ten years). It was an ordinary story, I met many men in the camps who had returned from abroad, and not only soldiers either. As for Vladimir prison, Novozhitsky had landed up there for failing to fulfil his norm in the camp.

Not long after being transferred to our cell Andrei decided to go on hunger strike—evidently he had been planning this move for some time. He wrote a statement into which he crammed a whole pile of reasons impelling him to go on hunger strike. He protested against his trial behind closed doors, against the fact that he hadn't been given a copy of his sentence, against being sent to prison for failing to fulfil his norm—he was too ill, he said, to fulfil it, and against the inhuman conditions under which political prisoners were being held in Vladimir jail. A few days afterwards Shorokhov also went on hunger strike. In his statement, addressed to the Central Committee of the CPSU and the Presidium of the Supreme Soviet of the USSR, he also protested against his closed trial, unjust and unfair sentence (whose text, like almost everyone else, he had never seen) and the starvation conditions in the jail.

Now we had two people in our cell on hunger strike. They were left where they were, in the same cell as us, although this was against the regulations: hunger strikers are supposed to be isolated. The prison authorities always break this rule—go hungry in the communal cell, watch your neighbors getting their skilly and munching their bread! Some men can't hold out—it's a real ordeal after all!—and give up their strike after three or four days. I too have endured that ordeal and will write about my hunger strike in the Karaganda camps.

Hunger strikers have one 'advantage': they can lie whole days in their cot without getting up. Now during the morning inspection the duty prisoner, in addition to his normal report: 'Cell no. 54, five prisoners, sir!' had to add: 'Two on hunger strike.' For the first five or six days after their statements nobody pays any attention to them. On the fourth or fifth day the officer says: 'Hunger strike? Well, and to the devil with you!' Or something juicier and more colorful. Then a warder glances through the peephole, sees two cons lying in their cots and bangs his keys on the door: 'Get up! Is it the cooler you want, you fucking bastards?' But seeing that they don't get up but just lie there without stirring, he remembers that they are hunger strikers and walks away from the door cursing. Another, though, doesn't immediately realize what's going on (how can he remember them all when almost every cell has one or two of them?), opens the door and goes up to the cots. Only at this point does he catch on; and then someone in the cell says sarcastically: 'Get him up, get him up, off to the cooler with him, who does he think he is lolling about like a lord?' The warder moves away again, cussing blue murder, and threatens the wag with the cooler (for 'arguing with a warder')—it's been done before, if the warder's mad enough. On the fifth or sixth day one of the warders will go up to the bed of a hunger striker and throw the blanket back from his face to check if he's still alive; and at the same time to see if he has tattooed his forehead.

The other men in the cell with hunger strikers get edgy and wound up to an unbearable degree. The indifference and even gloating of the prison officers drives you to distraction. Nobody cares two hoots about the prison regulations, and if you protest nobody bats an eyelid. It's absolute murder eating your rations in front of comrades who are on hunger strike. I myself always felt somehow guilty for not being able to help them and we always tried to swallow our food as quickly and inconspicuously as possible.

Novozhitsky and Shorokhov always turned their faces to the wall during breakfast, dinner and supper. All these days they took not a single crumb into their mouths. Sometimes they would ask for a drink—when you raised the mug of water to their lips they would take a few swallows and then turn to face the wall again. Another time one of the rest of us would be unable to endure it any longer and would try to persuade Andrei or Nikolai: take some of my ration, go on, you can eat it secretly; it's all the bloody same—you know they won't take you out until ten days are up; come on now, just a crust, the warders will never know. Novozhitsky usually refused politely, while Shorokhov would swear blue murder at you for your pains. And why not? Why interfere when things are tough enough as they are?

Every day they would bring bread and skilly to the cell for all five of us. The duty prisoner was obliged to ask a hunger striker whether he wanted his food that day. On getting a refusal he was supposed to return it to the warder. Thus the man on hunger strike was obliged to refuse his food three times a day; and the man on duty was also sickened at having to take part in this recurring torture. Novozhitsky and Shorokhov had both come to an agreement with us beforehand that each of us, when on duty, would hand back their bread and soup without asking them. We agreed, of course—this was the only service we were able to do for them. And that is what usually happens, even among the criminal cons, although the duty prisoner risks punishment if they find him out.

Andrei and Nikolai got terribly chilled, even though they lay on their cots fully dressed with their blankets pulled over their heads. But then even we who were getting our miniscule portions of food and were able to walk about the cell in our padded jackets—even we managed to get warm for a moment only twice a day, i.e. morning and evening when they brought the hot water. It was so cold in the cell that if you put the kettle of hot water on the floor it would go cold in a quarter of an hour. Yet these men were completely without food—or even hot water, for they refused to drink anything hot. Furthermore both of them, after several years of short rations in the camps, had just undergone a period of genuine starvation on strict regime in prison. Their bodies retained not a single drop of the reserves that a man has in normal conditions. And from the very first day of a hunger strike such a wasted organism begins to feed off itself.

Andrei no longer got up from his cot after the third day

and after the ninth day no longer spoke. Nikolai was able to get to his feet up to the eighth day after his hunger strike began; and he went on talking, although with difficulty, until the very end, when they took him away from us. Not once during the time they stayed in our cell did the doctor look in to see them. The nurse, as usual, used to come to the food trap every day (except Sundays) and ask her usual questions: 'Is anyone ill in here?'—and then, without so much as a glance at the hunger strikers, would continue to the neighboring cell.

The three of us who were left wrote protests practically every day, complaining that the hunger strikers hadn't been transferred to a special cell but were being kept in with us. And whenever one of the officers came in to see us we protested again. But the answer was always the same: 'Admin knows best where to keep them. We're still in charge here, not you.'

On the eleventh day after Novozhitsky had begun his strike, towards evening, a group of warders came into the cell. The duty prisoner made the necessary report. The warders went up to Novozhitsky and lifted the blanket. He lay there quite still in his bed, wearing his jacket, trousers and boots, and his face was like that of a corpse. The warders examined him to make sure he was still alive. Then the senior warder ordered one of us to collect up his belongings, and carry them out of the cell. I picked up Andrei's mug, bowl and spoon and together with Korolev went over to Andrei to help him out. He himself was unable to stand, we lifted him and assisted him into the corridor. He was so light that not even we, who were so exhausted and weakened that the two of us were hardly able to carry the sloptank, felt his weight at all. He was a living skeleton dressed up in the regulation clothing of a prisoner. A warder walked ahead of us down the corridor and let us into an empty cell. He ordered us to sit Andrei on the bare cot and Andrei slumped further and further to one side until his shoulder rested against the wall. I lingered there beside him, it was terrible to have to leave him there, half-dead, in an empty cell. But the warder drove me away:

'Scram, scram! There's nothing the matter with him. Nobody forced him to go on hunger strike, it was his own decision not to eat anything.'

I couldn't stop myself and growled back:

'And we, of course, eat like princes, I suppose!'

'Oh, I see your ration's got too big for you,' he replied, 'maybe we ought to clip a few ounces off.'

I got the message and kept quiet. The warder locked Andrei in and led us back to our cell. In there, meanwhile, the other warders had completed their search of Andrei's belongings and were conducting an ideological discussion with Shorokhov: why bother, they said, this hunger strike won't get you anywhere, give it up, you're only signing your own death warrant . . .

They ordered us to carry Andrei's things to his new cell. Korolev and I took the bedding, and truly the mattress was several times heavier than he himself had been. We found Andrei slumped in exactly the same position we had left him in: he was half lying with his face up against the wall. The warder ordered Korolev to lay the bedding out on an empty cot. And me he commanded to lift Andrei and support him under the armpits so that he did not fall. Then, on this body hanging from my arms, he carried out a search.

Afterwards we placed Andrei on the bed, covered him with a blanket and his reefer jacket on top of that, and went out. The warder locked the cell.

Although we had already heard from other prisoners that

hunger strikers were kept in their normal cells for up to ten or eleven days, we still hadn't been able to believe that such a mockery was usual or the norm (nowadays it is only seven or eight days). Now, however, we were to learn the truth of this for ourselves. And Shorokhov too, who was on his seventh or eighth day, now knew what an ordeal awaited him during the next four to five days. Nevertheless he still didn't call his strike off and on the twelfth day they took him away. Korolev and Ivan Mordvin were the two who took him. Nikolai looked a bit perkier than Andrei had done, in spite of the fact that he had gone a day longer and what's more had been on strict regime just before his strike because of his fight with Ivan.

I never saw Shorokhov again, nor heard what became of him. Novozhitsky, however, was brought back to our cell about a week later. To describe what he looked like is impossible. He had called off his hunger strike: you can starve and starve, but you can never persuade anyone in authority even to listen to your complaint, nor to go into it for you. . . . Nor do they let you die. The very day that Andrei was taken away from us, they began to feed him artificially. Another thing: both we and the two hunger strikers, Shorokhov and Novozhitsky, had demanded that they be removed from our communal cell, as is laid down in the regulations, because we all thought that this would save the hunger strikers from unnecessary torture. But it turned out that getting a separate cell was only a prelude to further cruel indignities. The artificial feeding itself was turned into a daily torture. What's more, I know from my own experience that the feeling of hunger doesn't disappear, nor even lessen: all you get is a sensation of heaviness in the stomach, as though some sort of alien object has been placed inside you. And then they had invented a supplementary form of torment—Andrei Novozhitsky told us about it.

Every morning the warders bring into the cell a ration of bread and a bowl of skilly and place them on a stool beside the head of the bed. Then they go out and leave the breakfast there half a day under the nose of the man on hunger strike. At dinner time they change the skilly and leave it there till the evening. The next morning they change the bread and say: 'Are you going to eat your bread today?' 'Are you going to eat your breakfast today?' 'Are you going to eat your supper?' And so on three times a day. We at least were able to shield our friends from this ritual.

One day the block officer went in to see Novozhitsky:

'Hunger strike? A waste of time, you can easily write complaints without going on hunger strike. Go on, complain, write, we won't deprive you of this right. . . .'

'But how and where can I complain about you beasts here?'

'We're not beasts, we act strictly according to the regulations. If you think we're breaking the regulations, go on and complain, it's your right . . .'

Novozhitsky, of course, received the standard answers to his protests, despite the fact that his protests were reinforced with a hunger strike: 'Correctly sentenced. Regarding the conditions of his internment in jail, this complaint has been passed back for local consideration.' Truly it makes you wonder whether a hunger strike is worth such answers.

Nevertheless, the fact that they have even been given some sort of answer fills some inexperienced protesters with hope. They call off their hunger strike and wait for the local authorities to 'do justice' to their complaint. So much the greater is their despair, therefore, when one of the prison officers informs them that what they consider to be 'inhuman cruelty' is really 'in conformity with the regulations'—and this is usually communicated to them with a maximum of cynical sarcasm and sneering commentaries. Very often, after this sort of final reply, the prisoner who has not yet recovered from his first hunger strike immediately starts a second, or else does something to himself that is exclusively conditioned by his despair.

Self-Mutilation

HERE IS one out of a number of similar stories, from which it differs only in its originality. It took place before my very own eyes in the spring of 1963. One of my cell-mates, Sergei K., who had been reduced to utter despair by the hopelessness of various protests and hunger strikes and by the sheer tyranny and injustice of it all, resolved, come what may, to maim himself. Somewhere or other he got hold of a piece of wire, fashioned a hook out of it and tied it to some home-made twine (to make which he had unravelled his socks and plaited the threads). Earlier still he had obtained two nails and hidden them in his pocket during the searches. Now he took one of the nails, the smaller of the two, and with his soup bowl started to hammer it into the food flap—very, very gently, trying not to clink and let the warders hear—after which he tied the twine with the hook to the nail. We, the rest of the cons in the cell, watched him in silence. I don't know who was feeling what while this was going on, but to interfere, as I have already pointed out, is out of the question: every man has the right to dispose of himself and his life in any way he thinks fit.

Sergei went to the table in the middle of the room, undressed stark naked, sat down on one of the benches at the table and swallowed his hook. Now, if the warders started to open the door or the food flap, they would drag Sergei like a pike out of a pond. But this still wasn't enough for him: if they pulled he would willy-nilly be dragged towards the door and it would be possible to cut the twine through the aperture for the food flap. To be absolutely sure, therefore, Sergei took the second nail and began to nail his testicles to the bench on which he was sitting. Now he hammered the nail loudly, making no attempt to keep quiet. It was clear that he had thought out the whole plan in advance and calculated and reckoned that he would have time to drive in this nail before the warder arrived. And he actually did succeed in driving it right in to the very head. At the sound of the hammering and banging the warder came, slid the shutter aside from the peephole and peered into the cell. All he realized at first, probably, was that one of the prisoners had a nail, one of the prisoners was hammering a nail! And his first impulse, evidently, was to take it away. He began to open the cell door; and then Sergei explained the situation to him. The warder was nonplussed.

Soon a whole group of warders had gathered in the corridor by our door. They took turns at peering through the peephole and shouting at Sergei to snap the twine. Then, realizing that he had no intention of doing so, the warders demanded that one of us break the twine. We remained sitting on our bunks without moving; somebody only poured out a stream of curses from time to time in answer to their threats and demands. But now it came up to dinner time, we could hear the servers bustling up and down the corridor, from neighboring cells came the sound of food flaps opening and the clink of bowls. One fellow in the cell could endure it no longer—before you knew it we'd be going without our dinner—he snapped the cord by the food flap. The warders burst into the cell. They clustered around Sergei, but there was nothing they could do: the nail was driven deep into the bench and Sergei just went on sitting there in his birthday suit, nailed down by the balls. One of the warders ran to admin to find out what they should do with him. When he came back he ordered us all to gather up our things and move to another cell.

I don't know what happened to Sergei after that. Probably he went to the prison hospital—there were plenty of mutilated prisoners there: some with ripped open stomachs, some who had sprinkled powdered glass in their eyes and some who had swallowed assorted objects—spoons, toothbrushes, wire. Some people used to grind sugar down to dust and inhale it—until they got an abcess of the lung. . . . Wounds sewn up with thread, two lines of buttons stitched to the bare skin, these were such trifles that hardly anybody ever paid attention to them.

The surgeon in the prison hospital was a man of rich experience. His most frequent job was opening up stomachs, and if there had been a museum of objects taken out of stomachs, it would surely have been the most astonishing collection in the world.

Operations for removing tattoos were also very common. I don't know how it is now, but from 1963 to 1965 these operations were fairly primitive: all they did was cut out the offending patch of skin, then draw the edges together and stitch them up. I remember one con who had been operated on three times in that way. The first time they had cut out a strip of skin from his forehead with the usual sort of inscription in such cases: 'Khrushchev's Slave'. The skin was then cobbled together with rough stitches. He was released and again tattooed his forehead: 'Slave of the USSR.' Again he was taken to hospital and operated on. And again, for a third time, he covered his whole forehead with 'Slave of the CPSU'. This tattoo was also cut out at the hospital and now, after three operations, the skin was so tightly stretched across his forehead that he could no longer close his eyes. We called him 'The Stare'.

In the same place, in Vladimir, I once happened to spend several days in a cell with Subbotin. This was a fellow the same age as myself and a homosexual. There were few homosexuals in Vladimir and everyone knew who they were. There was nothing they could earn there. He had been classed as a 'political' after being in an ordinary criminal camp and making an official complaint—thus 'letting the tone down'. One day, after having sent about forty or fifty complaints to Brezhnev and the Presidium of the Supreme Council and to Khrushchev and the Central Committee of the Communist Party of the Soviet Union, he swallowed a whole set of dominoes—twenty-eight pieces. When the whole of our cell was being led down the corridor to the exercise yard—he had swallowed the dominoes just before our exercise period—he clapped himself on the stomach and said to one con from camp maintenance who was coming the other way: 'Listen, Valery!' I don't know whether Valery really heard the sound of dominoes knocking together in Subbotin's stomach, but he asked him: 'What have you got there?' and Subbotin drawled 'Dominoes'.

The doctors wouldn't operate on Subbotin. They simply ordered him to count the pieces during defecation, saying that they would have to come out on their own. Subbotin conscientiously counted them each time and on his return to the cell ticked off in pencil on a special chart the number that had come out. No matter how diligently he counted, however, four pieces still remained unaccounted for. After several days of agonizing suspense he washed his hands of them: if they stayed in his stomach it was all right as long as they didn't interfere, and if they were out already, then to the devil with them.

'The Terrorist'

NIKOLAI KOROLEV was somewhat over thirty and was now serving his fifteenth year of imprisonment. Before his crime he had been living with his mother in a village near Tver. Both of them worked in the local kolkhoz and they worked hard there, from dawn to dusk. It was 1947. At that time there were practically no men in the villages, all the work was shouldered by women and by adolescents like Nikolai. Meanwhile the few men that remained in the village occupied all the important posts—chairman, foremen, stock takers. Usually they drank like fish and lorded it over the kolkhoz workers however they liked.

Nikolai noticed that his mother's eyes were tear-stained when she returned from work and at nights she would weep at home. He asked her what the matter was, but she only replied: 'Don't worry, Kolya, it's nothing. It's a dog's life, that's all. . . . ' But a neighbor told him that the foreman had got his knife into his mother and used to swear at her obscenely and humiliate her in front of the others.

One day Nikolai had been riding the oxen past the seed store. From inside came the sound of the foreman's voice—he was shouting, pouring out a stream of filthy language. Nikolai halted the oxen and went into the yard. Inside he saw his mother standing there, weeping, distressed and afraid, with her arms lowered, while the foreman sat on horseback in front of her, holding a switch and bellowing at her for all he was worth. Nikolai stepped forward:

'Leave her alone, you drunken pig!'

The foreman answered:

'Mummy's boy, what do you think you can do!' and poured out a stream of filth on him too. Then he leaned down from his horse and grabbed the peak of Nikolai's cap, intending, evidently, to pull it down over his eyes. Nikolai ducked, the foreman crowded him with his horse, and then, shifting his switch from one hand to the other, slashed Nikolai with it. The mother rushed to shield her son, put her arms round him and cried:

'Monster, monster! Crowing over us women's not enough for you, now you have to start on the children!'

Nikolai tore himself away from his mother and ran home beside himself with rage, with his mother's cry still ringing in his ears. Back in the house he seized his father's shotgun from the wall, loaded it and ran out into the street. The foreman was riding towards him, evidently on his way back from the stores. Nikolai raised the gun. He was hardly able to aim it for the mist covering his eyes. All he could see was the horse's muzzle, which seemed to be right in front of him, and so he aimed higher at some point above it. Having fired the shot he lowered the gun and went home without a single backward glance. Only when his mother ran up saying: 'Kolya, Kolya, what have you done?' did he understand that he had killed the foreman.

He sat at home and waited for them to take him. They came, took him out, put him in a van and took him first to the district headquarters and then to Tver, to prison. He was tried behind closed doors; not a soul was in court and no

witnesses were called. Killing a kolkhoz foreman was interpreted as an act of terrorism. And since terrorism was a
political crime, he was sentenced to twenty-five years. Nikolai
at that time was just eighteen.

Later he was sent to Vladimir, like me, for attempting to
escape. While doing special in camp ten he had got friendly
with an 'independent Ukrainian', Vasily Pugach, and the two
of them had participated in a group dig in the work zone. I
knew Vasily. He had been about twenty-five then, with a
twenty-five-year sentence round his neck, and his mother was
also behind barbed wire somewhere in Mordovia. He and I
had been in the same convoy to Vladimir and had both been
forcibly cropped—Pugach had also been deprived of his
luxuriant Ukrainian moustache. I had been very fond of
Vasily Pugach and therefore was well disposed to his comrade
and friend from the very beginning. And indeed, Nikolai
turned out to be an extremely nice fellow, calm and collected,
and that was of great value in a prison cell, where everyone
tends to be so nervous and on edge. He used to get letters and
parcels from his mother and I have already told how he
shared out the parcel, which not everyone was capable of
doing.

Nikolai asked me to write an official petition for him—he
hadn't really mastered reading and writing. I of course knew
that it was useless, but how do you tell that to a man who
has already spent fifteen years inside and has another ten left
to do? By that time the criminal cons with twenty-five-year
sentences had had them commuted to fifteen: that was the
maximum sentence under the new criminal code. But the
changes in prison sentences didn't affect politicals and to this
day they are serving out their twenty to twenty-five years.

I wrote a petition as best I could: that Nikolai had committed murder in a state of extreme disturbance; that this

murder could not be construed as an act of terrorism, because Nikolai had had no political ends in view; that he had been illegally tried behind closed doors and that a copy of his sentence was being illegally withheld from him. It ended with a request that his sentence be reconsidered and that his crime be requalified as murder and not terrorism.

I read the petition aloud. Nikolai listened to it together with the rest of the members of the cell. We decided to address it to the Presidium of the Supreme Soviet, to Brezhnev, I think it was. Then Nikolai put his signature on the bottom and the following morning handed it to the warder through the food trap. About three days afterwards they brought him a printed form informing him that his petition had been forwarded to Moscow. He signed this also and settled down to wait.

All the time he was in our cell he waited and then, when he was transferred elsewhere, wrote again and again. He sent off dozens of petitions asking for his case to be reconsidered. The answer was always the same: 'Correctly sentenced, no grounds for the case to be reconsidered.'

In 1963 I heard he was in a special regime camp, coming up to his nineteenth year of imprisonment.

Hard to Stay Human

SOON THEY started to break up our cell for some reason. The first to go was Novozhitsky. He was so weak he was unable to carry his own things. We helped him gather them up, carried his gear out into the corridor and said farewell. (We met again only in 1966, in camp eleven in Mordovia.) After that they removed Korolev.

For two days there were only two of us in the cell, Ivan Mordvin and myself. I found this very unpleasant, I couldn't forget the stolen sugar. And now on top of it all Ivan took it into his head to try and excuse himself. I listened in silence and then cut him short fairly sharply. He stopped after that, but not for long. The next morning he started a different tune—how he was due to receive a parcel. I can see him now: tall and skinny as a rake, in prison rig, with his hands in his pockets, pacing about the cell—three steps forward, three steps back—and talking without a break. Any day now he'd be getting a parcel with honey and butter and sugar. And he'd give me some of it too. And how he'd eat then. . . . I realized it was the hunger in him talking, but still I couldn't overcome my irritation: for God's sake, we were fed on the same skilly, weren't we, but I controlled myself, while he simply didn't give a damn for other people's feelings!

Luckily some new prisoners were brought in. First an old man, a religious believer, about 65 to 70 years old. He was called Pavel Ivanovich, but I've forgotten his surname. Then they brought an Azerbaijanian, Ilal-ogly, a taciturn fellow of about 35—short, dark, black-haired, and skinny like the rest of us. I don't know what he was in for, his Russian wasn't up to much. Three days or so later they brought Boris Vlasov—I particularly remember his arrival. The keys clattered in the locks, the door opened and a fellow on crutches came into the cell, accompanied by several warders. He went over to his cot, spread out his bedding and lay down, after which the warders immediately picked the crutches up and took them away with them.

It turned out that Boris Vlasov had been brought to us straight from the hospital. He had been in prison for ages now, and unable to stand the torture any longer had one day upped and swallowed two spoons, his own and a neighbor's. That wasn't enough, however. He also swallowed, piece by piece, a complete set of dominoes. First they dragged him off for an X-ray and then to the operating table. They slit open his stomach, extracted all the official property and stitched him up again. Then, still in hospital, Vlasov went on hunger strike. After fasting for a month he broke down. He called off the hunger strike and immediately slit the veins on his leg. They noticed in time, bandaged him up and now had brought him straight to our cell. He still couldn't walk and for the first few days the nurse used to change his bandages right there in the cell. A week later, however, he was able to hobble about on his own and began going to the medical post to get them changed—luckily it was on our floor and he had no stairs to climb.

Vlasov became friends with Ivan Mordvin. Both of them had fifteen-year terms, both were old hands, and for days on end they would natter on about the camps and prison: they had already forgotten about life outside and didn't even dream about it any more.

As time went on Ivan told Boris all about this and about that and one day came to the incident that had occurred in our cell. And then what did I hear but Ivan (and they weren't speaking in whispers but aloud, with no sense of embarrassment) starting to heap all sorts of abuse on Ozerov, Korolev and Shorokhov. No doubt if I hadn't been there he would have said the same sort of things about me. Not knowing our former cell-mates the others listened to Ivan and drank it all in, looking at me from time to time to see what I would say. At this point all the indignation that I had been feeling against Ivan, that had been accumulating since the very day of his arrival and that I had succeeded in suppressing till now, suddenly boiled up inside me. I cut him off sharply: he shouldn't lie about men behind their backs, he'd be too scared if they were there. Ivan had already lost his temper and called me some sort of dirty name in reply. I was even almost pleased by this, I took a swing and let him have it full in the face—now I'd found an outlet for my rage. I was so incensed that I was ready to tear him to pieces. Ivan grabbed hold of the kettle with the cooled remains of our hot water in it and swung it at me. I knocked it out of his hand and it clattered on the cement floor and rolled over, spilling water over the whole cell. Ivan and I grappled. I had managed to punch him several times in the face already and it was covered in blood: blood was running from his nose and oozing from his teeth and split lips. I don't know what I looked like, I was so enraged that I didn't feel any pain. I punched him again and he fell onto my cot. I turned and walked away, still quivering with rage, and sat down on Pavel Ivanovich's cot in order to get a grip on myself. But

just then Ivan jumped up and made a rush at me. I pushed
him away, got him down on the table and pressed him down
though I don't remember how. His foot came into my hand. I
grabbed hold of it and gave it a sharp twist. Ivan moaned. I
twisted still harder. Then suddenly I heard a crack. In a flash
I cooled down, my rage and fury might never have been, I
felt unbearably ashamed and sorry for Ivan. I let him go and
moved back from the table. Had I really just broken a man's
bone, with my heart stopped and my throat constricted with
rage? I was ashamed to look at Ivan and the other cons.

At that moment the door opened and the warders came
running in. There was nobody to drag apart by now so they
stopped and examined the cell and all of us. The duty wardress, a spiteful little old woman, pointed at me and Ivan and
began to explain:

'I was looking through the peephole'. (She was such a
dwarf, in fact, that she couldn't reach the peepholes and
always carried a little stool with her; she used to go from cell
to cell, place her stool in position and climb up to have a
look. And she was dangerous. You only had to feel a bit off
color or sleepy and lie down for a second and if she was on
duty she'd be sure to spot you and report you, and then
you'd be for the cooler.) 'I was looking through the peephole
and this one hit that one with the kettle . . . ' For some reason
it came out according to her that I had been the one with the
kettle. Still, who cared, it wouldn't make the slightest bit of
difference.

A couple of hours later we were both taken to see the
officer in charge of the block. 'How shall we take you in—
together or one at a time?' asked the warder maliciously. The
point was that when an officer is handing out punishments for
a fight—suspending shop privileges, putting you on strict
regime rations or strict regime in full—the accused often start

151

to beg forgiveness or cry, each blaming the other and trying to shield himself. Scenes like these give enormous pleasure to the warders and our escort, evidently, was anticipating a similar sort of spectacle, if only we asked to go in separately.

'It's all the same to me, I don't care if I don't go in at all,' I replied. 'They could just as well tell me in the cell what I'm going to get for it, that would be the best of all.'

'I don't care either,' said Ivan after a moment's hesitation.

The officer in charge of the block, Major Tsuplyak, was talking to the warders in his office when we arrived. As we were led in he broke off his conversation and looked in our direction, looking longer at Ivan. Evidently he remembered him.

'Number 54? A pretty sight you've made of yourselves. Stealing food again. A month on reduced rations for the two of them! Take them away, bring in the ones from 78 . . . '

Ivan stammered:

'Excuse me, sir. . . . '

But they pushed the two of us out and led us down the corridor and back to our cell.

The following morning we received only fourteen ounces of bread in our ration and only a single sprat for breakfast, without soup. The thing that bothered me most was that Ivan had been put on short rations because of me. What's more he found it harder than most to endure hunger. It seemed to him that he would never last out a month on strict regime food. He decided to put an end to himself. Two days after our fight he got hold of a razor blade from somewhere and slit both his wrists. This happened just after the bread had been distributed. Ivan had received his reduced bread ration and swallowed it down so as not to waste it (what if he were to die or get carted off to hospital with the bread still uneaten?) before slashing the blade across his veins. It was the time when breakfast was being served and so longer than usual went by without the warders looking through the peephole. Our cell got breakfast too. Ivan, who had fountains of blood spurting from both wrists by now, asked us not to touch his sprat. He threw up the bread he had just finished eating and the vomit mixed with the blood all over the floor. The rest of us, however, ate our breakfast as usual, feeling nothing except our hunger. Pavel Ivanovich, after wiping his bowl round with a crust of bread, placed the remainder of his bread ration in the box and began to pray. And that day perhaps he prayed a bit longer than usual.

At last a warder looked through the peephole and discovered what had happened. He summoned the nurse. She put the tourniquets on both Ivan's arms and started to bandage him up, talking away as she worked:

'Now what do you mean by going and cutting yourself like that? Who's going to say a good word for you when you're dead? These, I suppose,' she nodded in our direction, 'yes, if you're a good man . . . '

The warders stood around Ivan, smoking and talking among themselves. The senior warder threatened to give the whole cell a going over if Ivan didn't say what he had cut himself with. Then Ivan himself handed the razor blade over, so that we weren't all searched because of him.

The bandaging was finished, the nurse and the warders went away. Somehow or other we cleaned up the cell and scrubbed the blood and vomit off the floor. Ivan lay on his bunk, long, skinny and even whiter than usual, and covered in blood. His shirt sleeves were rolled up right to the shoulders and his arms swathed in bandages. Time for dinner came and they brought our skilly, with reduced portions for Ivan and me. Ivan was unable to stand and we handed him his bowl on the cot. He took it in his bandaged and bloody hands, drank it over the side, licked it clean and asked for his sprat from breakfast. Then he gulped it down greedily on its own—he had eaten his bread, every last crumb, in the morning.

Looking at Ivan I thought to myself: there lies a man who because of you went hungrier than usual; and because of you he wanted to die. What if he did try you with his greediness and his constant talk about eating, what if he did stoop to petty thieving—is he really to blame for it? And are you any better, do you think? Hurling yourself on someone who was just as defenceless and unfortunate as yourself! And anyway, if you're really so weak that you can't control yourself and your nerves, why don't you punch the face of one of those warders who insult you every day? Because for a luckless con you face only reduced rations, or at the most the cooler, while for a warder you can be shot by decree. That means you've been poisoned by fear and fear dictates your actions.

Then I thought about myself. What had I been reduced to by a few months in prison! When I first arrived in a cell I had thought I wouldn't be able to last a day in it. I couldn't even bring myself easily to use the sloptank. I went cold at the very thought of having to eat and sleep here, and of other cons eating and sleeping and evacuating themselves here . . . But now I could greedily swallow my sprat in the midst of blood and vomit and it seemed to me that there was nothing in the world tastier than that sprat of mine. A man pours out blood before my very eyes and I lick my soup bowl clean and think only about how long it is till the next meal. Did anything human remain in me, or in any of us, in that prison?

Ivan lay there for two or three days without rising. Then he began to get up and after several days they already insisted on driving him out for exercise periods and forbade him to lie down during the day, threatening him with the cooler. They read him a decree depriving him of parcels for four months for self-mutilation and introducing a razor blade into the cell. It was painful to look at Ivan—he had been so looking forward to a parcel! And on top of that, reduced rations! Every day at dishing-out time Ivan Mordvin would stand at the food trap and wheedle: 'Go on, just one little crumb more! Just half a spoon more!' Not once did they add even a fraction of an ounce, but nevertheless he would stand there three times a day and whine and weep at the food trap. At first every one of us, and I especially, felt sorry for him. But afterwards we all began to get irritated and annoyed. But no matter how we swore at him, Ivan continued to beg for more every day. He no longer had any shame, he could feel nothing but hunger, hunger, hunger.

Our Neighbor Powers

ONE DAY they announced over the prison radio that the American flyer, Gary Powers, was to be pardoned. Taking into account his frank and sincere admission of guilt, as they put it, and his good conduct, and also in response to the numerous requests of his family, a pardon had been granted to him.

This at once become the subject of discussions, arguments and quarrels in our cell. Powers had served not even a quarter of his term and here they were pardoning him; while we had to sit there from bell to bell, which meant that, according to them, Kolya Korolev, the 'terrorist', Pavel Ivanovich—in for his religion—or Andrei Novozhitsky, an unsuccessful fugitive—in short, any one of us was considered more of a threat and a danger than a capitalist spy.... However, some people also came to more realistic conclusions: one of our spies, they said, must have been caught in America and now the governments had agreed to make an exchange (subsequently I learnt that this was indeed the case: Powers was exchanged for Abel).

Powers' pardon aroused particular interest among us at Vladimir, because everyone knew that he was there in the same prison. A prison is always chock full of rumors and stories: they get passed on by look-outs—cons who work for admin—and are told around whenever the cells are shuffled. We knew that Powers occupied a cell for two on the second floor of the hospital block. Some had even managed to catch a glimpse of him and his cell-mate strolling in the exercise yard. Risking solitary in the process, they had hauled themselves up to the ventilation shaft in order to take a look at this exotic bird. They said that Powers and his companion wore all their own clothes instead of prison rig, that they were clean shaven—not like us, gone over once every ten days with an electric razor—and that their heads, on the contrary, were not close shaven but were covered with hair. Powers' companion was said to be either an Estonian or a Latvian, in any case from one of the Baltic states, and an educated man who spoke excellent English. This Estonian had been prepared as Powers' partner even before the trial was over. His sentence was twenty-five years and they had promised him that if he fulfilled the necessary conditions he would be pardoned and freed immediately after Powers. As for Powers, they said, it was obvious he wouldn't be in for long. And then, of course, they tempted him with special privileges. On the other hand, if he broke the conditions he would spend the rest of his life in Vladimir prison and even die there. (Incidentally, such life imprisonment is not unknown in Vladimir: one forester had been there for twenty years already after he had accidentally witnessed the slaughter of the Polish officers in the Katyn Forest.*)

But what sort of conditions were they? First, the Estonian was not to tell Powers about the real situation of the prisoners in Soviet prisons, but on the contrary should do everything he could to strengthen the conviction that all political prisoners were kept in the same conditions as they themselves.

* See note on page 35.

There were plenty of accidents that could happen: an emaciated figure in prison dress might somehow pop up while they were exercising, somebody in the hospital might suddenly shriek out (like the time we had heard it)—in such cases the Estonian was to think up plausible and convincing explanations for his American companion. Secondly the Estonian was told to say as little as possible about the ordinary way of life in the Soviet Union: let him keep Powers busy with conversation about the cinema, literature, sport. . . .

Powers had even been taken to Vladimir differently from us—no black marias or special prisoners' trains for him, he had never even seen such things. Oh no, his arrival in Vladimir had been by limousine direct from Moscow.

So that it was in vain, of course, that some of our prisoners hoped that when he was back home, the American flyer would be able to tell them there about our particular circle of hell. Powers was not allowed even a sniff of our real prison life.

Not everybody, though, would believe that Powers was being held under special conditions. I knew of one such 'disbeliever' whose name was Gennady. Gennady used to work himself up into a frenzy arguing with his cell-mates that this could not be, that once the prison rules existed they were bound to be the same for everybody. Naturally they made fun of him; and it was then that he swore that he would see Powers for himself and prove the truth of his words. So it came about that a few days later a comrade informed the warders that Gennady had swallowed two spoons, his own and his comrade's. It was nothing unusual. They made a search of the cell and needless to say found that two spoons were missing. Gennady was dragged off to the hospital block for an X-ray—via that very corridor where Powers' cell was situated. On his way past Gennady suddenly dashed to the door of the cell (he had found out the number beforehand), pushed the flap to one side and glued his eye to the peephole. And by the time the startled warder had recovered and dragged him away he had managed to see what he wanted.

Well, Gennady's fate after that followed its normal course: he was taken back to his cell and then locked up in the cooler for ten days—both for looking through the peephole and for organizing that trip to the hospital (the X-ray, of course, revealed nothing). But while he was back in his cell waiting for marching orders for the cooler he told his companions what he had seen in Powers' cell. Everything was the way the others had said it was: the hair, the civilian clothes, and an appearance that showed that there was clearly no shortage of food.

Of the cons in our cell only Boris Vlasov had seen Powers—also out walking in the exercise yard—and he confirmed that both Powers and the Estonian were held in special conditions.

Many men envied the Estonian his special conditions and the fact that he was now going to be released: if it had not been for Powers he would have had to sit there from bell to bell like the rest of us. But even more of the cons condemned him: sitting there alone with that American, how could he fail to tell him about the tortures being inflicted on all the other prisoners there?

In any case they envied him for nothing. We heard afterwards that the authorities refused to let the Estonian go, that they cheated him, and that after Powers' release, they moved him back to an ordinary cell under ordinary conditions, and that the next day he committed suicide. There was also another rumor that he really had been released. And another that he was moved to a different prison. I don't know which one was true. Only one thing is sure: that Estonian disappeared and nobody ever saw him again.

Beria's Men

AT ONE time a cell of former Beria* men used to exercise in the next yard to ours. The old fence that divided the yards was full of cracks and so we had a good view of them. They too were held under special conditions, not at all as we were. While exercising, for instance, they always walked about in their expensive overcoats and I never once saw them in prison uniform. I remember one of them. Short and stocky, he used to stride about the yard importantly in a warm overcoat and black Caucasian fur hat. There was another who also wore a Caucasian fur hat and a gray overcoat that somehow looked like a great coat on him. They used to say that the latter was not a Beria man but a general whose name, I think, was Schrönberg.

The Beria men's cell was next to ours and on our way to or from exercise we were able to see into it (while the members of a cell are exercising the doors are left wide open to air the cell, and we were always led out either a fraction before or after the Beria men). We could hardly believe our eyes. All the cells in Vladimir jail were so alike that if you blindfolded a con, led him into the wrong cell and uncovered his eyes, he

* Lavrenty Beria was Stalin's secret police chief. He was executed by Stalin's successors shortly after Stalin's death in 1953.

would automatically go to his usual place without even noticing where he was. But the Beria men's cell looked like a luxurious apartment to us. Their beds were covered with warm domestic blankets and a fetching tablecloth covered the table. They were allowed to lie down for as long as they liked during the day and they were allowed an unlimited number of parcels from their families. What sort of rations they got I don't know, or whether they were given the normal skilly, but in any case they had so many parcels that they could live on normal, everyday food.

How they were hated, those five neighbors of ours! 'Those bastards, queers and bloodsuckers used to live off our blood when they were free and even here inside they're not doing badly for themselves,' said the cons. There was even a rumor that they had done a deal with the government, with obligations on both sides: the Beria men would keep quiet about certain other important violations of 'socialist legality', in return for which they got special privileges in jail. They also said that the Beria men had been heard to say, either among themselves or to someone doing orderly duty: 'Well, what about Lavrenty Beria? Do you think he was the only one and that those men up there now had nothing to do with it? All decisions were taken unanimously. He's just the one they used as a whipping boy!'

Similar rumors and conversations in prison (and outside too for that matter) were reinforced by the fact that all the Beria men, and Beria himself, had been tried behind closed doors. Clean and honest actions are not done in the dark. If they had been tried publicly it may not have been necessary later to fill even a single cell in Vladimir with genuine state criminals . . .

Nevertheless, not long afterwards, in 1963, an enigmatic change occurred in the treatment of Beria's men. Their blankets were taken away, the cloth disappeared from the table and their cell became more like all the rest. Parcels for them were also limited to the usual norm: two a year of no more than ten pounds apiece. Instantly a change took place in the men themselves and in the relations between them. The calm, friendly atmosphere disappeared in a trice. The Beria men's cell became one of the most disorderly in the whole block. Hardly had these recent heroes finished the food from their last parcel than they fell upon one another over a stinking prison sprat. The sprats were usually given to a whole cell in a single bowl. The cons would then each take one in a special order, so that everyone had a fair chance. But the Beria men could never agree on who was to go first and so they always went out of turn and quarrelled.

In our cell at that time there was a fellow called Volodya. The moment he heard the servers giving out the sprats to the Beria men next door he used to jeer loudly about the friendship and solidarity shown by these prize sons of the people. Once or twice he got the cooler for it, but still he could never resist it. Not even wolves, he said, would attack one another, yet these savaged each other over a rotten sprat. They were worse than wolves.

Exercise

PRISONERS ARE let out for exercise once a day—for an hour on normal regime and half an hour on strict. You would think they would be in a tearing hurry to burst out of their stinking cells into the open air, and that it would be far more fun to move about an exercise yard than to take it in turns pacing a narrow cell. Nevertheless in winter the warders have to drive the cons out for exercise, nobody wants to go, although in the end they are forced to, for it's in the regulations. Exercise in winter is just one more form of punishment and torture, particularly for the old and the sick (the doctors excuse you from it only when you're on your last legs).

Twenty to thirty degrees of frost. All we have to wear over our cotton prison rig are our reefer jackets or quilted coats, and these are all tattered and torn, patched and patched again, washed and washed again. 'Older than Soviet power', as the cons say, or: 'Seven quarters have been buried in this jacket already' (a 'quarter' is a con with a twenty-five-year sentence). The remaining padding has gone into lumps and the wind blows straight through you. On your head you have an equally ancient padded cap with ear flaps. You have nothing to wrap round your neck—whoever had a scarf or a sweater, or warm underwear or warm socks, had it all taken away on the very first day. On your feet you have ankle boots over the thinnest and scantiest of already transparent foot-rags. Gloves are forbidden. We are all haggard and emaciated and haven't a trace of body heat, we have been too frozen in our cells. We stamp about the tiny yard, with our hands in our sleeves and our heads lowered, trying with our shoulders, if nothing else, to protect our noses from the frost and the wind. Some of the men, those who have no strength left at all, slump down in the corner by the fence and just sit there huddled up for a whole hour, slowly freezing.

Returning to the cell after an exercise period it is impossible to get warm for the rest of the day. And how can you? Hot water comes twice a day, morning and evening. It is so cold in the cell that when the kettle is brought you have to cover it with somebody's jacket and a blanket to stop it going cold in the twenty minutes before breakfast is brought. At night, in order not to freeze completely to death, you pile on top of you all the rags you can find. Nobody ever uses the mattress covers, which are supposed to take the place of sheets, the way they are intended. Instead of covering the mattress with it you put it on top, pile on your blanket, reefer jacket, cotton jacket and trousers and then crawl inside. But for me even that wasn't enough, I used to get right underneath. After all, it meant two layers instead of one and the mattress prevented draughts from underneath. And even then I froze, and I was only 24–25 years old. What must it have been like for the old men?

In my early days at Vladimir the exercise periods were far jollier than they became later. We used to be let out into the old exercise yards, which were fairly big—for three to four cells at a time. And only a ramshackle wooden fence separated us from the adjoining yard with another fifteen to twenty cons in it. At that time I got to know lots of cons from the other cells. You could even push a note to a friend through one of the cracks in the fence, though of course you had to make sure you weren't seen by the warder. The warder during this time used to walk up and down a raised board-walk overlooking the yard, while others would keep watch on us through the peephole. Still, they couldn't keep their eye on us all when there were so many of us.

But then one day they built new exercise yards in Vladimir prison. Each one the size of a cell for five, each one equipped with a door with a peephole, and with a concrete floor and concrete walls (those were plastered with roughcast so that nothing could be scratched on them). In other words, another cell only with the roof off. And they started taking us out one cell at a time. In winter it was intolerably cold in that concrete box. But in summer, although it was dreary and not a leaf or a blade of grass was to be seen, still the sun shone overhead and not even the warder on his boardwalk could cut off its rays or keep out the fresh, free smells.

On the other hand you lost your exercise period for the slightest infringement in summer. But in winter they never deprived you of it!

Tkach

I DON'T remember which cell this happened in: like all the other cons I was frequently transferred from cell to cell. As usual there were five of us: Richardas Kekshtas, Pyotr Glynya, Kostya Pintya from Moldavia, old man Tkach and myself. Tkach was a Ukrainian and had been inside, so he said, for seventeen years already—for belonging to a national liberation movement. Like the rest of us he started off in Mordovia and had then been transferred to the prison at Vladimir for failing to fulfil his norm, for his religious beliefs and one or two other crimes of a similar sort. The old man was a bit peculiar and no longer quite normal, or 'gone' as the cons used to say, putting a finger to their temple and eloquently twisting it round. Quite small, with a large bald patch on his head, a long emaciated face and incredibly huge ears, he used to sit on his bunk and spend all his time gazing tensely and fearfully at his cell-mates. He was afraid of everyone and everything. Whenever one of us joked that Tkach's ears weren't his own and must have been stolen, the old man didn't fully understand the joke and would smile at us timidly and ingratiatingly.

One day he secretly asked Kekshtas what sort of a man I was and why I was always silent—and it was true that I almost never talked. Kekshtas knew me very well, we had been inside together over a year by now, migrating from cell to cell, and he also knew my ingrown character and that my reluctance to talk was partly explained by my constantly increasing deafness. To Tkach, though, he said:

'Don't you know he's a cannibal? He's in for eating one old fellow just like yourself. There was one con sleeping here in this bunk of yours and he chewed off both his heels'.

The old man didn't want to believe him at first.

'You just watch out and see the way he looks at your ears', said Kekshtas, 'you'd better take care of them, otherwise he might eat them'.

Tkach was alarmed. I had only to sit down on the bench beside him and he would jump up and move to somewhere else. He even started to eat his meals in his bunk instead of coming to the table. At night he continued to go to bed with his hat on just as he had done before, because of the cold, but now he also started to wrap up his ears. Kekshtas had told me about his joke during one of the exercise periods and I played up to it. As soon as I caught Tkach's fearful glance upon me I would begin to stare at one or the other of his ears; and once, when he was sitting on the bench, I came up behind him and tweaked his ear. The poor fellow glanced round, caught sight of me and turned to stone. He clapped his hands over his ears, ran to his bunk and for a long time remained sitting there, unable to bring himself to lower his hands from his head. The whole cell rocked with laughter. Kekshtas, after he had recovered from his merriment, asked me:

'Well, tell us then, Anatoly, which are tastier—Tkach's ears or Volodya's heels?'

And I replied seriously:

'Tkach's ears, I should think: I'm sure if they were grilled they'd be as crunchy as a piglet's.'

Tkach looked at me in horror, he was thoroughly convinced now that he was facing a cannibal.

I should point out that Tkach believed in Kekshtas's story not only because he was cracked; everyone who had done time in Vladimir knew of cases even more horrifying than cannibalism. In one cell, for instance, the cons had done as follows: they had got hold of a razor blade somewhere and for several days collected up paper. When everything was ready they each cut a piece of flesh from their bodies—some from the stomach, others from the leg. Everybody's blood was collected into one bowl, the flesh was thrown in, a small fire was made from the paper and some books and then they started to half-fry, half-stew their feast. When the warders noticed that something was wrong and burst into the cell the stew was still not cooked and the cons, falling over themselves and burning their fingers, grabbed the pieces from the bowl and stuffed them into their mouths. Even the warders said afterwards that it was a horrible sight.

I can well imagine that this story is hard to believe! But later I personally met some of the participants in that terrible feast and talked with them. The most remarkable thing of all was that they were fully normal people. I am not Tkach and this is no cock and bull story. I myself saw Yuri Panov from that cell—there wasn't a clear place on his whole body. Apart from this instance when Panov and the others decided to feast on their own flesh, he was known more than once to have cut off pieces of his body and thrown them out to the warders through the food flap. Several times he slit his stomach open so that his innards came flopping out; he also slit his veins, went on prolonged hunger strikes and swallowed all sorts of odds and ends, so that they used to have to cut open his stomach and belly in hospital. . . . Nevertheless he emerged alive from Vladimir and went on to camp seven and later eleven. We used to talk about him to Yuli Daniel when he turned up in camp eleven and became friendly with our group. Yuli didn't want to believe it at first and then started to ask us to introduce him to Panov. But it turned out that he and Panov met each other not through us but through admin: Yuli landed up in the cooler and Panov was there too, and then they were all taken to the bath house. . . . Yuli told us afterwards that he almost fainted when he saw Panov naked.

And yet Yuri Panov was completely normal, not at all cracked, though it was true he was no political, although he was in on a political charge.

In our group in camp eleven we often discussed the problem of how to explain to people outside about all these incidents, which were difficult even to believe. Well, all right, suppose that all these people were abnormal. Why, then, should they be held in prison or in a work camp? Even according to the law they should have been transferred to a psychiatric sanatorium or handed over to their relatives for observation. And if nevertheless they are kept in prison and if all the doctors and commissions consider them normal, then what sort of conditions must they be that drive them to such savage acts? Outside the prison that same Panov wouldn't have dreamed of cutting off and frying his own flesh—unless he had truly gone mad. These are the sort of things that our society should ponder, except that of course nobody knows a thing about it. . . .

But let me continue with Tkach's story. For a certain time he believed I was a cannibal and carefully guarded his ears. Then one day we got food from the shop. All of us were allowed provisions to the value of one ruble twenty-five copecks—all, that is, except Tkach. He had nobody left at all who could send him money for the shop: some of his family had been driven out or shot by the Germans, others had been exiled in Siberia and had disappeared from view. We subsequently attempted to write to our own families to send money to Tkach, but all our requests were struck out by the censorship. And so we were obliged to share with the luckless old man. Pintya, Kekshtas and I had each bought two loaves of bread, a little margarine and some cheese or sausage. Each of us gave half a loaf to Tkach so that all three had one and a half loaves each. The same took place with the margarine and all the rest. After he had drunk a bit and started on the bread and margarine, Tkach said:

'No, Tolik's no cannibal.'

Kekshtas endeavored to keep the joke going:

'Do you mean to say that because he shares with you he's not a cannibal? He's cunning. I know him of old. He's just fattening you up. You don't think he'd feed you his bread for nothing!'

Tkach was on the point of believing him and looked fearfully in my direction, but I couldn't keep a straight face any longer and burst out laughing. Then Tkach laughed too and after him everyone else joined in. After that, although he still kept his cap on in bed, he didn't wrap his ears up any more.

This old man of ours was not only cracked but also very weak physically. He was always complaining about pains in his head, pains in his spine, pains in his heart. One day the two of us applied to see the doctor. During her rounds the nurse always asks through the food trap: 'Is anybody sick?' Almost all the cons complain about some ailment or other, especially in winter and then the nurse, not bothering to examine the patient, gives him some sort of powder. But if the complaint exceeds her competence she registers the con for a visit to the block doctor. The list is usually massive: practically everyone is sick. Then the nurse takes it upon herself, at her own discretion, to cross off the 'unnecessary' ones. The session with the doctor takes place in the presence of a warder and all the patients from one cell are taken together. Thus Tkach and I were taken by a warder to see the doctor. Unfortunately I don't remember her surname, but her first name was Galina. She started off by asking the old man her usual question:

'What's wrong with you?'

'Oh, doctor, I've got pains everywhere, help me.'

'You can't have them everywhere.'

'I've got pains all over, my dear. . . .'

'Venereal pains as well?' asked Galina sarcastically, exchanging glances with the warder.

'What's that?'

'I mean have you got pains in your trousers?'

'Oh, yes, yes, in my trousers too.'

'Shame on you, old man, getting mixed up with pederasts at your time of life.'

Only then did Tkach realize what the young woman meant. He told her that on prison rations not even young men could feel desire for a pederast, nor for a woman either. What he meant was that he was passing blood and suffered from sharp pains (in our cell only Pintya was without hemorrhoids, and then, probably, only because he was a 'new boy'—just in from outside). Galina told Tkach to drop his trousers, turn round and bend over.

'Yes, you've got hemorrhoids. How many times a day do you evacuate?'

'Once every two days, or sometimes three.'

'Well, what do you expect then? You should evacuate at least twice a day.'

'Evacuate what, my dear? The skilly? There's nothing in it but water.'

'I can't help you there, the food isn't my department. All I'm telling you is: with hemorrhoids you should evacuate twice a day. And also bathe the place with warm water. . . .'

Tkach complained about the pains in his head and spine. They measured his blood pressure—it was high.

'It's all right, everyone has high blood pressure at your age, and they also get pains in the spine.'

'Doctor, at least give me permission to lie down during the day.'

Galina wouldn't hear of it. If she let people like Tkach lie down she'd have to put the whole block on hospital regime.

Then I went through exactly the same procedure: 'Turn round . . . hemorrhoids . . . you should evacuate more often . . . bathe in warm water.' My ears were extremely painful, but Galina refused to look at them: 'I'm not a specialist, we don't have an ear specialist in the jail, you have to wait until they get one from town.'

In the two years I was there the ear specialist visited Vladimir jail just once. I managed to see him and he prescribed me hydrogen peroxide for two weeks. The drops didn't help me, of course, but there was no one to check up on this, and who knew when the ear specialist would be invited back to the prison. Anyway, not only Galina but I myself even could have prescribed hydrogen peroxide—you don't need to be a specialist for that. Galina, however, wouldn't do it. She was there not so much to treat the sick as to see that the formalities were carried out. I don't know whether today there are any doctors in the camps and jails who try to alleviate the sufferings of people who are in any case so unfortunate to begin with. There were once, but in the years from 1961 to 1966 I didn't meet any.

And so Tkach and I returned to our cell equipped with the valuable advice to evacuate more often and bathe ourselves with warm water. But how? Hot water was brought to the cell just before breakfast and supper, and it cooled in fifteen to twenty minutes. This meant that we would have to bathe our backsides just as our cell-mates were sitting down to their grub—and under their very noses. Such curative treatment had to be renounced.

Tkach grew worse and worse, he groaned with pain, froze and was unable to warm himself. If only they would let the man lie down, if only they would excuse him the exercise periods—it was the middle of winter! But no. We, his cellmates, appealed to the prison authorities; and we complained to the warders and the officers that the old man was weakening and that they might at least let him lie down for a while during the day. They told us that the doctor knew best who was fit and who sick. Tkach got so chilled that he couldn't bend his fingers any more and was unable to roll himself any cigarettes. Kekshtas used to make him enough in the mornings to last the whole day. I also tried rolling him some, but it didn't work, I had never smoked in my life. On the other hand I gave the old man all my tobacco, so that at least he had enough smokes. He grew very attached to us and was always afraid that they might take him out of our cell.

One evening they brought us our supper—the usual, watery mashed potato. As always we dealt with it in thirty seconds, licked out our bowls and were already starting to rinse them when we noticed that Tkach was still fiddling around with his.

'Hello, grandad,' said Pintya, 'I see you've got a piece of meat in your bowl by mistake. And seeing that you're toothless, you can give it to me if you like.'

Everyone laughed. Tkach finished his mashed potato,

poured some water into his bowl from the kettle, rinsed it sitting down and then went to the sloptank to empty it. Beside the sloptank the bowl fell from his fingers and rolled over the concrete floor, while he himself started to grope and feel for the wall—and then collapsed on the ground. We rushed over to him, lifted him and placed him on his cot. He seemed to be still alive. We started banging on the door and calling the warder. We heard his voice from the far end of the corridor:

'What's all that banging for? Is it the cooler you want?'

He came along and looked through the peephole. Learning what the matter was, he went to call the senior warder. About fifteen minutes went by, nobody came and we started to bang on the door again. The duty warder bellowed:

'Stop that noise! The senior warder will be here as soon as he's free—you're not important!'

After another ten minutes or so the senior warder came, unlocked the door and entered the cell.

'Well, what's going on in here?'

Once more we explained what had happened. He took Tkach's wrist and felt for the pulse. The old man was lying there without moving or breathing. But the senior warder was in no hurry to call the nurse or the doctor, he started to question us instead: how did it happen, who was doing what at the time, and who had seen what. Then he left with a promise to call the nurse. Another ten minutes passed and the nurse arrived, accompanied, as always, by a retinue of warders. She too felt for the pulse—there wasn't any. Then she soaked a piece of cotton wool in sal-ammoniac and held it under the old man's nose. It was no use. Tkach didn't move. She left the cotton wool on his upper lip and gave him some sort of injection. Tkach didn't come round. Then the nurse asked the senior warder to fetch the duty doctor from the hospital block. The doctor came, looked at Tkach, felt his pulse and quietly laid the limp arm across his breast. Then, after questioning us as to what had happened, she called the senior warder outside. She never appeared again, but the senior warder came back and ordered Kekshtas and me to carry the old man out. I took him under the arms, Kekshtas took the legs, and we dragged the body into an empty cell that was indicated to us. There the warder ordered us to lay the dead man on a bare cot and then hurried us out again. The cell was locked. I said to the warder:

'I suppose Tkach can lie on his cot till lights out now, can he?'

'Do you want to go in the cooler?' roared the warder as usual.

Tkach was dead. He had been completely alone, nobody had ever helped him and he never ever received any letters from anyone. But maybe he has relatives somewhere who lost touch with him and don't know what became of him. And so: old man Tkach starved for many years, suffered, fell ill, froze and died in Vladimir Prison in the winter of 1962.

Pyotr Glynya

GLYNYA HAD also been in a long time and always in prison—he had never been in a camp. His very first sentence, therefore, must have been direct to prison. But nobody knew what he had been sentenced for and it was absolutely impossible to understand him.

Glynya was formally insane and totally cracked. He was always muttering to himself and occasionally he would come out with a phrase like: 'I'm a Soviet agent!' He used to tell us quite seriously that Stalin himself had called him into his office and held a secret conversation with him, at which only Beria had been present. What the conversation was about, Glynya never said: evidently he didn't want to broadcast this important secret. He had been given some sort of task by Stalin and Beria and that was all.

Occasionally he talked as though he had a wife and daughter in Paris and would start to tell us all about France and Germany. None of us had ever been there so we couldn't check on how much of it was true or not. Anyway, you can't make much sense out of the ravings of a lunatic. Nevertheless he really did know German and apparently knew it well.

One day Glynya asked me to write him a petition to the Director of Military Prosecutions. My cell-mates also persuaded me: 'Go on, Tolik, write it!' I realized that what they all wanted to find out was what this fellow was in for. I was also curious and so I agreed: 'Go on then, tell me all about it.'

At this, Glynya started babbling such utter nonsense that there was no question of being able to make sense of it: some swamp where he had collected ducks' eggs and chased snakes, tasks given him by Stalin and Beria, Soviet agent, France, Germany, and again the swamp with the ducks' eggs.

And so we never did discover what it was that Glynya had been given 25 years for.

Vitya Kedrov

AT ONE time I shared a cell with a former criminal con named Vitya Kedrov. Now he was in on a political charge—'anti-Soviet agitation', I think—which he had acquired in a criminal camp. He had been imprisoned many times before and had been in those terrifying camps about which stories and anecdotes are now gradually beginning to appear. Thus there's no point, I think, in me retelling the recollections of Vitya and those other cons who had done time in the logging camps, the pits and the mines, in Kolyma, Norilsk, Vorkuta, Taishet, Magadan, Djezkaztan. . . . Vitya had lost the fingers of one hand—he had caught them in a circular saw. There was nothing new in this incident either.

Vitya tortured us in the way Ivan Mordvin had done in my other cell: for hours he used to stand at the food trap begging for something to eat. 'Keep me here as long as you like,' he used to whine, 'but don't kill me with hunger!' Naturally they never once gave him anything, but every day he would insist: 'Keep me here as long as you like, but don't kill me with hunger!'

We tried to shame him out of it—what did he think he was doing! He told me that in other cells they had even beaten him up because of it; and in our cell too it almost came to a fight. Nevertheless he just had to keep clinging to that food trap: 'Go on, give me something. Keep me here as long as you like, but don't kill me with hunger!'

The Bath House

WE WERE taken to the bath house at Vladimir once every ten days. There you got a change of underwear, a fresh so-called towel (which was just as much of a rag as the one you handed in), and on every other visit—that is, once every twenty days—a change of 'bed linen', i.e. mattress cover and pillow case. There they also cropped us—head and face at the same time, it was all the same to them. Over ten days, of course, we used to acquire quite a growth, so that we were afraid to look at one another. And we all looked so wild that anyone seeing us would be bound to think: 'Genuine desperadoes, wild beasts.'

In the summer we awaited our bath with impatience and counted the days, we couldn't wait to splash about in that water! And to have an extra walk in the sunshine, in the fresh air. They used to take us through the prison yard, with not a tree or a bush in sight, only the gray walls of the blocks with their barred windows and the bare asphalt underfoot. And nevertheless, sometimes you would catch sight of a pitiful blade of grass forcing its way upwards. But you couldn't go up to it, much less bend down: 'Not one step out of line. Keep your hands behind your back. No talking and no smoking.' That's what we were warned every time they took us to the bath house.

But although every step and every action in prison is anticipated and laid down, point by point, paragraph by paragraph, unforeseen incidents do sometimes occur. One day we were on our way to the bath house. We were passing the hospital block when we ran into the hospital director, a woman. Evidently she was on her way to work (it was about nine o'clock in the morning). Suddenly we heard a yell from the top story of the hospital block and something fell right at her feet. The woman bent over, looked at it, and spat. Just then we arrived opposite her and saw, lying on the asphalt, a bloody, amputated male member. Apparently some poor creature in the hospital had resolved to mutilate himself in that way and then, peeping out of the window, had tossed this 'present' to her through the ventilation flap. What, I wonder, had she done to him to provoke him to seek that sort of revenge.

The bath house had two sorts of facilities for washing—one a room with benches and basins, the others with showers in individual cubicles. We were sent in two cells at a time, one into the washroom, the other to the showers. To get a shower was tremendous luck and sheer bliss: you were able to wash properly, instead of standing in line for basins and then for water. You were able to stand there and spend the whole time scrubbing yourself, with the water pouring over you ceaselessly (although even then they used to push two or three into a cubicle meant for one). The only trouble was that this bliss always ended too quickly—you never had time to soap yourself a second time before the warders turned the water off and herded you outside again. That's why everyone tried to give himself at least one thorough soaping and to fill his dipper with a second lot of clean water, so as to rinse himself off at the end. If you managed it you were lucky, but sometimes you wouldn't even have time to get the soap off, and then you simply had to rub it off with your towel. In between baths the whole cell would be guessing: will it be the showers next time, or the washroom?

In winter, on the other hand, the bath house is just another form of torture. The newcomer, who still doesn't know about it, looks forward to having a thorough wash and warming himself up with hot water—after all, it's a bath, isn't it? If only it were like that! In winter it's so cold in the changing room that steam comes out of your mouth and the walls are sometimes covered with a white frost. You undress and stand there naked and blue, your skin covered in goose pimples. Then you wait there, in a filthy temper, for them to let you into the washroom, and you can feel the cold piercing you to the very kidneys. Afterwards you dress in that same icy cold and shuffle back through the frost to your block. . . . Old men were particularly afraid of the baths in winter and Tkach, for example, had to be driven there by force, just as he had for exercise.

Washing of any kind in prison in winter is real torture. Even washing during the toilet break. The water comes out the tap so cold that even I, a Siberian and a young man, used to feel my hands go numb and lose all sensation. Possibly, of course, this wasn't because of the iciness of the water but because of our permanent state of general exhaustion.

We were usually taken to the bath house by two warders, Vanya and Sanya. Vanya was short, dark and bad-tempered. His nickname was 'Gipsy'. At the slightest excuse he started bellowing, cursing, threatening and pummeling you. Sanya, his bosom pal, was the complete opposite: tall, white, leisurely and calm. He was calm when he stuck you in the cooler and calm when beating up a prisoner in the company of other warders. Sanya's nickname was 'The Beak' (he had a really enormous nose). And so it was usually Vanya the Gipsy and Sanya the Beak who took us to the bath house—if they weren't both together then invariably one or the other went along. Their greatest pleasure was to turn the water off in such a way that some of us were still covered in soap. It was they, too, who forcibly cropped the newcomers—that Ukrainian with the moustache I mentioned was one of their victims and the two of them had manhandled me too and held me down for the barber.

Equality of the Sexes

THERE WAS an official linen store in the bath house and in charge of it at that time was a woman of about thirty-five: she was a 'free' worker from outside and her name was Shura. Sanya the Beak was courting her. Courting her, did I say? Well, in his own way, of course—mauling her and pinching her. As far as we cons were concerned, who were forced willy-nilly to be present during their games, neither of them paid the slightest bit of attention. And anyway 'present' wasn't really the word! Naked as the day we were born, we had to wait there in the corridor to be shorn before going on to get washed. Shura never once missed this performance and used to sit there in front of us and mess around with Sanya. I think that having us naked men there looking at them even gave a special piquancy to their slapping and tickling. Or maybe they just didn't notice us—cons weren't really people, were they?

Apart from men warders we also had some women warders in our block. And they too used to watch us through the peephole and could come into the cell at any time. You could be standing at the sloptank to relieve yourself and it was quite possible that at that moment you were being watched by a wardress. And because of this, even though we were used to it, we constantly felt even more humiliated and embittered.

One day the following incident occurred in the cell I was in. One of the prisoners, called Yuri, went to the sloptank to relieve himself; and the sloptank stood right in front of the peephole. A wardress peered in and saw that a con was standing in front of her and blocking the whole cell (usually, if somebody in the cell was working at a tattoo or something else forbidden by the regulations, one of the others would stand 'on guard', blocking the peephole. By the time the warder had had a slanging match with him and then opened the cell, the 'working' cons would have time to clear everything away, hide it and adopt completely innocent expressions). The wardress, therefore, started to shout at Yuri to move away from the door. Her shouts brought the senior warder running and they opened the door, came in and suspiciously inspected us and the whole cell. The wardress pointed to Yuri: 'He's the one who was blocking the peephole.'

The senior warder threatened him with the cooler for breaking regulations. Then Yuri proposed that they either move the sloptank away from the door, or else put a peephole down lower:

'This way she couldn't see what I had in my hand and now I'll never be excused. . . .'

As usual the warders swore at us, threatened us with the cooler and went out. We had got off lightly—Yuri could easily have got the cooler for his impudence.

When the wardresses were on duty they also used to take us out for the toilet break. And they would watch through the latrine peephole to make sure that we broke no regulations. And male warders used to keep watch on women prisoners. And they too used to take them out for toilet break and peer through the peepholes into their cells at any time of the day or night.

At first the women politicals were kept on the second floor of our block. Among them there were dozens from the Ukraine and the Baltic states—in for 'nationalism'; and there were also religious believers. Some of them had been in Vladimir jail for ten to fifteen years or more. One day we were coming back from our bath and the women were returning from exercise, and we saw them at a distance. We also saw some old women being helped along by their younger companions. The women, just like us, had had all their warm clothes taken away and were also being driven out to exercise in winter in flimsy jackets and cold boots and also made to take cold baths and were also worn down with hunger. Prison regime was exactly the same for everyone, for both men and women. In this respect there was complete equality.

Prison Service

IN PRISON there are all sorts of unskilled jobs that have to be done outside the cells: cleaning, serving the food, stoking the boilers, and so on. Prisoners are appointed to do this work from within the block, so that the cleaners, servers and 'boiler-man' were cons just like the rest of us. In the store-room the assistant to the storekeeper, Shura, was an Estonian prisoner called Jan—he it was who did all the work for her, carrying bales about, changing our underwear and handing out the bed linen. Only when somebody received something that was in absolute tatters and impossible to put on, and then kicked up a fuss about it to Jan, did Shura herself intervene.

The cons on prison service lived in two separate cells, but also under lock and key the whole time, just like the rest of us. They were taken out only for the duration of their duties. They also got the same rations as the rest of us, except that they had an extra 4 ozs. of bread—22 ozs. instead of 18. Thus life for them was marginally better, they were 4 ozs. fuller and freer to about the same degree.

Nevertheless working in prison service was not easy, especially for the food servers. They, after all, spent their whole time trying to feed starving men—and what with? The kitchen would send along huge vats full of skilly, but when the servers started to ladle it into the bowls it turned out to be all water. Yet in every cell the cons would be crowding up to the food trap and begging for some of the thicker stuff, and then would listen to hear what sort of skilly was being poured into the bowls at the next cell. Each prisoner thought that his neighbor was getting a better portion. If somebody got a potato in his bowl two days running they immediately suspected the server of favoring one of 'his own'. And it went without saying, of course, that the server always had thick stuff out of the bottom and lived only for his belly. What this thick stuff was thought to be, God only knows, when the whole vat had nothing but water in it, without a solid grain in it.

Some of the cons on prison service were widely respected, you could see that they were honest and fair to the highest degree. Others were regarded with suspicion and distrust, and some even with hatred. Threats were made: 'Just you wait till we're in the same camp together and then I'll get even with you.' I remember a certain server called Roman who came from Vladimir to camp seven. On his very first day in the canteen, Kolya Grigoryev—also an old Vladimir hand—poured a bowl of hot soup over his head; and later that same Roman was secretly beaten up—he must have given good cause to be hated.

Religious Prisoners

THIS IS the term used to describe prisoners who have been jailed for believing in God. They aren't the only people who believe in God, there are other cons who believe as well. But religious prisoners are the ones who have been arrested and tried precisely because of their religion. And what variety there is! Moslems from the Caucasus and Central Asia, Orthodox Christians, Baptists, Jehovah's Witnesses, Evangelists, Sabbatarians and many others.

Our newspapers sometimes carry stories about the crimes of various fanatical sects and about ritual murders, the torturing of children and so on. I find them difficult to believe. How many people did I see at Vladimir or in the camps who belonged to these various sects and not one of them had even committed a murder. They were all dead against killing and the use of force. And of the religious prisoners in the political camps not one had ever been convicted of murder. Those accused of murder are usually tried for 'anti-Soviet propaganda'—if, for example, they say that all political power including Soviet power, comes not from God but the devil, or from harboring and distributing anti-Soviet literature. Like the rest of us they are tried in secret, and only the ones tried for murder are brought before an open court. Then they say of all religious believers and members of sects: 'Look what they're like—fanatics!'

The fanaticism of religious prisoners is expressed only in their insistence on retaining their own religious beliefs and customs. They are extremely quiet and humble people, old men for the most part of about 60 or over, although there are young ones among them as well. Their attitude to imprisonment is somewhat different from that of the other cons: they take consolation from the fact that they are suffering for their god and their faith and they are patient in bearing their sufferings and pain. Once I heard some of them sing the following song:

'. . .The Savior bore His cross with nought but prayer,
He did not complain to the Father about His foes,
His was a marvellous example of suffering,
For the flame that burned inside Him was holy love.'

And nevertheless these men, who were humble and obedient in everything not touching upon their faith, were dispatched to Vladimir—for failing to fulfil the norm, for refusing to work on religious holidays. Here, in the cells, I was thrown together with large numbers of them. Almost every cell had its Evangelist, Sabbatarian, or Jehovah's Witness, and in some cells there were several together. The prison authorities humiliated them in every possible way. I had seen that on my very first day. Many believers had a rule that they must wear beards, yet they were all forcibly shaven while wearing handcuffs.

And what about fasting? You might well wonder how fasting could possibly come into it when in general there was nothing to eat, when day in and day out consisted of nothing but one long fast lasting for years on end and when men were half dead with exhaustion! But most believers wanted to observe the rules of fasting even here when the right time came around, and that when in prison you eat what you're given! 'Even with a microscope you won't find any fat in prison skilly', we argued with them, 'every day's the same!' 'Ah, but you never know,' they replied. 'A little bit of fat is supposed to be included according to regulations and maybe they put it in.'

The warders knew this. And so on fast days they would serve the skilly first to those cells with believers in them. In a full vat, perhaps, there would be one little blob of fat floating on top—so why not make sure that it went into the bowl of someone who observed the fasts? That way he wouldn't eat it and nobody else would get a chance. Generally speaking the religious believers, knowing they would be served from the top of a full vat, were afraid to eat for fear of committing a sin. And when they had tumbled to this trick of the warders they started refusing any hot food at all on fast days and abided by bread and water.

In the starvation conditions prevailing at Vladimir not everyone had the strength to keep up the fasts and refuse food. Then the warders and officers would start to jeer at them: 'You're talking a load of old rubbish when you say you believe, what sort of God is that, it's all put on!' And whenever a religious prisoner went to the doctor in prison they would say: 'Don't come to see me, sign up for an examination with that God of yours and let him make you better.'

The Mentally Sick

I OFTEN heard various cons say that if you thought seriously about it, there wasn't one normal man amongst us. In such inhuman conditions and seeing the sort of things that we were forced to see, it was impossible to preserve a sound mind. Especially at Vladimir.

But apart from this universal deviation from the norm, there was hardly a cell in Vladimir Prison that was without at least one con who was well and truly 'cracked'. Some used to gabble nonsense, while others made up all sorts of untrue stories about themselves. And there were also violent ones. I don't know whether they first cracked up as a result of long years of imprisonment or whether that's how they were when they were jailed, but sharing a cell with them was sheer torture. And the authorities purposely didn't segregate them. On the contrary: if there were two lunatics in one cell, they would be split up and put in separate ones so as to poison the existence of two cells instead of one. And it was useless to complain.

In one cell there was a con called Screwy Sanya. By day he was quiet and meek, sitting on his bunk without talking to anyone and plunged in thought the whole time. When lights out was called, Sanya would lie down and wait till all the

others were sleeping. Then he would get up, go over to somebody's cot and urinate all over his sleeping cell-mate. What's
more he tried, if possible, to make sure it went in his face,
and this every night. They tried keeping watch over him and
took it in turns not to sleep. But the whole thing was impossible: all cons had to be in bed after lights out, it was forbidden either to stand, to sit or to read lying down. Just try not
to sleep, especially when you can't catch up during the
day. And so it came about that the 'watchman', more often
than not, awoke soaking wet. They also tried beating Sanya,
although they realized he was a sick man. But if the warders
found out about it, they would whisk the culprit away to the
cooler while Sanya, as before, continued to do his business
every night.

In another cell there was a completely quiet lunatic who
never touched anyone. He even bore himself with a special
kind of dignity and looked down on the others. His peculiar-
ity, however, was that he insisted on mixing all his food with
the contents of the sloptank. Whenever dinner or supper was
brought, each man would take his bowl and sit somewhere to
eat. He, though, would go over to the sloptank, lift the lid,
scoop some of the contents into his bowl and begin diligently
to stir it. But that wasn't all. He would then walk round to
everyone in the cell and press them to have some: 'Try it. My
mummy used to make my porridge that way when I was
small, it's very tasty!' Then he would stick it under their
noses while they were trying to eat. Afterwards he would sit
at the communal table and eat it, forgetting all his dignity
now and champing away, smacking his lips and covering
himself all over in 'mummy's porridge'. After dinner he
would pour water into his bowl, rinse it round and then
drink it.

There were also the sort of lunatics who used to tear all their clothing off and walk about the cell naked. Whatever clothes they were given they would rip them to shreds and stuff them into the sloptank. At least they weren't sent out to exercise. But they never lasted long. They caught pneumonia and died.

The Man Who Hanged Himself

AT ONE time I shared a cell with a fellow called Sergei and he told me about the following incident concerning himself.

Once he had spent fifteen days in the cooler and he came out half dead, 'holding on to the wall'. He thought and he thought: how could he improve his conditions a bit, if only a fraction, if only for a short time? The best would be to go to hospital, but how? He made up his mind to 'hang himself'— not completely, not so as to die, but enough to be taken to hospital.

At that particular moment he was alone in the cell. He tore his mattress cover into strips, plaited them into rope, made a loop and prepared to hang himself. There was a lamp over the door of the cell, set back in a niche with a grille over the front. Sergei calculated the time when the warder would be walking away from his cell, climbed up on to the sloptank, tied the rope to the grille, put the noose around his neck and waited. And everything happened just the way he had calculated.

The warder came back to the peephole, looked inside and saw a con's stomach directly in front of him. He guessed at once: 'The con has hanged himself!' As he began rattling his keys and unlocking the door, Sergei slowly slid off the sloptank. The rope went taut and he hung there, but he still hadn't lost consciousness because the noose hadn't tightened. Sergei knew in advance that he wouldn't have time to be strangled: the warder was already opening the door and entering, and soon would be taking him down. He was already choking as he felt the warder take him by the wrist, feel for his pulse and realize that he was still alive. But then, instead of taking him down, the warder began to pull on Sergei's legs in order to draw the noose tighter. And Sergei lost consciousness.

He came to his senses in the block's medical post. When he was fully conscious again he questioned the nurse on how he had come to be there. The nurse knew nothing of the fact that Sergei had only half hanged himself or that the warder had tried to finish him off. And it came out that only an accident had saved him from death. Just at the time when the warder was in his cell another warder had come into the corridor from the stairs. He had come on business. The man in the cell had then let go of Sergei and called the other to come and help him get the hanged man down. With the two of them there, one of whom would be a witness, he no longer dared to go ahead with the murder. They were all afraid of one another and always informed on each other.

Sergei pointed out 'his' warder to me. It was our senior warder nicknamed 'Ginger'—a real angel without wings. Courteous and good mannered, he never shouted or swore, but spoke with a voice of sweetest balsam.

Now I understood why Sergei twitched all over whenever Ginger came into our cell.

Cell No. 79

I was kept for a time in cell no. 92 and opposite ours was cell no. 79. We usually exercised together, all ten of us, and got to know one another fairly well. I particularly liked one of their prisoners whose name was Stepan. He had been a geography teacher at home in the Ukraine and had already done 13–14 years in jail when I met him, out of a total sentence of 25. He was such a calm and restrained fellow that I envied him.

One day the Legal Inspector of Prisons came into our cell and asked his usual question: 'Any complaints, any questions?' And registering our silence left immediately. He used to make a visit to all the cells. In the early days a few of the cons had gone to him with complaints and protests, but the response was exactly the same as to letters to the Central Committee, to the Public Prosecutor of the USSR and the Presidium of the Supreme Soviet. And so the cons stopped.

Out at exercise the following day we asked the cons from cell 79 whether the Legal Inspector had been to see them.

'Yes, I'll say he has. He and Stepan are old pals.'

Evidently the Inspector had entered cell 79, caught sight of Stepan and looked startled. Then he spoke familiarly to him and asked:

'Are you still here then?'

'As you see!'

The Inspector wriggled and squirmed, said goodbye and went out.

Stepan then told them that they had once shared a cell together for two years in this same jail. In 1956 the other man had been rehabilitated. And now they had met once more in a prison cell, though no longer as two cons but as con and authority. But what could Stepan say to him, this Legal Inspector, about what could he complain? The Inspector knew it all already and had seen for himself, for he wasn't blind.

In the same cell with Stepan were two former criminal cons, Sergei Oransky and Nikolai Kovalyov, nicknamed Vorkuta. They were 'former' criminals only in terms of their charge, for they had merely been re-tried on political grounds and had had their sentences lengthened, as was usually the case. In everything else they were dyed-in-the-wool criminals, corrupted, disorderly and completely senseless.

Both of them, as was customary, were tattooed. Sergei Oransky had on his forehead in tiny, almost imperceptible lettering: 'Slave of the CPSU', while Vorkuta was absolutely smothered in tattoos, with not a clear place to be seen either on his face or body. Later he was put into our cell for a while and I saw how he removed one of the tattoos from his forehead. This is how he did it.

First he took a razor blade and slashed the place all over. Then he began to knead the slits apart with his fingers, rubbing away for ages, all smothered in blood, until what covered his forehead was not so much skin as some sort of bloody shreds. Then he sprinkled his forehead liberally with permanganate of potash—it was issued specially for this purpose at the medical post. The permanganate of potash ate into the wounds and Vorkuta writhed and howled with pain. The following day his forehead was swollen, black, seared by the permanganate of potash and beginning to go septic. But a short time afterwards the skin began to peel off and new skin formed over the wound. The tattoo was gone and in its place remained a huge, ugly scar.

Nevertheless many men with tattoos preferred to get rid of their 'anti-Soviet slogans' in this way, rather than be operated on in the hospital. There they simply cut the skin out without giving any form of anaesthetic, so as to persuade cons not to repeat the process. Sergei Oransky also got rid of his tattoo himself.

After his 'operation' Vorkuta said that the scar would stay big only for a while and afterwards, in the camp, would be tanned by the sun and the wind and become almost unnoticeable. We laughed: 'You would need to be born all over again for your tattoos to be unnoticeable.' Nevertheless he also removed the other tattoos from his face. The scars so disfigured him that he was horrible to look at. Neither time nor sun helped: even after three years you could hardly call his face human.

Both Vorkuta and Sergei used to slash their wrists and Sergei used to slit open his stomach and let his guts fall out, and also swallow all sorts of rubbish. One day the following incident occurred in their cell. One of the inmates was a Hungarian called Anton. I don't remember his surname, but everyone called him The Magyar. The Magyar asked Vorkuta if, the next time he slit his veins open, he would collect the blood in a bowl instead of letting it run to waste on the floor. Vorkuta was taken aback at first and then agreed: 'Why not, why shouldn't I? I shall lose it just the same.'

And so the time came for Vorkuta to slash himself again for the usual sort of reason and The Magyar held up his bowl to catch the blood. The other cons in the cell didn't see this. As soon as they learned that Vorkuta was going to slash himself, they turned their backs and stuck their noses into books. They couldn't help but notice that somebody was moving about behind them, but interfering in such cases was out of the question. Nobody knew of The Magyar's deal with Vorkuta and nobody guessed that he was an interested party.

The Magyar collected half a bowlful of blood, crumbled his bread into it and then started to drink this pottage. Turning round at the click of the spoon, Stepan and another Ukranian called Mikhail saw the following little scene: there sat The Magyar on his cot with the bowl on his knees, scooping up the bloody soup with his spoon and greedily gulping it down. His lips and chin were drenched in blood, blood dripped from his spoon and he kept raising and turning the spoon over in order to lick it clean with his tongue. Realizing what was afoot, Mikhail didn't even make it to the sloptank, but threw up on the spot.

They told us about this incident and said The Magyar had explained to them, without a trace of embarrassment: 'Well, the blood was going to be shed anyway, why let it go to waste?'

Later that same Magyar resolved to go on a secret hunger strike. A secret hunger strike is far more terrible than the usual open one. It usually means that a con has come to the absolute end of his tether and really intends to die. He didn't make any announcements, didn't refuse his food and always accepted his bread, skilly and dinner. But none of it went into his stomach, he secretly handed it round to his cellmates. So it went on for over a week. And all this time, just like the rest of us, he was obliged to go out for toilet breaks and exercise periods and was forbidden to lie down during the day. I used to see him every day in the exercise yard while this was going on and I saw him literally turn into a shadow. How he managed to get up the stairs I will never know! The rest of us all had to hang on to the wall as it was.

On one of these days we were being taken out for our exercise period in the normal way. The Magyar was walking behind me. Suddenly I felt a shove in the back—and he slumped down on to the concrete steps, turned a somersault and rolled down the stairs to the vestibule, where he remained lying. The warders chivvied us and prodded us past him. He lay there like a corpse, with wide-open, glassy eyes.

The next day we learned from cell 79 that The Magyar was alive. Then he was dumped back in his cell and continued his hunger strike, which was official now and not secret.

Return Journey

UNEXPECTEDLY FOR me I was sent back to the camps a year before my prison term was due to end. At that time, at the beginning of the summer of 1963, they started sending quite a lot of cons away from Vladimir—those who only had a short prison term still to do. Who knows, perhaps they needed the room for new arrivals?

In the transit cell I met up with Anatoly Ozerov again, he was also being sent back to Mordovia. During his spell in prison he had gone almost completely blind and it was painful to think how he would now have to grope his way about the camp with a stick, like Blind Sanya. But then I too had gone almost completely deaf and Ozerov was probably regarding me with the same sort of pained sympathy as I him. 'Yes, Tolik, we're not the men we were when we came,' he said.

Burov wasn't there. Could they be making him do the full term?

Black marias, identical prison coaches, the same old transit prisons, only this time in reverse order: Gorky, Ruzayevka, Potma.

At the Gorky transit prison we were taken for a bath. Inside the bath house, in the changing room, sat a duty officer who examined us before we entered the wash room: had anyone tattooed himself on the train? Those with tattoos on their bodies had them copied down—the officer made a list of what and where things were written. Then came the turn of Vorkuta (he too was going back to the camp). Naturally the officer had enough work for an hour! Vorkuta stood in front of him in his dark blue briefs and slowly turned round and round. When the list was finished, the officer said: 'That's the lot, I take it. We haven't left anything out, have we?'

'Yes, we've left out Khrushchev,' replied Vorkuta.

'Khrushchev, where?'

'Khrushchev on my prick.'

'What do you say? Do you want a spell in the cooler?'

'You asked me where Khrushchev was tattooed and I merely told you the truth: on my prick.'

'Show me!'

To the roar of laughter from the other cons, Vorkuta lowered his drawers and showed him: tattooed in large letters along the full length of his penis was: 'Khrushchev'.

'Handsome, isn't it?' said Vorkuta innocently, stroking his Khrushchev tenderly. 'But he's lonely on his own, poor fellow. What he needs is Furtseva* for a bit of collective leadership.'

Lowering his head the officer completed the list.

The bath house at Gorky transit prison is excellent, the best I have ever seen. All the cons praise it and the fame of the Gorky bath house has travelled to all our prison camps.

As usual we travelled the whole way behind tightly closed curtains. They hung between the glass and the bars. From outside you would never have guessed that those ordinary curtains concealed stout iron bars, and that behind the bars

* Mrs. Furtseva is Soviet minister for cultural affairs.

203

were pale faces all covered in coarse stubble. And we, for our part, couldn't see outside.

In Savansk a soldier in the corridor threw back the curtain immediately opposite our barred door. We all rushed to look out. On the platform stood an old woman with a sack, pitifully dressed and wearing bark sandals—a countrywoman of the astronaut, Nikolayev.

PART THREE

Back in Camp

WE ARRIVED in Potma at the beginning of summer and spent several days in the transit jail there. We had to go before a medical commission to be classified for the kind of work we could do. Everybody except Stepan was classified A1, while Stepan, with one leg cut off above the knee, was put in the second or possibly even third category. Our other ailments—hemorrhoids, ruptures and so on—didn't weigh in the balance.

Already here, in the Potma transit prison, I was struck by certain changes and innovations. One block was crammed full with prisoners on special regime and they were all wearing a striped uniform. This uniform is still in use and the cons wearing it are called 'stripeys' or 'tigers'. At Potma at that time they were mainly religious prisoners—for some reason they were now being segregated from the rest and all going on special regime.

After about three or four days we were loaded into 'Stolypins' and distributed around the camps. I landed up in camp seven, together with Ozerov. The station was Sosnovka, not far from Potma.

We were marched from the station under armed guard—tommy gunners with dogs walked ahead, behind and to either side of us. But the road gave me such pleasure that I even forgot about the guards. How fine it was to walk down that simple, trodden road and through a hamlet with a wood standing just behind it! Grass grew on both sides of the road—I hadn't seen any for two years. And now some little wooden houses came into sight and although I knew that guards and warders lived inside them, still the very sight of those peaceful cottages with their two or three windows brought a feeling of joy and relief. As we walked along we filled our lungs with the fresh, tree-scented air and we knew that tomorrow and the next day we would be breathing that same air all the time, and no longer the stifling air of the cells and the exhalations of the sloptank.

And here was the camp, exactly the same as all the other camps: watch towers, barbed wire, perimeter fence, searchlights. . . . Ah, what the hell! At least it wasn't prison with its gray walls and muzzled windows! We waited about forty minutes at the guardhouse. Roll-call, counting, recounting; then we were called out in groups, searched—and let into the camp.

A crowd of cons was waiting inside the guardhouse—those who worked the afternoon and night shifts had come to meet the regular convoy. No sooner had I stepped down from the porch than I was ringed with prisoners and peppered with questions: who was I, what was I in for, how long? But the first question was: 'From Vladimir, eh? You can see that! You'd go to the grave looking better.'

The very first thing they did was take us to the canteen, continuing to question us on the way: do you happen to know so-and-so? Or so-and-so? Do they still stop you from lying down during the day? Did you see Powers? Who's the governor now—Grishin or Tsuplyak? The canteen at camp seven was the same as everywhere else: bare, painted tables, long benches, serving hatches at one end and a stage at the other, with a dais and a large white cloth for a cinema screen. Above and behind the stage and all around the canteen walls hung slogans, placards and photo-montages. But the surroundings were of little interest to me now.

I was made to sit at a table where several cons from our convoy were already hard at work with their spoons. We newcomers were surrounded by a crowd of local veterans, cookhouse hands and cooks in their gray and white overalls. At once a bowl of noodle soup was pushed in front of me and a whole pile of cut bread was placed at my elbow, then they thrust a spoon into my hand and said: 'Eat, dig in.' I stirred the soup with my spoon. It was thin and fatless, even though the cooks had served us with the thick stuff from the bottom. But it seemed to me on that occasion that not even at home had I eaten better noodle soup.

'Well now, brother, is it the same as at Vladimir?'

I replied that you'd get five Vladimir helpings out of a bowl like that.

I wasn't aware myself of how I had emptied the bowl in a flash. At once they took it away and brought it back again brim full: 'Eat up, eat up!' I realized that if I finished this they would bring me yet another. I felt embarrassed at eating so greedily and decided to recoup on the bread. The slices of bread had been cut the full width of the loaf; one slice took me four bites to get through; I was trying to stuff a whole mouthful of bread in one go with each spoonful of soup; and therefore I had to keep stretching out my hand for fresh slices. But this too began to make me feel ashamed. I managed to slow down and not take the bread so often, and when they offered me a third bowl of soup I refused, saying that I was already full. In truth I felt that although I had stuffed my belly full, I could have gone on eating and eating.

As we stood up to leave the canteen the local cons suggested that we take some bread with us. Supper was at five, but at four they served hot water and that way we would have something to eat with it. We almost wept with gratitude.

Such generosity with the bread continued at number seven for about another month or two, you could eat as much as you wanted. But after that, they too started rationing it. But in the camp it didn't matter so much, as I will explain later.

After dinner I went for a walk round the zone. After feeding me they left me alone to look around. The first thing I noticed was the abundance of greenery: there were lots of trees and shrubs, and flower beds had been laid out round the huts, though the flowers hadn't come out yet. There were equally many slogans and placards, but I ignored them and didn't look at them, admiring instead the trees and the grass. There were lots and lots of cons about the zone, in fact there were over three and a half thousand men in the camp, and therefore there were plenty of people about, even during the day when the first shift was at work.

I also noticed that the cons were all dressed identically now, in black cotton tunics, similar trousers, and with black uniform caps on their shaven heads. Two years ago it had been different, then you had been able to wear your own clothes in the living zone. On that hot day, it is true, many had bare heads and wore their tunics flapping open, while a few, stripped to the waist, were even tanning themselves in the sun. (Later, during my last year in camp, we were thoroughly persecuted if we took such liberties and were forced to keep our tunics on no matter how hot it was: 'You're not on holiday now!')

I strolled about in the hope of meeting old acquaintances, but none turned up. A few I recognized by their faces, remembering that I had seen them, I thought, at camp ten, but I couldn't really say I knew them. After all, I had only been there a few months before landing up in jail. And nobody recognized me. Many looked round, it is true, and asked: 'Just out of Vladimir?' And when this was confirmed, remarked: 'I could see you were.'

I went to the barber's. Here there were five con barbers hard at work and long lines of people waiting in front of each one. Once again, though, I experienced an extraordinarily friendly and solicitous attitude towards me on the part of others: guessing that I had just come from prison, they immediately let me go first, without waiting. I sat in the chair of a lame Lithuanian barber and while he shaved me questions rained down on me from all sides. They came from both barbers and customers and the Lithuanian repeated everything into my ear to make sure I understood. How pleasant it was to sit with a clean towel around my neck and to feel for the first time in two years the touch of a shaving brush and soap. Overcome with pleasure, I closed my eyes and tried to let my mind go blank.

After my shave I walked out of the barber's shop, running my hand over my freshly shaved chin and not finding the usual stubble! And just then I caught sight of a familiar face. Tapping his way past the barber's shop with a stick came Blind Sanya, that same Sanya I had met on my first day in camp ten, just over two years ago. My exalted mood vanished in a trice. What was I feeling so pleased about, idiot? I was still in Mordovia, wasn't I, the camp was just as much a prison, only with the walls pushed back a bit and the sky visible overhead.

By four o'clock I also had time to glance into the library. It was full of people and there was nowhere to sit, so I merely walked up and down. As in the canteen and outside there were placards everywhere, together with newspaper and magazine cuttings, quotes from the classics and slogans, slogans, slogans: 'He who doesn't work shan't eat'; 'Today's generation of Soviet citizens will one day live under Communism'; 'Communism is the bright future of all mankind'; 'Lenin is always with us'. The largest number of sayings and quotations came from the speeches and reports of Khrushchev; wherever you looked you saw 'N. S. Khrushchev' looking back at you, together with his face on various photographs and cuttings.

But it was time to go to headquarters for my first interview. A group of new arrivals was already waiting outside HQ and was constantly being joined by more people coming up. We discussed the work that lay ahead of us and who was likely to get what. We had no choice in the matter: we would have to go where we were told. They called us in one by one and each con as he emerged again would say: 'Eighth company', 'twenty-seventh', 'foundry'. At last my turn came.

A spacious office contained what seemed the whole of admin: the Camp Commander himself—Lieutenant-Colonel Kolomytsev, his various aides and deputies, majors, captains, lieutenants, young and old. I was spoken to by some major with tattoos on his hands and with a scar across the whole of his cheek and upper lip. (The cons told me later that this was the Deputy Camp Commander, Major Ageyev, nicknamed The Lip, a terribly foulmouthed officer and a great trouble maker. They said he was the brother of that other Ageyev who had beaten us in camp ten, that he had been disfigured by some criminal con in revenge and that he himself was a former criminal con. I don't know how much truth there was in all this but he certainly used to behave like a thug, foully cursing everyone to beat the band and bellowing from one end of the camp to the other; on the other hand he was never insulted and never punished cons if they gave as good as they got and it seemed that he even liked it.) Anyway it was this same Ageyev who asked me all the standard questions, inquired whether I was intending to escape again (naturally I said no, I would sit out my term) and informed me that I would work in the emergency gang as a loader.

'What sort of gang is that? And what work is it?'

A young lieutenant explained to me that this gang unloaded coal, logs and timber from railway wagons and loaded them again with finished products. I said:

'But I'm deaf, how can I work on loading and unloading? I won't hear the commands and I'll be crushed to death.'

'Never mind, you'll hear if you try hard enough,' replied the lieutenant, 'we've got worse than you working at it.'

This was my company officer, Lieutenant Alyoshin. That evening I had an interview with him above in his own office. Again I heard the same old sickening questions that I had to answer every day: name, charge, sentence. And then a new question:

'Do you repent, are you sorry for what you did?'

'All I need to be sorry for here is not that I tried to escape, but that I failed.'

Alyoshin was silent in response to this and then briefly outlined my duties and the camp rules and regulations. Soon I was to get to know them in practice.

Meanwhile I set off for my hut and my section in order to get myself organized. It turned out that our section was the best in the entire camp: the cots stood not in a double circle, as in all the other sections, but in one. I was shown where to put my cot (it was a lucky place, they said: a twenty-five-year-termer had slept in this spot and only yesterday had been freed after doing twenty-one years), where to get a sack for my mattress and where to get all the rest of a con's camp equipment and clothing, including a cap like the ones I had noticed earlier. This black cotton cap was somewhat reminiscent of a fore-and-aft cap with a peak and was called a 'Cuban' in the camps, while in camp ten we had still worn forage caps à la Stalin. The cons used to joke that in this too Khrushchev was eradicating the cult of Stalin and currying favor with Fidel. Tomorrow I too would have to put on this black prisoner's uniform and keep it on for the next three years.

Later our orderly, Andrei Trofrinchuk (also a twenty-five-year prisoner, a Ukranian from Kiev, he had already done sixteen to seventeen years, in general there were lots of cons with twenty-five years in number seven at that time) took me into the work zone to stuff my mattress. At first they didn't want to let me through the guardhouse in the clothes I was wearing, but then Andrei persuaded the warder and we passed through. Just as we had entered the work zone a flood of women came walking the other way—they were free workers in good clean clothes. The working day had just finished in the office and the other institutions where they worked, and almost all the office workers were the wives or daughters of officers and warders. The women passed Andrei without so much as noticing him, looking straight through him as if he were made of glass. With me, on the other hand, many of them exchanged greetings. I was astonished and Andrei explained laughingly that they must certainly have taken me for one of 'theirs', a free worker, because I wasn't dressed like a con, and the fact that I was on my last legs wasn't noticeable at a distance.

We came to a shed where some cons were using a planing machine to turn miscellaneous planks and blocks into shavings—these were 'feathers' for the camp mattresses and pillows. We picked out one of the drier bales of shavings, filled the mattress cover and pillow case and set off back for the living zone (at the guardhouse they searched us, of course, and the sacks of shavings—everything was back to normal).

The whole of our gang was already back in the hut. The men had returned from work, eaten their supper, received their food from the shop and were now drinking tea. The ganger, Anton Gaida, came over to me and told me to take the paper packets that were on the table. It turned out that every con in the gang had put aside from the food he had bought a spoonful of margarine and a handful of toffees, so that now I had my own food and just as much as the rest of them. Everybody persuaded me to take it without being shy, for they all knew what Vladimir jail was like and some of them had been there themselves. As for the shop, I'd have to wait a good month and a half till I could use it, till I had earned five rubles from my work. But there was no hope of lasting out on nothing but camp rations, it was only at the beginning that it seemed you could eat your fill in the canteen; once you got on a bit and had to work, though, you soon found out that without food of your own, without the shop, you would be kicking the bucket.

Thus they persuaded me to take the food, explaining at the same time what sort of life lay ahead of me. Deeply touched by their thoughtfulness and sympathy, I took the packets and carried them off to my locker.

As I began to get a closer look at my gang-mates I suddenly saw a familiar face and managed to remember who it was. He was a con called Ivan Tretyakov, who had travelled with me from Taishet via all those transit jails to Mordovia. At the end of it, though, I had been sent to number ten, while he had come straight here to seven. He was pleased to see me too, and also that we would be working in the same gang. Examining me closely, he said that I was unrecognizable,

that he himself would never have known me—I had changed
enormously since 1961, I was so far gone I was terrifying to
look at. And moustachless too, what had I done with it,
eaten it in desperation? We gossiped away and exchanged
information about our former travelling companions. Then
Ivan suddenly stopped short, excused himself and dragged
me over to the corner, to his cot, to drink tea. Again I felt
ashamed of my starved appearance. I had already eaten
plenty that day, but my eyes still looked insatiably hungry
and probably it showed quite plainly.

Ivan fetched two mugs of hot water, took some bread,
margarine and toffees out of his locker and offered them to
me. We sat on his cot drinking our hot water and talking,
recalling all our convoy ordeals. Ivan showed me some photos
of his family—his wife and two daughters. They lived in
Balkhash and the elder daughter was already married.

I remembered Ivan's past. He and his family had originally
lived in Western Byelorussia and when the Germans came
Ivan had joined the police. There was a man from the same
village in camp seven and he later told me that when Ivan
was a policeman he had never run wild or oppressed people in
any way, but had simply done his duty. Ivan himself now
deeply regretted it, but never sought to excuse himself,
merely explaining his error by the fact that he had to find a
way of feeding his wife and children.

Well, I don't really know what happened in those times
during the war and I can't pretend to judge, but I do know
that both in the convoy and here in camp, Ivan behaved like
a decent fellow and a good comrade. Everybody thought the
same of him in our gang and because of this they immediately
treated me not only with sympathy but also with trust:
Tretyakov would never be friends with a stool pigeon! And
you had to be careful, because often the authorities would

transfer their stool pigeons from camp to camp and pretend that they were simply newcomers.

Anyway, after the Germans, Ivan went into the Soviet Army and fought with them to the very last day—after which they sentenced him to twenty-five years inside. For a while he was transferred to a free colony at Balkhash and was joined there by his family, which remained there still. But he himself, like the majority of the settlers, was locked up in a camp again and then sent to Taishet. It was there that the two of us met.

Ivan suddenly remembered something and said:

'By the way, Tolik, you were a bad prophet.'

'What do you mean?'

'Do you remember the two old men who travelled with us from Taishet—Ivanov and another one with gray hair and a big beard, a Volga German? You prophesied that they would soon go free and that you would see them off when they left. Do you remember? Well, you can go and say hello to Ivanov tomorrow, he's here.'

'And the German?'

'Yes, the German left,' replied Ivan, 'feet first. He told you, didn't he: "I shall be here for the rest of my life, Tolik. I shan't be released, I shall die behind barbed wire." Well, he died in here.'

Ivan and I talked right up until lights out. He advised me to join his team unloading coal and timber. The work in the other team was slightly easier—loading finished products, unloading barrels, spare parts, cases of paper, but on the other hand you couldn't earn much for the shop in that team, while in the 'big' team you at least got credited with an extra twenty rubles a month, and sometimes even more. What's more, you weren't got up so often at night—it was rarely more than once. I agreed and it was a simple matter to arrange it with the ganger.

For my first three days the ganger didn't call me out to work, he let me rest and get my strength back. The whole gang had agreed in asking him to do this. It was done, of course, without the knowledge of admin. I was marked down on the chart as working, otherwise I would have ended up in the cooler as an absentee. Only in the emergency gang were such tricks possible. There were sixteen men in the big team, of whom twelve were needed for unloading. Thus four always remained behind. At the next call twelve cons would have to go again—the four who had rested plus eight from the first twelve, and so on, by turns, with four cons always left behind in the living zone. And so I was left behind for three whole days, but I had to steer clear of the company officer, of course. And then by the fourth day I had been carried long enough on the backs of others and it was time to bend my own.

My first time out was in the early evening—we were called out to unload a wagon of timber. The logs were loaded in a double stack, end to end, with a 'cap' of logs over the joins to stop them shifting, and all the work was done by hand. At first it went easily: we set up our 'roller' (a simple log with a hook on the end to hook on the side of the wagon), several men climbed up on top and started shoving the 'cap' off, while the rest used crooks to roll the logs away from the wagon. You just had to shove and away they rolled. The hard part began, however, when we got half way down. All of us had to take hold of the log together and at the command: 'one, two, three!' had to raise it aloft and throw it over the side of the box-shaped wagon. As for the bottom logs, there was no hope of throwing them out and they had to be dragged and pushed out at the back.

By the time I had helped unload this one wagon I thought

I would never get back to the hut. The work itself was killing, and on top of that I was completely out of condition after two years in Vladimir jail. I could hardly walk. But the boys cheered me up: it was nothing to worry about, I would soon get used to it. Back in the hut I collapsed on to my cot and went straight to sleep, without even eating. I awoke what seemed like a minute later. When I had gone to bed the others were taking off their clothes after work. Now, when I opened my eyes again, they were still undressing, noisily discussing the job, the timber and the 'frisk' at the guardhouse. My body ached all over, as though I hadn't slept at all, yet it turned out that the night was already over and the gang had just returned from its third call—twice more during the night they had been out unloading wagons. On me, however, they had taken pity, not wanting to wake me.

With difficulty I got out of bed and was hardly able to straighten up, I had pains in my waist, arms, legs, neck. I went out to get washed and I couldn't even walk straight—my legs wouldn't bend and the whole of me was swaying. And I waddled like a duck as I went. I was kidded for ages afterwards about that duck's waddle of mine.

When I came to the washroom I was told that a con had just hanged himself in one of the section washrooms, he was cold when they cut him down that morning. He was a Latvian or Lithuanian with a twenty-five-year term. He had already done sixteen when he was re-tried for a possible reduction to the new regulation fifteen. But the court refused, leaving him nine more years to do. So he hanged himself.

New Designs

The new year comes and with it new designs
The camp is ringed with a barbed wire barricade
Stern eyes keep watch, regard us from all sides
And hungry death is everywhere on guard
> (Sung to the tune of a favorite old tango
> from the twenties and thirties)

GRADUALLY I REALLY did get used to the work and I settled down in camp seven. And I learned of changes other than the obvious ones that I had been so quick to notice before. Since the autumn of 1961 the situation in the camps had taken a big turn for the worse and it still continues to get worse with every succeeding year. So what was the regime like for political prisoners between the years 1963–65? And since it has remained the same, what is it like now in 1967?*

First, the prisoners have their heads shaved and are not allowed to wear their own clothing or footwear. The con is forced to spend his whole time in the black cotton camp uniform, with heavy ankle or knee boots on his feet (women too) and in winter a padded coat or jacket (reefer jacket) on top of his cotton tunic. If a warder catches sight of a con in a civilian shirt or a cap, he will chase him all over the zone until he catches him and takes it away, after which the con is dispatched to the cooler. The same thing happens if they find any civvies on your cot during a search. The huts are

* Considerable documentary evidence shows it to be the same in 1969.

searched frequently and usually when the cons are away at work. Those waiting for the second shift are usually chased out during this time. Everything is turned upside down, they rummage through your bedding and your lockers and read through all your newspapers and letters and anything you might have written. What they want, they take.

The writing of letters is limited to two a month. And the fact that you can receive as many as you like, and from whoever you like, is just one more proof of what it is the authorities are afraid of. All the means at their disposal are used to limit information about the camps, so that the public knows as little as possible about what goes on there. Furthermore the prisoners are warned that it is forbidden to write about the camp organization and the rules to relatives. All letters are examined by the censor. You have to hand each letter over in an open envelope. If he doesn't approve of something in it, he sends it back to you. And letters from outside are opened before arrival. Sometimes one or two sentences are blacked out. Some letters disappear completely: the censor confiscates them and adds them to the prisoner's file, or else simply refuses to hand them over. Who can you ask about them? The minister of communications?

You may also receive printed matter: books, magazines, newspapers, Soviet only. Not even Polish and Czech are allowed. Not even humorous ones. Many of our cons knew or had studied foreign languages. In the camps you can find an expert in almost any language you care to name, from English down to some remote Indian or African dialect. Some of them know half-a-dozen languages, so that there are plenty of teachers available. But the only books and newspapers you can get in these languages are ones published in the Soviet Union. And the same goes for text books.

It is also possible to have soap, toothpaste and notebooks

sent in printed packets. And handkerchiefs. All printed packets are prodded and felt, closely examined and minutely studied before being passed on.

In the big camp, of course, it happens that a con gets away with wearing a sweater under his uniform tunic and puts on a normal cap or beret instead of that sickening 'Cuban'. Sometimes a pair of socks gets through in a printed packet, or a warm scarf. But this is the result of an oversight on the part of the censor or warders—it's not so easy to keep an eye on everything and everybody when you've got three-thousand-odd different men milling around under your eyes. And a con who commits a 'violation' in this way takes good care not to be seen and gives all officers the widest possible berth.

Receiving food or even smokes from outside when you're on strict regime is completely forbidden. No parcels, no packages. The con has no right to them. The camp administration has the right to permit parcels as a form of reward for exemplary conduct, to show that a con 'is responding to corrective training'. But even then only to prisoners who have completed half their term. That means you serve at least half your time without parcels and after that you may or may not be allowed a 'concession'—one 10 lb. parcel once a quarter, 40 lbs. of food a year, or just over 3 lbs. a month! And after this you have to work till you drop, bashing out your norm, and not once break a single one of the camp regulations. And needless to say, that's not all. A prisoner, for instance, gets fed up with admin and says:

'I've served half my time, I always do the norm and I haven't broken the rules—why can't I have a parcel?'

And the company officer clarifies the matter.

'Well, well! So you haven't broken any rules! But we punish for breaking the rules and concessions have to be worked for, concessions have to be deserved.'

It is well known what 'deserved' means: suck up to the powers that be at all times and in all places, beginning with the warders; cooperate with admin, be an 'activist', prey on your comrades, become a stool pigeon. And in general it means that you're thrown on the mercy of the camp authorities. For a food parcel means a lot in camp. Even those pitiful 3 lbs. a month. And each time, every three months, you have to ask for your 'reward': you go to the company officer, make your applications, get in return a sermon and—nine times out of ten—a refusal.

Applications since 1965 have grown very rare. Now you have to appear before a commission consisting of your company officer, the camp commander, representatives of the KGB and PEU (Political Education Unit) and the KGB Security Officer for the camp. This lofty body sits in judgment on whether a con shall be allowed his 10 lbs. of food, or whether he has failed to deserve such magnanimity.

The majority of prisoners serve their whole term without receiving a single parcel. In all my six years inside I received only one package from my mother—10 lbs. of food—and that was when I was lying in the camp hospital. One girl I knew sent some apples. They were a birthday present. I only learned about it a month afterwards, from one of her letters. I wrote back telling her she was naive to think that a prisoner in Mordovia was allowed to eat apples. Maybe she had been reading about prison parcels in the newspaper, in an article about some 'difficult pages'. My letter was confiscated and added to my file and I was called in by the KGB and warned that for writing like that I wasn't far from having my sentence extended. I expect the apples went rotten on their way back to my friend.

If a parcel should weigh a couple of ounces over 10 lbs. together with its wrappings it is sent straight back again. If a parcel comes from a friend and you happen not to recognize the sender's address on the box, it is sent straight back again.

Well, and what about a prisoner's rights? There is his right to correspond (with limitations and censorship). His right to have visits from relatives—I will write about these a bit later. His right to buy up to five rubles' worth of food in the camp shop, though only with money earned inside the camp. If he has nothing left after deductions have been made—too bad, he can make do without, even if his relatives are prepared to send money. Not on sale in the camp shop and forbidden because of the regime regulations are: sugar, butter, tinned meat and fish, bread. All you can buy is tinned vegetables or fruit (hardly anybody buys these because they are too dear, they take your whole five rubles), cheap sweets and margarine. There is also soap, cigarettes, cheap tobacco, toothbrushes, envelopes, notebooks, and you can buy camp clothing if you like—not that anybody does on five rubles a month.

But all these rights are no better than a dream, a mirage. Admin has the right to deprive a prisoner of all of them. This is done for violations, and who can say that he commits no violations—if admin wants to find some? And so they take away your rights—to the shop, for instance, for a month, two months, three. And then you have to get by on 'basic'—on camp rations that have been worked out on scientific principles to be just enough to keep you from dying off.

The daily norm is 2,400 calories: 25 ozs. of bread, 3 ozs. of cod, 2 ozs. of meat (the sheepdog guarding the cons gets 1 lb.), 1 lb. of vegetables—potatoes and cabbage, about 1 oz. of meal or noodles, $\frac{3}{4}$ oz. of fat and $\frac{1}{2}$ oz. of sugar. And that's all. It adds up to one and a half times less than a normal man needs on light work. You will say: what about the shop? But then they deprive you of the shop! Keeping strictly to all the rules and regulations they condemn you to an empty belly!

But anyway, not even all of this finds its way into the prisoner's bowl. A cart, for instance, comes into the compound carrying meat for the whole camp, 300 lbs. for three thousand men. You look at this meat and you hardly know what to think: is it carrion, or something still worse? All blue, it seems to consist entirely of bone and gristle. Then it goes to be stewed and you're lucky if half an ounce finds its way into your mouth. You're eating cabbage and you can't make out to begin with what it is: some sort of black, slimy, stinking globes. How much out of the established quota gets thrown on the rubbish heap? And in spring and summer the cookhouse hands can't even bring themselves to throw out the bad potatoes any more, otherwise there would be nothing to put in the soup. And so they throw in the black and rotten ones. If you go near the cookhouse in summer the stench turns you over. Stinking cod, rotten cabbage. The bread is like we had in the war. In number seven we had a bakery in which we baked two kinds of bread, black for the camp, white for outside. Sugar, though, you would think was foolproof. It won't rot, you don't have to measure it. But then they give it to you damp so that it weighs more. And they give you ten days' ration at a time—5 ozs.—because if they gave you your 1 oz. daily, it wouldn't so much be a question of having nothing to eat as of nothing to see.

During six years in camp and jail I had bread with butter twice—when I received visits. I also ate two cucumbers—one in 1964 and another in 1966. Not once did I eat a tomato or an apple. All this was forbidden.

Every month you have 13–14 rubles of your wages deducted for food. Outside now as a free man I go to a cafe where dinners are cheap. Cabbage soup costs me 23 copecks, a main dish 25–27 copecks without meat, a dish of stewed fruit 7 copecks, and then I have 4–5 copecks' worth of bread. That means 60 copecks a day on dinner alone, or 18 rubles a month. And breakfast and supper costs about the same. Thus I alone spend about 50 rubles a month on food, almost the whole of my salary, and you wouldn't say I was eating well. But a con spends 13 rubles!* Even if he ate only canteen soup once a day and his 25 ozs. of bread, that would take almost the whole sum, and he'd have three rubles a month to pay for all the rest. No subsidies are allowed for prisoners, they have to pay for all their food out of their own paltry wages. Everybody can figure that out and see what sort of grub that must mean. And then basic's nothing in comparison with the cooler and a reduced quota of food. Reduced—that means 1,300 calories, one third of what a man needs: 14–18 ozs. of bread, skilly that's all water and cod once a day—the usual 3 ozs. or perhaps less. And not a grain of sugar, not a shred of meat, not a granule of fat. At the same time you still have to go out to work, and if you're unable to and refuse, you'll be tried and stuck in the clink.

It happens that starving cons who have longed for years for a touch of green or a fresh vegetable sometimes get hold of some seeds and sow them in the compound, say carrots or onions in some distant corner. Sooner or later, however, the warders always see them and kick them out. It's not allowed! Caucasians have more success with their edible sweet grass. It grows to the cons' advantage: the warders can't recognize it or distinguish it from other grasses.

And that is what strict regime looks like today. Strict regime, for the most part, is for political prisoners, because

* At the official rate, there are 1.11 rubles to the dollar and 2.16 rubles to the pound sterling, but a more realistic rate would be three times as many rubles in each case. There are 100 copecks in a ruble.

among criminals only the persistent offenders get put on strict regime, or those who commit a crime or a violation already in the camps, and even then not for their whole term—they do a stint on strict regime and then go back to normal regime again. For criminals and civil prisoners strict regime is the harshest form of punishment. But for us politicals it is the mildest, our imprisonment begins with this, because it is the minimum awarded by the courts. From strict regime political prisoners can go only on to special regime or to the clink. And that is even worse.

Work

WHILE I WAS at camp seven I tried almost all the different sorts of work there were. We had a big output of furniture—out of three and a half thousand cons practically all, with the exception of some of the invalids, worked in the factory. We had a sawmill, a cutting out shop, a machine shop, assembly shops, a finishing shop, our own foundry, a blacksmith's shop, our own timber yard and our own builders. Only the skilled craftsmen and supervisors came from outside. All the workers were prisoners.

For a month or two I worked in the finishing shop. It was full of unhealthy fumes, the stink of varnish and acetone, and the workers used to suffer from dizziness and vomiting. True, the finishers used to get a supplementary ration consisting of 14 ozs. of milk a day, and the foundry workers too. But as often as not the milk didn't come every day. And then many cons tried to share with their friends, who otherwise after five or ten years without it would forget even the taste of milk. So how could you possibly drink it all on your own?

The foundry, at the time when I worked in it, was absolute hell. It was used for smelting and casting spare parts out of an alloy consisting of zinc, aluminum and copper. The furnace was an old one with a poor ventilation system, so that your lungs would be filled with zinc fumes, gases and smoke and you would run out with the sweat pouring off you to take a few gulps of fresh air.

The law decreeing a shorter working day for unhealthy types of work doesn't extend to prisoners—you still have to do a full eight hours. When you come off the shift you are trembling from head to foot, as in a fever, and then you have to wait outside the guardhouse for an hour for roll-call. After I left they built a new foundry, so I don't know what it's like now. But our norms were impossible to fulfil. And all the time they were being raised, while our rates were steadily lowered. Some cons, in order to earn more, used to pitch in in pairs and then book it down to only one of them. Thus one would be credited with 150 per cent, while the other would get only 20–30 per cent, which was okay, just so long as you weren't put on reduced rations. Then the first one would share his bonus with the second. Or maybe he would leave it in his own name and accumulate money for the shop. After a few months, half a year or a year of such work, one man at least would have something to take out with him when he was released, enough to see him through for a while. And then, once outside, he would try to help his friend still in the camp. But this was a dangerous game: the authorities might take their cue from such a 'star' and raise the quotas for everyone else.

Some have to go without their dinner and work two shifts in succession. They would still only be booked for a single shift, but a working day of 14–16 hours would enable them to turn out up to 150–170 per cent of the norm. Thus they killed two birds with one stone: their pay was higher and they earned the approval of admin. For generally speaking admin knew of these various tricks. And with regard to overtime they sometimes had a direct agreement with some of 'their own' cons: these would then be listed as the star workers and on the basis of their performance the norms would be raised for everybody else. 'If he can do it, then you have to as well!'

It is generally thought, I suppose, that production goes up at the expense of mechanization, but in fact any increase is at the expense of the con's sweat and blood. In the finishing shop the norm was originally to polish six 'Yugdon' radio-gram cabinets, but while I was there this was pushed up to thirteen. In 1964 the norm for 'Radius-V' television cabinets was four, and in 1965 six. But the work stayed exactly the same: a wad of cotton wool soaked in acetone with which you polished the cabinet by hand until you had brought it to a high sheen.

Basically, however, I worked as a loader in the emergency gang. I have already described the first job of unloading I did and that is how it continued day after day, with five to seven wagons to unload every twenty-four hours. In the autumn and winter our clothes would never have time to dry out in the drying room before the next call came and we would have to pull them on, still wet, and go out. The work was so heavy because there were only sixteen loaders for the whole factory.

Even worse than timber was the coal. It used to come in a steady stream, great mountains of coal would be piled on both sides of the track and there would be nowhere to put the latest consignment. Two or three wagonloads would arrive and they would be practically invisible behind the heaps. That meant it was impossible to open the hatches: there was nowhere to shovel the coal and it would all slide under the wagon. Like the timber, therefore, it had to be thrown over the sides, only much farther away, of course. And in winter it would be frozen solid, we would have to break it up with crowbars before unloading it. Even before that, though, we would have to roll the wagons into position ourselves ready for unloading, because the track was poor and they wouldn't let the locomotives on to it. So we'd have to heave and push a wagon of 62 tons 200 yards up the slope, and at least an hour would go on that. But neither the time nor the work involved in this was taken into consideration or paid for, because it was held that our gang was working 'with assistance of light machinery', and the fact that we, a gang powered by 14–16 cons, had been harnessed to a wagon in place of a locomotive wasn't entered in the records at all. And the whole of our 'light machinery' in unloading consisted of crowbars, crooks, staves and a roller.

In the spring of 1965 they equipped our timber yard with a crane for unloading timber. And at once a part of the loaders was transferred to the factory, for fear that we might have a bit less work to do. The remainder now had to go on call every time and couldn't take turns any more. And the work was just as hard as before: we still had to shovel the coal and every now and then the crane had a breakdown. And you couldn't put the crane on special regime as a shirker.

In general, though, a prisoner's work differs little in essence from work outside. I'm a free man now and since April 1967 I have been working as a loader—we do the same uncredited overtime and we also push wagons about from store to store, and our earnings are about the same: 70–75 rubles (if you don't do extra work). The only difference is that you get a bit more to eat and the deductions from your wage packet are bigger, especially for childlessness. In the camp, too, you pay the same taxes (and they also make deductions from cons for childlessness!) and then 50 per cent of the remainder is assigned for maintenance of the camp and its staff—from warders to the administration and doctors; and it also goes on hut maintenance and supporting the sick and invalids. Out of the remaining 50 per cent they take 13 rubles for food and you have to pay out several rubles a month for that wretched camp uniform that is issued on deferred payment. And out of what's left 5 rubles goes on the shop (if you're allowed). . . . So that you won't get rich as they imply in the advertisements: 'Save up and buy a motor car!' God grant that in the course of your term you can save enough for a suit and a pair of boots.

It's no different, however, outside.

There was a time in the camps when, just as elsewhere, we had a wave of 'work on a social basis'. The company officer would call in a number of activists among the cons and prompt them to some new valuable initiative. In our library we had a librarian and in return for his work he received, although it was tiny, something that could nevertheless be called a salary. Under pressure from admin the prisoners organized themselves in shifts to look after the library voluntarily, in their free time. The librarian was dismissed ('You can hang around hungry if you like, you don't have to work, you're an invalid. Otherwise go and pitch in at the factory.') But that was only a library! Later we were forced, 'on a social basis', to renovate our own hut. And why not? After all, ordinary workers go and build houses for nothing in their free time. But then if workers go to work on such social projects (and who knows whether they go voluntarily?) they stand a chance of getting a flat in that building, while in our case it turns out that we're forced, 'on a social basis', to repair our own jail! And we repaired it: if you refused you got no parcels and a black mark on your record.

Our cons also built a new Visitors' Hostel for free in their spare time. Some of them even volunteered for this project, because the old hostel really was very bad and small. A mother or wife would arrive and would have to wait around for two weeks or more. And some of them had a long way to come, so that their holiday wasn't long enough and they had to ask for unpaid leave from work, and then they would spend the whole of their holiday time in Mordovia, standing around outside the guardhouse. Because of this a large number of wives couldn't come at all. But now admin had suddenly turned generous: here's the material, now build it yourselves.

The cons built a new hostel with 20 rooms in it and were overjoyed: now my wife can come too! Even though they were working for the camp, still it was somehow for themselves as well.

But when it was finished admin took 12 of the 20 rooms for its staff. Here they set out their desks and hung up their curtains. So the cons, 'on a social basis', had been putting up offices for their jailers! Still, they did at least leave 8 rooms for family visits and at least the waiting got shorter: now it was 8–10 days instead of the former two weeks.

Admin and **HQ** got a double advantage from this unpaid work: first they would be praised for their success in 'educating' the prisoners; but second and more important—they made considerable savings. For no matter what happened 50 per cent of the cons' wages would be deducted to pay for all the repairs and building work in the camp. And in this way they both deducted the money and got their building work free. Admin, moreover, used to be liberally rewarded for any savings they made, while the cons, of course, got sweet blow all.

But the biggest evil of camp work is not that it is cruelly heavy, nor that you work for virtually nothing, for a morsel of bread, or for even less. The main reason why you hate this work is because it's slavery, arbitrarily enforced and humiliating, and all the time you have those parasitical warders standing over you, grudging you the crust of bread that you've earned with your own sweat.

My Testimony

When I was released and came to Moscow, I would always stop by the windows of shops selling furniture and radio and television sets. There inside would be a polished table, a handsome, shining wardrobe and familiar cabinets: 'Radius-V', 'Yugdon', 'Melodia'.

So you buy yourself a new wardrobe and you sit there in the evening in your cosy room, in front of the television set. You've paid 360 whole rubles for that TV of yours and now you are going to enjoy your right to a bit of comfort and relaxation. That television set has cost my friends our sweat, our health, roasting in the cooler and long hours during roll-call in the rain and snow. Look closely at that polished surface: can you not see reflected in it the close-shaven head, the yellow, emaciated face, and the black cotton tunic of a convict? Maybe it's a former friend of yours?

The Cons' Economy—Double Entry Book-keeping

'Yes, but wait a minute', some of my readers will say, 'if those were the conditions you lived under in Dubrovlag, how is it the whole lot of you didn't just bite the dust? We know that there used to be really terrible camps: Kolyma, Vorkuta, Taishet. There they used to die like flies from exhaustion, 'goners' would literally tremble in the wind, dysentery and scurvy were practically universal. But at least you haven't got that any more and I don't understand, there's something wrong somewhere.'

Old Kolyma and Vorkuta hands who have remained prisoners to this day explain it as follows: the grub is the same or even worse, there are no parcels, and the shop privileges are limited and often withheld altogether; in the logging camps, the pits and the mines no con would have lasted even a season under present conditions, he'd go under. At least the work is human now. That's one thing. And the other is that there were millions stuck in the camps in those days, there was hardly anyone outside to help, and in any case how could they in those hungry days of the war and postwar period?

And there is a third reason which I will now explain.

If men aren't dying of starvation in the camps of Mordovia, this is because there exist all sorts of illegal, forbidden ways of getting hold of food. For the con here isn't shut up inside four walls like he is at Vladimir. Work truly saves the compound from hunger. And the reason is that all sorts of free workers also work at the factory, such as supervisors and foremen, and the trucks that bring loads into the compound are driven by drivers from outside. All this company also finds it hard to make ends meet on the wages they get. Of course they are warned against us in various ways. We are said to be cut-throats and desperate criminals. But this sort of propaganda has little effect. When they mix with the cons the free workers soon see that the cons are just the same as they are, and that in general they think the same. . . . Every one of them realizes that if he were to speak his mind out loud he would be inside too, a con like all the rest.

Free workers value the opportunity to work in the compound because of the bonus they get on top of their wages. They get 15–20 per cent added on 'for danger'—a danger that is less than outside, where the workers can easily get blind drunk and end up by crippling or killing their foreman. So the bonus is prized. But even then the wages aren't high enough. And it is here that the possibility of trading with the prisoners arises, of speculating on the side, which is more profitable in camp than anywhere you care to name. True, there's a danger of being not only fired but also arrested and charged. But on the other hand, how difficult it is to resist temptation!

The most profitable trade of all is in tea. It's easy to smuggle in—easier than butter or sugar—and the rake-off is big. For a packet of tea costing 38–40 copecks in the shop a con will pay a free worker 1½–2 rubles. Ten packets means 15–20 rubles of clear profit—as much as a foreman gets for five days' work in the factory. Once the tea is inside the compound it passes through several more hands, bringing a profit to each new proprietor.

A camp trader, say, buys some tea in bulk from one of the free workers and then splits it up and sells it to his friends in $2\frac{1}{2}$–3 ruble packets. After that it becomes currency. One con has done a deal with a warder and when his wife comes she brings him thirty-odd pounds of foodstuffs (out of which the warder, of course, gets a bribe). Not only does he not starve himself, but he starts to barter his vegetables for tea, and the tea he sells to a 'dealer'. Another is himself a 'dealer' and sells his shop food for tea. And so on and so forth.

If the officers find out that some of the cons have tea, they will turn the whole zone upside down. And if they find any they put the owner in the cooler. But that, of course, doesn't stop anyone.

In our gang we had a prisoner called Konchakovsky. The whole camp knew that he traded in tea. He had an agreement with one of the drivers and the latter used to bring him about 50 packets at a time. Konchakovsky used to hide the tea in the work zone. He didn't sell it himself, though, but did it through an intermediary, Sanya the Beak (the exact double of the warder at Vladimir jail), who was also in our gang. Sanya would find a buyer among the cons and sell him a couple of packets, usually still in the work zone. That way there was no risk of being picked up during the search at roll-call and no loss through having the tea confiscated. And it was up to the buyer to smuggle it through without being caught. The most common method was to hide it in your boot, spread out over the whole sole. After all, they could hardly make everyone take his boots off at roll-call, otherwise they would need the whole day to search everyone, and when would the cons get their work done? And anyway the

237

warders used to get bored and they too used to hustle while on duty. Sanya the Beak also used to take tea through to the living zone on occasion. The price was 2–3 rubles a packet (this depended on demand, but was never less than 2 rubles), while Konchakovsky paid the driver 1½ rubles a packet.

This group went on speculating over a period of several years, but still it came to grief in the end. This happened in about 1963–64. Probably they were given away by some warder or officer whom they failed to bribe properly. Certainly such a major enterprise can't get by without bribes: the driver, for instance, bribes the warder at the gate and treats him to vodka or gives him presents.

As for the warders, it is difficult for them to resist. Sometimes they even complain to the prisoners themselves that although the work's not dirty and you're not likely to rupture yourself with it, still you have to eat and drink and feed the kids and the pay's not much. And even the officers, although they've got more to fear, are unable at times to resist temptation. Thus gradually a whole lot of people get to know about this commercial enterprise but keep quiet about it in return for a kick-back. If a lone prisoner with tea gets caught it's the cooler, but big speculators are left alone. And so it goes for as long as everyone is paid or until the participants fall out. Then somebody squeals, there's a search and the culprits are caught redhanded. Then comes the trial and a sentence for speculation. That, evidently, is how Konchakovsky's group came to grief.

Four of them were tried in court: Konchakovsky, Sanya the Beak, the driver and the shop assistant who had sold the tea to the driver and shared the rake-off with him (within the whole territory of Dubrovlag, shop assistants outside were forbidden to sell more than one or two packets to one person at a time). All of them got 3–5 years of camp. Sanya and

Konchakovsky, moreover, being sent to do theirs in a special regime camp. Konchakovsky came off worst of all: he had already done 14 years out of a 25-year sentence and had hoped to be released in a year owing to the reduction in the maximum. But now there could be no question of that: to his remaining 11 years they added a further 4, bringing it up to a full 15. Thus having done 14 and with 15 still to go, he would have a total term of 29 years! And now special regime too! Some price he paid for his tea and the benefits it brought with it—money, butter, sugar, vodka and the shortlived indulgence of the authorities.

In 1965 the warder Vasya Vasek came to grief by trading in tea. He was a really savage animal who used to go to extremes during the searches, yet he himself was a speculator. Probably his savagery was his undoing and one of the cons betrayed him for it. The only thing that happened to Vasek, however, was that he was dismissed from his job. Generally speaking, if one or other of the warders gets caught, they try not to bring charges in order to avoid publicity.

Vodka is also a profitable commodity—you make about five rubles clear profit on a pint. But it's harder to smuggle, of course, like tinned food. But nevertheless both manage to find their way into the compound by way of the free workers.

The camp bakeries and shops are also a great help. Wherever there's a bakery you can have enough bread—provided the money is there. The bakers (who are cons) always 'arrange' to have left-overs and these they sell. At camp seven five two-pound loaves of black bread used to cost a ruble, or you could have three loaves of white bread (baked for outside) for the same. The cons would either settle up with the bakers when they bought it or else pay a sum in advance. I used to pay 10 rubles in cash in advance and then take the bread when I needed it until I had used up my credit. The bakers used to share their profits with their civilian supervisor from outside.

The shop, too, always had a brisk trade going. The civilian who ran it always used to bring in more food than was necessary for the camp. He did it supposedly secretly. A share used to go to the quartermaster who let him bring his stuff into the zone, and then he also used to bribe the officers, who pretended they didn't know about it. And after that, of course, it was simple. At camp seven we had two selling points, the so-called shop and buffet. Basically they were both the same and in both places the cons paid not cash but with vouchers (not in any circumstances is the con allowed to have money in his hands). The man selling the stuff was a civilian from outside, but the buffet keeper was a con and it was through him that trade was conducted—not in vouchers but in cash. All the food was three times as dear, of course, but what can the con do? He will pay five times the price if there's something going.

Where do prisoners get their money from? From outside, of course. You bring it back from a meeting with one of your family or in some other way. A whole host of stratagems have been thought up for doing this, but I won't describe them— let the cons go on using them for a bit. One thing only can be said: they knew how to look and we knew how to hide. Furthermore we have a fundamental interest in the matter, for us it's a question of life and death, whereas for them, when all's said and done, it's only a matter of duty.

In any case admin isn't really interested in cutting off all the streams of food and money into the compound from outside. A hungry con, a 'goner' is a poor worker, and who's going to keep the factory going then? If the plan's fulfilled the whole of admin is rewarded and that's not something you want to lose. Certainly not. That's why, in general, they hunt lazily, mainly to keep the con on tenterhooks and also to exhibit the necessary degree of diligence to their superiors. There are, of course, people who enjoy their work—these try their very best and work hard.

On the whole these camp fiddles keep everybody going. It saves the cons from starving to death, helps hard-working civilians to feed their families and assures the bosses of a suitable standard of living.

And even the worst-off cons, those who receive nothing from outside and never take part in these trading deals, even they gain from them. For instance, there's no point in a man like Konchakovsky drinking his skilly every day and he's certainly not going to make a rush for a smelly sprat; sometimes he doesn't even finish his bread. And there are plenty like that in the camps. Maybe they aren't so rich as Konchakovsky, but they're still more or less comfortable, with a thing or two tucked away in their lockers. And so the penniless con gets hold of a spare helping of skilly, or sometimes even a spare bit of bread. One man I knew used to say: 'Yes, that way it's possible to live.'

But without these backdoor supplies strict regime would be just the same as Vladimir Prison or special regime.

One day, I remember, we had 'vinaigrette' for supper. Nobody ever refused this, not even a camp millionaire: it might be rotten underneath, but it had vegetables in it! We came back tired from unloading something, soaking wet, hungry as wolves, and at once rushed to the canteen. But the cooks always dish out vinaigrette strictly according to ration, because absolutely everybody eats it and there is never anything left. Two spoonfuls is the ration, no more. Kolya Yusupov looked into his bowl and went off the deep end: 'You work not even like a donkey, but like an elephant and they feed you like a rabbit!' What use to him, this six-foot giant of a loader, were these two spoonfuls of silage and this blob of revolting sprat? It was as the cooks used to say: 'Be grateful that it's not like this every day. If everybody came to the canteen every day you wouldn't last longer than a couple of months before kicking the bucket.'

And that is the whole secret of the prisoner's existence today.

Everything Here is Just Like Outside

THE HUT is chock full of people, they've rounded up as many as can be found. Behind a table sits the presidium, the chairman is conducting a general meeting of the company. The presidium is made up of prisoners—beside them sit the company officers. Democracy! On the agenda are elections to the Council of the Collective. Does anyone have any proposals?

Some con or other gets to his feet and reads out a list, the assembled prisoners take yet one more yoke on their necks, for the benefit of admin, and go back to their work. But at least it's quick.

Another time there's a new craze: the men are proposed and elected one by one, with a 'discussion' of the candidates. The same tame prisoner gets up:

'I propose Ivanov.' We all know him as an exemplary production worker of exemplary conduct. He takes an active part in the life of the collective (not camp! Such words are never uttered at meetings—we're nothing but a friendly collective, and that's all!) and he participates in amateur art activities.

Literally the same thing, word for word, is said about Sidorov and Petrov, except that perhaps the wall newspaper takes the place of amateur art, or the IOS—Internal Order Section, or something else of that sort. And although 'we all know' that he was a *polizei* (a collaborator who was a policeman in the German Occupation) sentenced for bloody crimes, we all vote 'for' in order to get away as quickly as possible.

Why do we do it? The answer is simple. For in fact the candidates are proposed not by prisoners but by admin through its previously prepared stooges. Whether you want it or not, the bosses will insist on getting their own way and only those that admin wants to have will end up in the Council. On several occasions it has happened that the voting machine 'seizes up'—the cons refuse to vote for some complete rat. Then the company officer stands up:

'Hey you, why are you refusing to vote for our activist?' he will say to one of the 'uncooperative' cons.

'Because he's a stool pigeon, a rat and as slippery as an eel.'

'It doesn't matter, it's not going to be the way you want it but the way I want it,' replies the candid officer. And he drags the meeting out ad infinitum until they elect the ones he has chosen.

Anyway, what difference does it make who you elect to the Council? It is never allowed to act of its own volition, to go against the decision of admin, to refuse to carry out its demands: it acts under admin's control and admin always has the right to dissolve a Council it disapproves of or to expel any con from its membership. Thus this organization hasn't even a semblance of self-government, nor indeed a semblance of anything. Everyone knows that the Council of a company or camp collective is nothing but a willing instrument, a bludgeon in the hands of the authorities, and with the aid of this bludgeon the authorities can terrorize any prisoner they want—and make it look as though it's by the will of the other prisoners. It may be that this produces an impression outside the camp that, say, the prisoners themselves have insisted on their comrade being punished. Inside the camp, however, everybody knows exactly what this means.

There are also idealists among us who say: 'Look at us. We chose these scum ourselves and then complain. We need to have decent men in the Council'—and they volunteer to join. Sometimes admin doesn't object: come what may the Council will do what it's told to do, while on the other hand the cons can't keep needling them with: 'You've only got *polizeis* and stool pigeons on the Council.' How does it all end? With the rout of the idealists, as usual: either they themselves seize on the first pretext to leave the Council or else they are simply expelled.

The function of this organ is an extremely unsavory one. Every single decision it takes is a blow against the prisoners, either all together or some of them individually. One day it's a decision to repair and redecorate the huts in the cons' spare time—so when you've finished your eight hours of compulsory slavery you can use your free time to build a prison for yourself and others. Another day they discuss and condemn somebody's behavior and force another man to work beyond his strength, knowing that he is sick and not in a condition to maintain his norm. And then how does such a discussion end? 'We beg the administration to deprive such and such a prisoner of shop privileges and parcels, to place him on a reduced quota of nourishment and to confine him to a punishment cell.' When jailers do this sort of thing it is at least understandable, but who among the prisoners will consent to condemn his comrade to starvation? Only swine of the lowest possible kind!

And so you get a situation that is the only one acceptable to the authorities and yet for all that very ugly: the Council of the collective is actually made up almost exclusively of former *polizeis*. Earlier they collaborated with the fascists and now with the adminstration of our camps for political prisoners—after all, it's all the same to them, as long as they can have a quiet life and get out as soon as possible. Even outside they manage to get on better than the rest: they are released with excellent character references, all the official organizations help them, they take a careful look round, adapt themselves—and prosper. They might even make the grade as minor bosses somewhere.

When you say to a company officer: 'Just look at who's working with you!' he starts to squirm like an eel in a frying pan. And truly it's embarrassing. We don't, of course, know about all the members of the Council or what they were sentenced for (and we wouldn't be interested in the first place if they were to behave themselves decently). But then one day the court comes to examine their terms, if they've 'earned' it. These sessions are open. And at this point it emerges that one 'activist' collaborated with the Nazis, another worked on a special punishment squad, and a third was in the same business.

Thus I learned accidentally at camp ten that the chairman of the Council of our company collective had also been an 'activist' in a Nazi death camp. During the trial he broke down and wept. 'I didn't do anything wrong, I only opened and closed the crematorium doors.' God knows, maybe he really wasn't a traitor there, but merely served so as not to go to the gas chamber himself. . . .

What goes for the Council of the collective is equally true of the IOS—it has the same reputation, the same composition and the same aims: to assist admin to terrorize their fellow prisoners. And the reward for this is the same: parcels, a good reference—'responding favorably to collective training'. The IOS is the Internal Order Section, the camp militia. The same as the 'Kapos', the prisoners chosen to police the others, in the Nazi concentration camps.

Perhaps someone who doesn't know may be wondering what is wrong with the prisoners maintaining order among themselves, after all you get upsets and fights in camp, and brawls and drunkenness—and there are criminals there too. But the chief function of the IOS is not to maintain order, but to keep watch over and spy on the prisoners and to inform the authorities on who says what and who has forbidden contacts with outside. And again to deprive the con of his shop, parcels and visits, or rather, to 'beg the administration to deprive. . . .'

The members of IOS wear a red armband on duty with the three letters printed on it, and not long ago a new rule was introduced: now they must constantly wear a red diamond on their tunic or reefer jacket, because the armband is only for when they are on duty—and when a warder in the zone has to identify his faithful aides in a hurry it is usually too late—after all, they serve out of fear, not conviction.

All the bosses, especially higher up, are very proud of themselves: everything here in camp is just like outside—self-government, the prisoners are being reformed, they keep order themselves, how's that for putting faith in the prisoners? Maybe they've forgotten about the 'Kapos'. Maybe they don't know how prisoners are recruited for the Council and the IOS? Maybe they don't know, higher up, who it is that enters these camp organizations? The camp administration knows perfectly well—these are the same 'Kapos' and *polizeis*, and the percentage of 'reformed prisoners' depends directly on the number of skunks in the zone.

The prisoners loathe them. Seeing the red diamond with the letters IOS on it they say: 'Ah, the skunk has come out for a stroll!' (and on top of that you get a badge—you put it on, sell yourself, everybody turns away from you and there's no way back). But resisting a con with an armband is punishable in just the same way as resisting a warder—you end up in court. Just like outside.

A Mordovian Idyll

In the autumn they started driving us out under a double armed escort to pick potatoes. We went willingly—who knows, maybe we would get to eat a baked potato if the guards turned out to be human and didn't stamp out the fire. Only cons nearing the end of their sentence were allowed to go, that way there was less danger of escapes. One day I went along too.

Leaving the compound for the first time in two years I looked at the free life outside as at a totally different and forgotten world: houses along the streets, free people, free horses, non-working dogs (excluding the ones guarding our column, of course), chickens scratching in the dust. There was a sign up outside a club: 'Dancing'. Good God, do you mean to say that here, no more than a hundred yards from our huts, people are dancing, listening to music, making love?

We passed some schoolboys carrying satchels. They skipped past our column without even looking at us, coolly made their way past men who were being guarded by tommy gunners and dogs. It was clear that the local people had long been used to such a spectacle. . . .

There was the club itself, a squat, ramshackle structure on a crumbling foundation. And next to it the camp commander's mansion, looking particularly sumptuous in comparison with the miserable cottages surrounding it. All around it ran a high fence and there was a gate with a sign on it: 'Beware of the dog'.

'What's he got the sign for?' quipped one of the cons, 'all he needs to put is the master's name and that in itself would keep everyone away.'

PEU–Singing, Dancing and Sport

FROM TIME immemorial, from the days of Stalin's camps, there have been 'spontaneous activities' in camp. Who knows, perhaps they really were spontaneous once upon a time, men gathered together and sang and read poetry. They say they even used to act in little plays, put on shows and perform operettas. They say the theatre in Vorkuta even came into being as a result of this kind of spontaneous activities. It existed first of all independently and then under the patronage and supervision of the CEU—the Cultural Education Unit, whose organizers placed more faith in the cons than in themselves where questions of art were concerned.

Now it is no longer the CEU but the PEU—Political Education Unit—and it doesn't so much patronize the arts as control them and run them. And in general it's no longer a spontaneous activity but a form of forced labor—another one to add to the extra work you have to do.

And why is this? Not one concert program can get by without the help of the PEU. 'Help', did I say? The PEU runs the damn thing from start to finish! And you're lucky if, between the anthems and the marches, you can squeeze in a lyrical song or two, a romance, or a poem by Pushkin, Blok or Essenin. In the first place a concert is supposed to 'educate' its listeners; in the second it is supposed to offer evidence that the participants have been fully 'reformed'; and in the third it has to please the commission and help our camp 'outspit' its neighbors in the competition (and how do you do that?—'The golden grove was ablaze' is problematical, you don't know whether it's good or bad, it depends on your taste, but 'Lines on my Soviet passport' is absolutely bound to please everybody without question); fourthly, the concert itself just might as well not take place, to hell with it, but you need a tick in the right place on the report. This it is that determines everything: the program, the people who take part and the attitude of the cons to 'spontaneous activities'.

And so the company officer starts recruiting people for the choir or the poetry reading circle. Some he approaches himself, others are called into his office. One is promised a parcel, another a good character reference (when I say 'promised a parcel' I don't mean that he gets some sort of extra parcel—no, I mean his lawful, regular one, which he still has to 'earn'). The poetry lover answers: 'To whom would it occur to sing on an empty stomach?' And the master of diction replies: 'Get fucked with your amateur activities before dinner.' There are some, though, who agree. A few for the parcel, but this makes an unreliable group, and too slippery: a man turns up to all the rehearsals, gets his parcel—and you can't get him on the stage whatever you do. The basic membership of the choir and similar groups is made up of cons with twenty-five-year terms—they hope to get known, earn themselves good character references before they go to court, and then maybe their sentences will be cut.

And so a concert is announced. The next job for the warders and educationalists is to round up an audience. And here they really get on their high horses when the necessity arises. Why aren't you going to the concert? Sick? Have you got a doctor's certificate? Oh, so you don't want to go? Why not? You don't like it? What don't you like? You won't answer? But the con is bound to answer for he is obliged to be polite to all representatives of admin and the camp security services. Violation! One, two, three such violations and your shop privileges are stopped—not for not attending the concert, oh no, that's a voluntary matter, but for 'disrespect to . . .'

Newcomers go to the concerts—out of curiosity. I too went along several times to get an eyeful. What a joke! If the PEU chief, Major Sveshnikov, had specifically wanted to demoralize the cons with negative propaganda, he couldn't possibly have bettered this. On the stage a choir of policemen sings 'The Party is our Helmsman' and 'Lenin is always with You'. From the auditorium comes loud guffaws and whistling. The warders bellow: 'You'll get the cooler for interrupting the program!' The choir, even though it's full of old men, sings loudly to drown the racket in the audience. And pretty much in tune—they are mostly Ukranians and Ukranians know how to sing. What do they sing? Once they gave a rendering of 'Buchenwald Alarm', but for some reason admin didn't like this very much.

It's the same story with sporting arrangements. Force is applied (moral, of course—the same parcels and references) to get the cons to join the sports sections, where they are obliged to participate in athletics tournaments. When you see these sporting competitions you don't know whether to laugh or cry. Old men, all but legless already, run up and down or leap about the stadium (no more and no less—under the sensitive leadership of Camp Commander Pivkin the parade ground was turned into a stadium, now camp eleven has it's 'pivkins' too), their skinny, crooked legs with knotted veins clothed in baggy shorts and their mouths gasping for air. Having run the required distance, they are checked off by the company officer and then hurry off to their bunks to lie down and rest a bit.

. . . On the other hand, what singers and guitarists there really are in the camps! Sometimes we'd get together in the evenings after work, in some corner of the compound, and what songs we'd strike up—underground songs and old ballads, all accompanied by the guitar. Once the Estonians organized a concert of their folk music. And we had literary evenings—in honor of Shevchenko or Herzen. Somebody would talk about the writer and others would read Shevchenko's poetry in Ukranian. Yet others would read their own poetry or translations into Russian. But all this, of course, went on not only separately from the PEU but in secret from admin—at such evenings, after all, each man said what he thought and read what he wanted.

There were even more amateur sportsmen who were genuine and admin usually left them alone and didn't persecute them. I myself went in for soccer and there were also lovers of table tennis and skating. The basketball always used to attract large numbers of spectators; there were high class teams of Lithuanians, Latvians and Estonians, lads who were the pick of the camp, young, tall and agile. The only thing was that they all had shaven heads.

PIS—Political Instruction Sessions

AT SEVEN o'clock in the evening the canteen closes and the cons working on the first shift wander out all over the zone. The time from now until lights out is our own. Some go to the library, some to the volleyball court, some sit in the hut and write letters home, domino fans settle down around some tables or other, friends gather to talk or to argue, and some simply walk up and down inside the fence on their own—a hundred yards in one direction and then about turn and back again—eyes down and thinking about something.

But today is Thursday, the day of our political instruction session. At seven on the dot every single man has to be back in his hut: attendance at the political instruction sessions is one of the con's most important duties. Nevertheless, everybody does what he can to slip out of this duty. What's the good of it, what's the use of it? Just sit there like an idiot and listen to your company officer, stammering and stumbling over every other word, as he reads you a regulation 'lecture' from previously prepared notes in an exercise book. The majority of the company officers are completely uneducated, particularly the older ones, and are not able to prepare even this sort of talk on their own—and anyway they wouldn't be trusted to: who knows what they mightn't blurt out in their ignorance? Each talk is prepared by Sveshnikov himself. Before each session he dictates it to the company officers, who painstakingly copy it down in their exercise books (I can just imagine how many grammatical mistakes there are in those notes!) and then interpret it to us.

What do we get from such a talk? We are all quite capable of reading and understanding the newspapers ourselves, the clichés and slogans there have long since tired and sickened us, dating from when we were still free. The majority of the prisoners have completed high school, many of them also had a higher education and have doctoral dissertations to their name, men who have learned to think independently, who have made special studies of philosophy and the works of Marx, Lenin, Hegel, Kant and contemporary philosophers and sociologists: willy-nilly, 'politicians'.

It's sheer farce when the company officer, repeating somebody else's words parrot-fashion and unable to make head or tail of his own notes, conducts a political discussion with them on the level of class four in school. And in our camp, which was a political camp, even the criminal cons knew and understood more than the company officers, for they would listen to the conversations of the other prisoners and join in their arguments. I myself entered the camps completely ignorant. I had had only eight years of schooling and the most I could say was that I tried to think for myself, without prompting. But once I had decided to sort out what was what, why should I want to listen to the company officer's burblings? I had read the whole of Lenin, volume by volume, and was now starting on Plekhanov.

Having been along a few times out of curiosity, I didn't go to political instruction sessions any more and for this I was constantly having my shop privileges taken away. During the whole of my time inside I wasn't allowed a single parcel.

I remember my first chat with the company officer on this theme. Alyoshin called me into his office:

'Sit down. Marchenko, you've only just come back to the camp from prison and you're already breaking the camp rules, why? You were transferred from prison before your term was up, weren't you? Are you in a hurry to go back there and get a sniff of the sloptank?'

I replied that I saw nothing in these talks that was interesting or useful to me. Then, seeing that I couldn't be swayed by threats, he attempted another tack:

'The others go! Do you consider that you're cleverer than the others? That you know everything already?'

'No, I don't think at all that I know everything already. On the contrary, I know too little, and that's why I value my time. I have never considered myself cleverer than the others. But I'm certainly no more stupid than the people who run the sessions. The fact that others go is their own affair. I decide for myself and I'll carry on deciding.'

Alyoshin started telling me that attendance at political instruction sessions was obligatory. I could go and not listen if I liked, so long as I came and sat for the regulation two hours. But like it or not, I would be forced to give in: 'If you don't give in I'll punish you.'

'Of course I don't mind going to the sessions now and again just to see this comedy for myself, but—compulsorily every week? Under duress? I didn't ask to come to this camp of yours and I don't want you to "educate" me. What's more I'm a political prisoner, maybe I have my own opinions, my own point of view on facts and events, maybe I'm an idealist, a religious man. After all, it's not a discussion you're inviting me to. If I begin to say what I think at your talks you always answer me with threats of force—the cooler, a new trial, prison!'

In short, prisoners are driven to the political instruction sessions by threats of punishment. If you don't go—no shop, no parcels, visits are cut short, you get a bad character reference: '. . . .persists in his errors, isn't responding to corrective training. . . .' So that only those who value their parcels or references go 'voluntarily'. But the majority of prisoners in the camp have nothing to lose: they've already been deprived of the shop for something else; their next visit's not due for a long time—next year; they've still a long way to go until their term is half over, so there's no hope of having any parcels; they're in admin's bad books anyway, so the character reference has gone to the devil; and they've just got to sweat it out from bell to bell, because only the cons with 25 years can hope to get their sentences cut. Cons such as these don't go. But it is essential for everyone to go, the company officers are required to ensure a hundred per cent participation in political education. And you can't blow up the figures in your report—Sveshnikov himself might come round at any moment, or another officer squeal on you. And so you have to tie yourself up in knots all the time.

. . . .Ten to seven. They close the library at this time on Thursdays and drive everyone out of the reading room. But on the volleyball court the ball is still flying from end to end, the dominoes are still clicking on the domino table and cons are strolling about here and there. The door of the staff offices opens and a crowd of about 30 company officers comes spilling out into the zone. They are on their way to 'catch' their cons. Warders are running about the zone winkling cons out of various secluded corners. Several officers approach the volleyball court:

'Stop the game, it's time for political instruction!'

Nobody answers and the game continues. The cons appear to be deaf. Then one of the officers or warders runs up to the player with the ball.

'Give it to me!'

The con silently tosses the ball to another con. The officer goes across to him but the ball is already being held by a third, And so it goes on until it reaches the most timid con. He himself won't take the ball over to the officer, but now they have taken it away so what is to be done? The warders lose no time in dragging the culprits off to the cooler—not for refusing to attend the political instruction session but quite legally for insubordination to an officer.

The same thing happens with the domino players. 'Stop the game! Give me the dominoes!' And it ends the same way: the officer scoops up the dominoes from the table and several men are dispatched to the cooler.

At last they've rounded up everyone they can find; and some have come themselves. The session begins. The officer mumbles into his beard, following his notes, while the cons occupy themselves in various ways—finishing off letters or reading books. The officer tries not to notice this. Only if they read or write openly in the front row does he suggest to them that they move farther back, so that Sveshnikov doesn't see them should he happen to come in. Sometimes this responsible job—reading out the notes or a newspaper article, or an article from the magazine 'Kommunist'—is entrusted to one of the 'activist' cons so as to give the appearance of prisoner participation in the political instruction sessions. These activists usually turn out to be semi-illiterate old men who can barely read, so that collective work is hardly possible. And on extremely rare occasions the company officer steels himself to ask someone a question on the subject of the previous week's session. But whom? That one over there is no good, he's illiterate and can't string two words together; and that one's even worse—he's too literate.

On the other hand the cons themselves, having been forcibly driven to the session, often pepper their instructor with questions of their own, mainly about material matters. 'You say that we have to live honestly without deceiving the state, but how can a family get by on 50–70 rubles a month? What salary do you get? You just mentioned the increasing prosperity of the workers—how do you relate the concept of 'increasing prosperity' with the rise of food prices and the raising of the norms in industry?'

This last question was asked by Kolya Yusupov one day when I was there. Our company officer was lost for words and then said: 'You, Yusupov, misunderstand our political situation. You purposely draw attention to individual shortcomings which are only temporary.' All the cons laughed and I asked:

'How long does your "temporary" last and on what time scale is it to be calculated? We know, for instance, that the decree on censorship was accepted as a "temporary" measure and even for a "short time" only. That was approximately fifty years ago and the censorship is still with us. . . .'

'Your sentence was too short, Marchenko, it ought to be extended. And there are one or two more here, I see, who would like a spell in the cooler!'

'We're convinced, we're convinced!' roared the cons boisterously.

The session ended and the cons dispersed, cursing all 'instructors' and 'propagandists' to kingdom come. Everybody laughs at them, even the stool pigeons.

Big Bosses and Little Bosses

Power comes from the people . . .
But on what does it feed?
Where does it lead?
What does it breed?

Bertolt Brecht—'Songs'

As soon as word goes round that Gromov is on his way to the camp there's a terrible hustle and bustle. It's no joke—Gromov in person! The camp commander runs in circles and hustles the company officers, these hustle the warders and the lot of them together, of course, hustle the cons. There is a general clean-up, an exhaustive search of the huts and you start to overfulfil all the norms. Are you sneaking off work? The cooler! Are you improperly dressed, has your hair grown a couple of centimetres? Haircut! No shop privileges!

Gromov is feared like the plague—and by everyone: free workers, officers, even the camp commander; and also the local inhabitants. In all the settlements from Potma to Barashevo, in all the camps—male and female, criminal and political, special regime, normal regime, strict regime—everyone trembles at the mere mention of Gromov's name. He can do anything, he is a feudal prince in these parts. Colonel Gromov is Commander in Chief of the whole of Dubrovlag. And the main thing is that you never know what he is going to praise you for and what will cause him to blow up. It can happen that what inspires his gratitude the first time will bring a tongue-lashing the next.

Here he was now, leaving the staff offices at camp seven for the zone. He was accompanied by a deferential retinue consisting of aides from HQ and the camp bosses. The officers divided their time between casting apprehensively obsequious glances in Gromov's direction and glaring at the cons—there mustn't be any violations or disturbances. Nevertheless they weren't watchful enough. Right outside the offices an old man, leaning on a stick, came up to Gromov and started telling him something. Whether he was complaining or perhaps asking for something I didn't hear. All I could hear was Gromov snapping at the camp commander: 'This won't do!', before moving on impassively.

Confusion overtook the retinue. One of the company officers went up to the old man and scolded him in a loud voice:

'Why didn't you say so earlier? Come to my office tomorrow and we'll sort it out for you.'

The old man, thanking the officer profusely, hobbled away in the direction of his hut. At that moment Gromov turned and roared:

'Where? I said to the cooler with him, the cooler! This won't do! You've let your prisoners get out of hand, they won't even let me pass! Why didn't you make it clear that he should register to see me when I'm receiving prisoners and should come at the proper time?'

While he was thus dressing our camp bosses down, two warders ran up to the old man, snatched his stick from his hand, threw it away and dragged the poor fellow straight off to the cooler—and he had just been overjoyed to think that Gromov had interceded for him.

Gromov came to us another time because our plan was on the rocks. He must have really blown up the staff inside, because when Ageyev scrambled out into the zone behind Gromov he was as red as a beet. He had been ordered to send all the invalids to the factory, that is those cons who were unfit for work but somehow managed to do little jobs around the living zone, acting as orderlies, keeping the compound clean and so on. For a beginning there was to be a general muster of invalids, they were to be rounded up into a single hut for a meeting to be held. Gromov was giving instructions as he walked and Ageyev, absolutely quaking with fear, was running alongside and asking:

'Comrade Colonel, what shall we do with the bed-ridden? Carry them to the meeting or leave them?'

'Carry out your orders, major!'

And so it was everywhere, no matter where he appeared. The officers would scurry about with their eyes bulging out of their sockets, petrified with fear, and punishments would rain down on us poor cons from right and left. When Gromov used to come to us (much later) in the hospital at camp eight, Major Petrushevsky himself, the Chief of the Dubrovlag Medical Department, who used to pack medical orderlies off to the cooler in droves—the windows were all dusty, there were cobwebs in the corners and coal was falling out of the stove—Petrushevsky himself used to trot at Gromov's heels and then look sideways into his eyes to see whether he was angry or satisfied. And it goes without saying that a day or two before Gromov's arrival we orderlies were transferred from our blocks back to the communal huts—God forbid that he should ever discover that the con orderlies were living two and three to a room: what luxury, maybe they'd like to have separate flats or their wives to be sent out to them?

One day Gromov came to the hospital with a commission

from Moscow—representing the Ministry of the Interior. The commission proceeded through the wards, the doctors answered questions, the director of the hospital, as usual in Gromov's presence, smiled ingratiatingly, nodded her head and hastened to agree with everything he said. Nobody, of course, even looked at the cons—patients and orderlies—or asked them any questions. But in one ward the patients spoke up for themselves, complaining that it was cold. Gromov didn't deign to answer them. But a visiting colonel, taking a look at the thermometer on the wall (it was 15 degrees in the ward), went over to one of the bunks: 'Who are you, where from, what's your name, what were you sentenced for?'

The patient replied. He had an ulcer and had only just been brought in from the camp in a very serious condition. His name was Sikk, he was from one of the Baltic states and he was in for 'nationalism'. After hearing all this the Moscow colonel shouted so that the whole block could hear:

'And you have the nerve to complain that you're cold! People like you should be kept out in the snow, and not in hospital! The whole lot of you Baltic people are enemies and gangsters! You fought against us with weapons in your hands and now you're asking us to coddle you!'

He went on bellowing like that for ages. Gromov stood there the whole time completely calmly, without interfering, and in no way hurrying to support his superior. On the whole he always behaved independently and didn't suck up to anyone.

On the other hand he found an excuse on this occasion to pick on another prisoner, a doctor's assistant named Ryskov. Ryskov was not a bad fellow, a Moscow journalist and poet, though physically not very strong. For that reason some of his friends among the cons had helped him to get light work in the hospital, as a doctor's assistant (he had had some medical training). It seemed to Gromov that Ryskov held himself with a dignity not prescribed for a con—and he answered questions without a hint of servility. He called Ryskov into the office and questioned him as to who and what he was and why he was here in the hospital. Ryskov replied that he worked there.

'Why do you talk so provocatively to your superiors?'

'I don't talk provocatively, but simply the way I do to everyone else.'

There was nothing to pick on and nothing to justify the cooler. Nevertheless, Ryskov was sent back to camp with the next convoy, to do general work. In such cases there's no point in asking why. Admin knows best, admin makes its own arrangements.

Gromov has been serving in labor camps for a very long time, ever since the time of Stalin. In those days he was commander of a camp that was building an oil refinery at Omsk. In Mordovia you can still meet cons who used to work in that camp. I shared a cell with one who had been foreman there. Listening to his stories used to make your blood run cold. Anyway it's well known what camps were like in Stalin's time, in the fifties! And now Gromov was in command not just of one camp, but of the directorate of a whole network, with dozens of camps under his control. The methods had changed a bit, but he himself was still the same and just the same despot that he had always been. All that had changed was that he had gone up in rank and was now a colonel. Doubtless he would be a general by the time he retired.

On the whole a great many camp personnel had toppled from their posts since Beria was shot in 1953. The lower ranks had been simply dismissed or demoted. To the bigger (and older) fish it was suggested that they accept an early retirement and these retreated with their fat pensions to have a well-earned rest in the Crimea, cultivating the vineyards that had been confiscated from the Crimean Tartars. But even those dismissed or demoted former MVD* men managed to set themselves up in comfortable little jobs, with good rates of pay, in or around the remaining camps. They became production managers, supply managers, warders and even just foremen—anything to get back into a camp where you were paid not for the work you did but for squeezing cons to the very last drop. They settled in there and bided their time. They were confident that their experience would be needed again, that they would be recalled. And they were right.

They themselves admit that they received in some cases advice, in others instructions, from 'above' to send in official complaints and petitions asking to be restored to their posts and for their good name to be rehabilitated. Naturally each of them wrote that he had served faithfully and honorably, that he had been slandered and treated unjustly, that he had never exceeded his powers but had acted only on orders from above, and that he promised to do the same in the future. Slowly and on the sly they began to be restored to their posts and to return to their favorite form of work. They took out their uniforms—which hadn't yet had time to fade—and again appeared in the roles of camp commanders, company officers and aides at Dubrovlag HQ.

Former members of Stalin's cadres at camp seven included the Commander, Kolomitsev, and his deputy, Ageyev. One of our company officers for a time, after Alyoshin and Lubayev,

* Ministry of Internal Affairs. Beria used it to consolidate his position after Stalin's death by fusing it with the Ministry of State Security, but the security service was separated from the MVD after Beria's downfall.

was a former lieutenant-colonel who had been reduced to the ranks and subsequently rehabilitated. A con who had been imprisoned in Mordovia since 1949 told me about the Chief Officer's deputy at camp seven, Shved, that Shved had taken an active part in the mass shootings of cons while they were on parade. At that time they used to lead all captured Ukrainian 'secessionists' into the forest, ostensibly to gather firewood, and then gun the whole column down under the pretext of an 'organized mass escape'. Thus the cons knew that if they were taken out to gather firewood there would be no return. And the cons on parade started refusing to go into the forest. Shved, who was then a major, used to go up to the prisoners who refused and shoot them point blank with his revolver—the con who told me this had seen it with his own eyes. Shved was later dismissed and reduced to the ranks, but afterwards returned to work in the camps, although without his former rank.

In my time he was merely a senior sergeant, although already pushing fifty. He was an extremely brawny Ukranian, calm and leisurely in his movements, with a singsong Ukranian accent (about which we always teased our Ukranians: look, we said, you're always complaining about 'big brother' Russians taking it out on you here in Mordovia, but what about this beloved countryman of yours? He makes mincemeat of both you and us, without distinction). Shved was short, stocky, round-faced and bullnecked and both his face and his neck were always red—the cons said it was from the amount of our blood he had drunk, like a bedbug. Insofar as he was deputy to the Chief Officer he wielded great power. And he used to do everything he could to make life unpleasant for us.

We in the emergency gang used to have to go to the work zone three or four times every day, and sometimes even more.

267

As soon as the wagons were brought up for loading or unloading we would have to go out—day-time, night-time, at any time of the day or night and in all weathers. And so Shved thought himself up a little amusement: long before the wagons were ready, Shved would call us out to the guardhouse. When we arrived there would be no warder—he had gone off to the work zone to hunt for 'malingerers' who might be sleeping in odd corners during working hours. We would hang around, growing steadily more irritable, and a whole hour or more would go by before we could get to work. Having done our stint and unloaded the wagons, we would set off 'home' again—and again the same thing would happen, we would have to wait for more than an hour, come rain, come snow, standing by the guardhouse gate. All this when we might easily be called out again in another three to four hours! Shved would come out of the guardhouse to gloat. And when we complained would reply:

'What can Shved do? I can't tear the warder in two so that one half goes looking for loafers and the other half stays in the guardhouse. We're short of warders, you're costing the state too much already.'

One evening I was called to the guardroom to see Shved: during one of the searches a civilian cap had been found under my pillow. That meant I faced an explanation and most likely punishment.

After knocking on the door, I entered the office. Shved was sitting there playing draughts* with a warder. Two more warders were just sitting around. They glanced at me and went on playing. I just stood there. After about three minutes had passed, Shved tore himself away from the board: 'Company?' I replied. There was silence again and then, after another move: 'Gang?' Again a pause, a move and then the question:

* Checkers.

'Surname?' I answered the questions and stood there waiting.

At last the game finished. Shved had won and beamed with gratification. He carefully packed the pieces into their box and then, before turning his attention to me, spoke to the warder: 'Slip down to the visitors' hostel and put an end to that visit there, he's had long enough. And tell Tarasova she's not to let any food through, not even an ounce. Then bring the prisoner here—I'll search him.' (Shved usually searched the cons himself after visits—either he didn't trust the warders or else he just loved the work.) Then he turned to me:

'Do you know what you've been brought here for? Do you want to guess?'

'Why should I guess, you'll tell me yourself.'

'What are you doing with a cap of a civilian model? What have you thought up to answer?'

I hadn't time to reply before the other con was brought in from his visit—an old man of about sixty. Shved stood up, went over to him and said banteringly:

'Well, grandad, did you hold the old woman's tits for a bit?'

The old man was lost for words for a moment, but then nevertheless responded:

'That's all over for me, I'm too old.'

'You should have called me if you couldn't manage it yourself. I would have come down and done her a favor.'

'Yes, but she's an old woman too. . . .'

'It doesn't matter if she's old. I wouldn't have turned my nose up at her. What's your score?'

'Eleven years to go.'

Shved burst out laughing.

'You mean you hope to live another eleven years? I'm not talking about your sentence, blockhead—how old are you, I said. Never mind, let me search you'.

269

Shved removed the 'Cuban' from the old man's head, felt it all over, seam by seam, and then laid it to one side. Meanwhile the old man had already taken his tunic off. Feeling it carefully, Shved asked in friendly fashion:

'Tell me right away, grandad, how much money have you got on you?'

'What money? I haven't got even a ruble. Once a year the old lady's allowed to come and she can't even give me a lump of sugar.'

Shved replied just as good-humoredly: 'It's nothing to do with me. The law's the law. If the law says a prisoner's not allowed to have sugar, lard and other kinds of food then that's the way it has to be. The law has to be obeyed. If Shved's told tomorrow that parcels are allowed, Shved will let a whole wagon-load in.'

My skin used to crawl at the tone of his voice and those abominable jokes. 'The law's the law. . . . If Shved's told not to send the cons out to work, Shved won't send them. . . .' I could see him so vividly intoning these sayings of his, pacing up and down with his revolver on parade, that my fists clenched involuntarily.

Shved had already felt his gray undershirt all over and ordered the old man to take his boots off. Grunting and groaning, the old man removed his felt knee-boots and gave one to the sergeant. The latter groped around inside the boot, found nothing there, took out the inner sole, examined it and pinched the leg of the boot—there was nothing. Just as calmly he examined the second boot and when he fished out the inner sole his face lit up with a happy smile: a ten ruble note had been glued to the under-side. Shved started to shame the old man:

'And you said you had no money on you! An old man, a Christian too, no doubt—aren't you ashamed of telling lies?'

The old man was silent, he had been caught red-handed, there was nothing he could say. Shved meticulously peeled the note from the inner sole, smoothed it out, laid it on the table and went on with his search. He felt the trousers that the old man had just taken off, ordered him to drop his underpants, turn round, turn back again and squat on his haunches (in doing which the old man almost toppled over) and then examined the underpants. There was nothing else hidden anywhere. But Shved was pleased: he knew that no con would come away from a visit empty-handed—they were all the same, all swindlers and liars!

With relish he wrote out a report, signed it, gave it to the warders to sign and then ordered one of them to give the ten rubles back to the old woman and get her to sign for them. The old man, meanwhile, was already getting dressed and mumbling something about being allowed to have no food and no money, not even if you were dying of starvation.

But Shved had already lost all interest in the old man and after rapping back at him as he walked away: 'I'll deal with you later' turned his attention to me. Evidently he was now 'tired' of working, for he told me curtly that he would write out a report on me and hand it to the Chief Officer, let him deal with it and punish me himself.

'You can go.'

The old man and I left the guardroom together. When we had gone some way from the guardhouse I took the old man to task: how was it he hadn't found a better place in which to hide his ten rubles? The old man grinned cunningly:

'It wasn't me who was diddled, it was Shved.'

And he explained to me where the trick lay. His visit had been from his wife and son-in-law, and his son-in-law had already knocked around a bit—including ten years spent in the camps at Kolyma. His wife, too, had left the camps only five years beforehand and they were both well used to visits. While still at home the son-in-law had concealed 25 rubles in the heel of one of his boots and here had exchanged boots with the old man.

'These are my son-in-law's boots. We know Shved was bound to suspect I had money hidden somewhere, so we put the tenner in the sole on purpose. He's now pleased with himself and I've got something to add to my regular fiver.'

After so many years, how could he fail to learn how to pull a fast one on the warder?

The marketing director of the furniture factory at camp seven was Chekunov. They said that earlier he had worked for the MVD but was later demoted. We, however, only knew of him from work, for it was with him that we in the emergency gang had to deal: he was in charge of the loading and authorized our worksheets. He and the chief of the timber yard (for unloading) constituted our immediate bosses at the factory and on them depended our work and our pay.

This Chekunov not only never let the least bit of extra pay through on to the worksheets, but would even refuse to pay us for work done. We, for instance, used to push both full and empty wagons from place to place by hand—it was heavy work, but we never got a penny for it. Not only that but Chekunov even used to sermonize: 'What, do you expect to get money from the state for nothing? To squander the people's wealth, plunder the state? I as a Communist am guarding the people's property!'

And suddenly there came a rumor: Chekunov's been caught for misappropriation, Chekunov's going to be tried. It turned out that he had been writing off good furniture as defective; after first setting himself up, he had supplied all the officers of Dubrovlag with furniture on the cheap and all the representatives of local government absolutely free. And in general he had been up to various machinations with defective goods: whenever furniture came back after being damaged in transit, he would write it off as defective, then get the cons to repair it and send it out again as new. I think that's how it was, or maybe he found some other way of lining his pockets, but in any case he was a natural swindler. Somewhere or other along the line, though, he failed to share with the Party boss, the latter then informed on him and thus our Chekunov was awaiting his trial.

We celebrated too soon, however. It didn't come to a trial initially; all he got was a strict reprimand from the Party. And the Party chief was thanked for his vigilance. Once again Chekunov returned to the ranks of the bosses, once again we had to listen to him ranting: 'Sitting on your arses at the people's expense?' And a little later the Party chief was removed and transferred elsewhere.

But evidently he wouldn't rest and wrote a letter to Moscow—not only about Chekunov this time but also about his cronies, who were covering up for him. Willy-nilly the local authorities had to take the matter up properly. Chekunov was their man through and through, but it was better not to tangle with Moscow. He was relieved of his post and charged. But they didn't stick him in jail before the trial, like the rest of us, but left him at liberty while the case was being investigated. He covered his tracks, did deals with the witnesses, shot his furniture off to various friends. And he also came to the camp, to the work zone, to talk to us in the emergency gang—but of course in quite a different tone from before, politely and even kindly, insisting on the conversation himself, so that it was clear he was afraid of something.

Later the trial was held. All the free workers from the factory and the offices went to hear it, even abandoning their work in order to do so. They told us afterwards what had happened. Chekunov got three years on modified regime and was to serve this term here in Mordovia. That meant he would come under some officer whom he himself had supplied with free furniture, would be free to go about without armed guards and would get parcels every month. Living off the fat of the land! Life in camp for Chekunov wouldn't be just easy, but seventh heaven.

More often than not, however, it never gets as far as a trial, they try to hush everything up, not wash their dirty linen in public. One of our camp bosses, for instance, built himself a great big house on the side—using government materials and free labor: cons. He set himself up with furniture from the factory and lived like a lord. But it still wasn't enough, his greed was too much for him and he came to grief over some further manipulations. They didn't put him on trial but suggested he should apply for his pension. He sold his home, loaded all his belongings into packing cases and departed for some place in the south, where he settled down to live out his days in peace.

Everybody knew he was a swindler. We cons learned about it from the free workers, and anyway it was all the warders could talk about: just look at that skunk—feathered his own nest very nicely with not so honest labor and wouldn't even give us firewood from the factory.

The cons needled the officers for ages afterwards about it: what's this about teaching us to live by honest labor while your own boss is a thief—and what's more wriggled out of everything without being punished? At first they tried to persuade us that it wasn't true, but then gave up—how could you hide it anyway?—and merely got out of it by saying that 'every family has its black sheep'.

Not one of the camp officers or employees can resist fiddling something or other. Taking stuff out of the compound, for instance—that doesn't rank as pilfering. How can it? It's nothing, it's government stuff, and the government won't go broke (at this point they somehow manage to forget their political instruction sessions and little talks; those are just the necessary words, the correct things to say, and anyway they're one thing, but here we're talking about trifles, small stuff, some three cubic yards of firewood, and that's a different matter entirely). Even less would it occur to any of them to 'ask' a con to work for them, whether in or out of working hours—it is crystal clear that the con is dying to do favors for his bosses.

Our company officer, Lieutenant Alyoshin, 'asked' his cons to load him up a truck of firewood. It's true that this meant not only loading it up, but sawing and chipping it first. But who would refuse? For on that same Ageyev depended such questions as whether you were to have shop privileges or not, or parcels, or visits—in short the whole of your camp existence. So we sawed and chopped it and loaded it under the watchful gaze of a warder (he had to watch the lorry being loaded in case somebody was hidden underneath—at the guardhouse too they would thoroughly prod the whole load with a pointed iron rod and examine it from all sides). The truck rolled up to the guardhouse. And who should turn up at this moment but the commandant of the compound.

'Where'd you get that wood? Who's it for? Where's your receipt?'

The warder sitting on top of the wood handed him the receipt to show that the wood was paid for. The commandant looked from the paper to the truck and back again:

'Christ, the fucking bastard, he's signed for one yard and loaded up four! Turn your lorry round and start unloading! Unless Alyoshin pays up at the cashier's.'

Alyoshin came up and a first-class row broke out. There

was a parade just at that moment, a crowd of cons were standing by the guardhouse and they rocked with laughter as they listened to the exchange. The conversation went like this:

'You've got a fucking brass neck, you great prick! Signed for a yard and taking out four.'

'Well, it's all the fucking same to you, isn't it? Is it yours or something?'

'I don't give a fuck, turn the fucking truck round, or else pay for the rest!'

'Wait a minute, what the fucking hell are you shouting about?'

'Fuck off with your "wait a minute!" Turn it round!'

And so on for about fifteen minutes to the general merriment of the cons. I don't know how long it would have continued, but at that point the Camp Commander came over to the guardhouse (Kolomitsev had already retired by that time and been replaced by Dvoretskov). Both of them dashed to meet him, the commandant with a complaint and Alyoshin with a request to be allowed to take the wood out. The Camp Commander was at a loss. He didn't really want to offend Alyoshin, but it was awkward to give him permission in front of the cons. He neither agreed not disagreed, but excused himself by saying he was busy, that they would have to sort it out themselves, and walked away. Alyoshin spat, gave a wave of his hand and ordered us to unload the three extra yards. He would make up for it later, there was no point in paying out money unnecessarily.

That same firewood later caused me to have a personal skirmish with another company officer. The incident occurred in the autumn of 1965, not long before my departure for hospital in camp three. I was working on night shift in the foundry at the time. I came back one morning from work, drank my skilly and lay down to sleep. I was absolutely dog tired from work, my ears were hurting, my head aching, and I couldn't even fall asleep for the pain. Then, when I had just dozed off, I was woken by the orderly:

'Go to the company officer, he wants to see you.'

How reluctant I was and how hard it was to get up! While I got dressed I kept wondering to myself what it was all about, why was I being called? I couldn't think of anything I had done to give cause for going to the cooler. I thought and thought and decided that an answer must have come to one of my complaints about my illness.

Knocking on the door, I entered the office and the company officer said something that I couldn't hear properly—I had a steady roaring in my ears. The orderly bent down and whispered to the officer to speak louder. The latter repeated loudly:

'Go to the factory with the orderly. You must go now.'

Half asleep, I was able to make very little of it and I stumbled to the guardhouse. Several cons from our gang were already waiting there, they were also from the night shift. Well, they led us, as usual, through the gate and only when in the work zone did I suddenly come to my senses and ask:

'Hey, where are they taking us? And what for?'

'What for, what for? To load wood for the company officer, of course.'

God, what a fool, stumbling off like a donkey to break my back for an officer! I was so infuriated, both with myself, the orderly and the officer—and with the whole world—that I turned round and walked back. But it wasn't so easy! Who was going to let me out of the work zone all on my own? I would have to wait at the factory until they finished with the wood. So on top of everything else I was going to have to go without my dinner: I was in the work zone now and my dinner would be in the living zone. There was nothing to be done. I found a secluded corner and flopped down to have a sleep—I was damned if I was going to slave for my jailer.

I dozed off—and again was woken up. A warder was digging me roughly in the ribs:

'Aha, skiving off, eh? Let's go to the cooler!'

I tried to explain to him that I wasn't on duty, that I had done my stint and was resting, but he wouldn't listen to me and dragged me off to the guardhouse. It was useless to resist. All right, I thought, it will all be cleared up at the guardhouse. But just for the purpose, the warder who had searched us and taken us into the work zone wasn't there. I tried again to explain that I'd only just come off work and would have to go back that night—what a hope! He took me straight through the guardhouse and into the cooler. To kick up a fuss, insist, call for the company officer—all this was to invite a certain 10–15 days in the cooler for disorderly conduct and resisting a warder. I gave up in disgust and lay on the bare boards. For dinner I had the cooler skilly, with no bread. Then round about four o'clock, I was let out: they checked with the records office and assured themselves that I was working on the night shift. All they said when they let me out was: 'why the bloody hell did you have to sleep in the work zone?'

After supper I was again called in to see the company officer.

'Why did you leave the others and refuse to work?'

After everything that had happened I was fighting mad and in no mood to restrain myself. I said that although I was a con, not a man, nevertheless I neither desired nor intended to wait upon my jailers. And there was nothing said in my sentence about acting as laborer to company officers.

'But nobody forced you to go, you were only asked to help. If you didn't want to, you shouldn't have gone. And the others didn't refuse, they volunteered to go.'

'Yes, of course they volunteered—otherwise you'd find an excuse to stop them getting any more parcels. A prisoner's got to earn his parcels—and that means by sawing your fire-wood, doesn't it?'

The officer said he had no time to argue with me now but would deal with me later. I could go and get ready for work. I left convinced that I would get no shop privileges that month. And so it was.

Khrushchev Gets the Boot

IN THE autumn of 1964 we were on our way to dinner from work when we saw the following little scene: three warders dragging a con off to the cooler while he struggled and yelled so that the whole camp could hear. Many people in the zone knew this prisoner, he was a former criminal con, a rowdy and even violent fellow. As he was being dragged through the whole camp, the cons who passed him asked:

'What for?'

'For Khrushchev, you cunts, for Khrushchev!'

Soon afterwards we learned what the matter was. Now the story is well known to all the cons in Mordovia, just like the story of Kolya Shcherbakov's ear.

It turned out that Khrushchev had been ousted and we in the camp still didn't know about it. The camp administration, however, had hastened to put an end to the cult of Khrushchev. Early one morning, long before reveille, they had roused the camp artist—a con—from his bunk and brought him to the staff offices. The top brass was already there, and not just the camp KGB but their superiors. The artist was ordered to erase the name of Khrushchev from all the placards as swiftly as possible, while all the cons were still in their huts. There was far too much work for only one

man, however, for the whole camp was plastered with placards and slogans and on all of them was written: N. S.
Khrushchev. Therefore they summoned several 'activists' as
well—stool pigeons, members of the Internal Order Section
and Council of the collective. And this special task force set
to work.

It was clear that they still wouldn't finish before reveille, so
they hurried to expel the former head of the government
from at least all the more prominent places: inside the staff
offices, on the outside walls of the offices and in the area
immediately surrounding the offices. Over the cinema screen
on the open-air stage hung a lengthy red banner: 'Under
Socialist conditions every man who leaves the path of labor is
able to return to useful activity.' And in even bigger letters
the signature: 'N. S. Khrushchev.' This banner was very high
up and couldn't be reached without a ladder—which was the
last thing you could expect to find in a prison camp! While
they were getting a ladder and moving it into place, reveille
was sounded and the stage was surrounded by gaping prisoners. And when the artist started to scrape off the name of
Khrushchev, everybody at once guessed what was up. And
what a scene there was! Whistles, hoots, curses—many were
inside because of Khrushchev, including almost all the criminals. Nobody from admin dared show themselves to the
prisoners that morning, but just sat tight in their offices.

But now the time came to open the library and here they
suddenly remembered that all the walls inside were plastered
with newspaper and magazine cuttings and photographs and
placards. Something had to done quickly. And then they
called in a number of low skunks—well known to admin—
about whom it was known that even if they couldn't be
forced they could always be bought.

One of them was invited into the office of Sveshnikov, head

of the Political Education Unit (he himself talked about this afterwards in great detail). Sveshnikov took several packets of Indian tea from his desk and spread them out for the con to see:

'Go to the reading room, destroy all the photographs of Khrushchev in any way you like—and this tea is yours.'

Before the criminal con lay the tea. This in camp terms was a whole fortune—you could buy quite a few people with tea.* Sveshnikov and the other officers present from the KGB all knew this and were thoroughly confident of success. They looked at the con and he looked at the tea. Of course he was calculating in his mind how much tea there was—in a minute he'd agree. Or else he'd bargain in the hope of adding to it. The con transferred his gaze from the tea to the officer and then back to the tea again. At last he said in a business-like tone:

'Tea makes everything possible. But . . . you know, officer'—this to Sveshnikov—'you've got such a lovely arse as to make any woman jealous. You've fattened it at our expense. Let me just shag you once and in return I'll bring you twice as much tea and every single photo in the camp of your faithful Leninist.'

Naturally they dragged him straight off to the cooler. And as he went he bellowed to the whole camp and everyone he met on the way:

'Look at these cunts! Not so long ago they were kissing Khrushchev's cock and arse themselves and now they want us to take his mug off the walls! I got seven years added on for Khrushchev, you nancy boys, they made me a political because of him! You should be letting me go now! But no, because of him again you're dumping me in the cooler!'

* This is a reference to 'tea addicts'. A very powerful stimulant can be brewed from tea.

We in the emergency gang had been working since before dawn and not having been in the zone that morning still knew nothing. Thus we heard the news about Khrushchev's downfall, interspersed with obscenities, from the mouth of the unfortunate criminal. He continued to yell the same in the cooler and could be heard all over the camp.

But of course they found people ready to sell themselves for tea—'tea makes everything possible'. They appeared in the reading room and set about tearing down the placards and cuttings in front of everybody, to the accompaniment of general laughter. This important operation soon became a game. A con would go up to a photograph, wet his index finger with spit, give a push and a twist and there would be Khrushchev headless on the photograph, while his head stayed on the con's index finger. Then the con would creep up on one of his friends, strike suddenly with his finger, and the friend's forehead would be decorated with that all-too-familiar physiognomy. In the noise and confusion they started to tear down the pictures of other members of the Central Committee and government too: Brezhnev's body suddenly acquired Khrushchev's face, and vice-versa. And they managed to destroy practically all the photographs of Podgorny, explaining afterwards with an innocent expression on their faces: 'Sorry, I got mixed up, they all look so much alike.'

A day or two later they started to 'reshape' the reading room. The disturbances died down of their own accord. But then new ones took their place: cons who had been sentenced because of Khrushchev started demanding to be set free. They said that in camp eleven they even packed their bags and moved on the guardhouse: 'We were imprisoned for criticizing Khrushchev and now we've been proved right. Let us go!' Instead they were dispersed, of course.

In order to calm the prisoners down a bit they started calling in everybody who was in for Khrushchev, one by one, to talk to the KGB. There they were advised to write to the Presidium of the Supreme Soviet petitioning for pardons; the latter, so the argument went, would be bound to respond to such petitions, now it was merely a question of letting them know of your existence. The calculation was a simple one: by the time the cons had written their petitions and sent them off, and then waited for some kind of reply, two to three months or even half a year might go by. In the meantime the agitation would die down; and in any case the answers would come in bit by bit—while some were reacting indignantly to the refusals, others would still be waiting and hoping.

Many prisoners to whom it was suggested they write refused: 'What pardon? We were proved right, we ought to be rehabilitated'. But the majority nonetheless begged for pardons—anything to be released, who cared how it was done? And who would want to spend any more time than was necessary in camp?

Perhaps a few of them really were rehabilitated—I don't know of any such cases and never heard of any. Even pardons, at camp seven at least, were granted to only a handful out of hundreds, and only to those who had not more than a year left to serve and had good references from admin.

One of the men to be pardoned a few months before the end of his term was Sanya Klimov, my neighbor at the time of my meeting with my mother. After that meeting I got to know him better and learned that he had been charged under Article 70 'for criticizing Khrushchev'.

Klimov had been a building worker formerly. One day he and his friends had picked up a couple of bottles on pay day and gone into a restaurant. This was just at the time when the price of butter and meat had gone up, so the dinners must have gone up too. They behaved rowdily and loudly criticized Khrushchev: first it was the damned vodka going up, now it's butter and meat. By the time we overtake America the bread will be dearer too. In other words it was the normal sort of workman's conversation. Sanya, most probably, talked louder and more sharply than the others—and he was just unlucky. Some KGB man must have been in the vicinity, or a party worker. Sanya was picked up within minutes, there in the restaurant, and his friends whisked off as witnesses.

Now he wrote a petition for pardon and at least got out before the end of his term. But a fellow from our emergency gang, Potapov, another Sanya, is inside even to this day, although he too was in for Khrushchev.

Sanya Potapov had been an active Komsomol worker and a convinced Leninist. He served in the navy and was Komsomol Organizer of his unit. After demobilization he became secretary of the Komsomol town committee in Lipetsk. He married an equally convinced and enthusiastic Komsomol worker who was also a Komsomol secretary. An exemplary family came into being, a genuine Komsomol cell—two secretaries. And a child was born—also a future Komsomol member.

But the trouble was that young Potapov was an honest and thinking sort of fellow. To begin with, mixing with the young workers, he saw that they weren't burning with enthusiasm at all, that many of them were dissatisfied with their life and their pay and used to make fun of Khrushchev almost openly. He started to meditate on the situation in the country, on the role of politics in economic life, and came to the conclusion that the current policy was wrong and the methods of management no good (after 1964 they came to be characterized as 'voluntarist').

Sanya tried to talk about these things in the town committee where he was secretary, but he was called to order, as they say, and put in his place. But he was no longer able or willing to suppress his views and so he embarked on underground activity in the spirit of the best models to be found in our own literature: he started to write leaflets and distribute them round the town. By day he would work in the local party headquarters, delivering lectures and reports to the youth of the town, and everything in them was 'proper' and 'acceptable'. But coming home in the evenings he would sit at his desk, take paper and pen and write out one of his leaflets: that Khrushchev and his Central Committee were following an anti-people's policy that threatened the country with economic collapse; that an adventurist foreign policy was bringing us to the verge of catastrophe; that the raising of food prices and the raising of work norms were cutting the workers' wages back at both ends. These handwritten leaflets he would stick up in prominent places during the night or put into people's letter boxes.

One day one of the members of the town Party committee caught Sanya just as he was dropping a leaflet into his box. He knew Sanya very well and now he knew who had been supplying him with regular leaflets. But he didn't run straight off to tell the KGB. Instead he tried to persuade Sanya that this form of activity was useless. It would make no difference, he said, for our people were incapable of acting decisively and incapable of standing up for themselves. 'You will just become a useless victim,' he said to Sanya. And then he warned Sanya that if he continued to put leaflets in his letter box he would go to the KGB. He himself understood the situation even better than Sanya, there was no need to convince him, but he had no intention of going to prison for nothing: 'My life and my freedom are too dear to me.'

After this Sanya continued to write and distribute his

leaflets, but missed out the home of his friend. And so it went on for about two years. All this time the KGB was searching for an 'anti-Khrushchev organization' and couldn't find one—they couldn't even imagine that all this was being done by one man. In 1963 the military commission started calling in everyone in Lipetsk liable for military service and proposing to them that they either write their curriculum vitae or fill in a questionnaire. Sanya realized that they were collecting samples of handwriting and attempted to change his own as best he could. Whether this didn't help or whether he was betrayed isn't clear, but soon afterwards he was arrested. He was tried, like most of the rest of us, in secret session, and condemned, under Article 70, to four years in camp. Then he was brought to Mordovia.

Sanya suffered a great deal on account of his family. By 1963 a second child had been born. After his arrest his wife, of course, was kicked out of her job in the Party committee and found work as a typist. But how could a typist feed two little children on her salary alone? What's more she was often ill and had to spend long periods in hospital, for she had a weak heart. And if it hadn't been for his and her parents, goodness knows how they would have got by.

Knowing of his difficult family situation the camp KGB, even before Khrushchev was toppled, had called Potapov in several times and suggested that he write a statement admitting that he had wrongly interpreted the policy of Khrushchev, that he had slandered him and had now repented. Then they themselves would see about getting him pardoned. But Sanya always refused. Then, when Khrushchev was removed, they called him in again together with the rest to petition for a pardon. Sanya said:

'How can that be? Some months ago you suggested to me to write that I had been wrong and was repenting. Now it turns out that I was right, that I was correct in criticizing Khrushchev, yet I still have to beg for pardon. What do you want me to write in my petition?'

Their reply was: 'Isn't it all the same to you, just so long as you go free?'

He refused to write and is still doing time in camp eleven. But even of those who did petition, far from all of them were released. Particularly the ones whose cases were similar to Potapov: they were refused on the grounds that 'agitating against Khrushchev they were also agitating against the Central Committee' or on the grounds of 'the special gravity of the crime that was committed'.

A Visit

'MARCHENKO, YOUR mother's here', said a fellow from a gang
that worked outside the camp. Returning from work they
had seen an elderly woman standing by the guardhouse and
eagerly staring at the passing cons. As usual they asked her
who she had come to see. She said Anatoly Marchenko, her
son, and also managed to add that she had been waiting for
three days already to see my section commander and get him
to sign a permit for a visit.

I hadn't seen my mother for many years. I had gone away
to work on construction sites, then I went to the camps,
escaped, was caught again, sent to Vladimir prison. . . . Six or
seven years had gone by. I had left home an eighteen-year-
old youth, strong and fit, and now I was already a con with a
sizeable stretch behind me, deaf and sick. And what had
happened to my mother during these years? She had written
me letters, or rather not written them herself but dictated
them to the girl next door, for she herself couldn't write.
There was little I could learn from them about her or father.
I knew only that father still worked on the railway, that my
kid brother had grown up and was due to go into the army. I
knew, or felt, that my mother loved and felt sorry for me,

that she grieved. And now my legs even wobbled when I realized that I was about to see her again.

It is difficult to convey what a con feels, knowing that his mother is nearby, and that he can't see her or help her. Why she had travelled thousands of miles to get here from Siberia; she had had to make preparations, endure three to four days of hard travelling, and now she had spent three days knocking on doors, walking around the camp, hoping against hope to see me or at least find out something about me. I was overwhelmed with rage, it rose in a ball in my throat. I tried to suppress it, to keep it inside, to remain at least outwardly calm, for if I allowed myself the luxury of addressing various cutting remarks to admin, both I and my mother could say goodbye to any visit.

I went to the deputy camp commander, Major Ageyev: for the first time in all my stay there I decided to ask admin for something. And although I made a great effort to keep calm, I didn't make a very good job of it. As a result of my agitation, my suppressed fury and the necessity of having to ask for something, I was incapable for several minutes of uttering a single word (I in any case tend to stutter, and when I'm worked up the words just refuse to come). At last I mastered myself. I asked that my mother either be given permission to make a visit or else be given a refusal, so that at least she wouldn't have to worry, to linger on in uncertainty and to wait in vain.

As it happened, I was lucky: my company commander, Lubayev, was away, he was off for two days at the end of his spell of duty. There was somebody to put the blame on, and besides, the officers always had their own little scores to settle. Lubayev wouldn't have given me a three-day visit for anything in the world and he would have forced my mother to wait in line for fifteen days (the lines for visits were enormous at that time, some people had to wait for two weeks and more and it even happened that they went away empty-handed—not everyone, after all, has the time to wait so long, or can pay for a room and afford the expense of food for a fortnight). Ageyev evidently knew that I was on bad terms with Lubayev and allowed the visit just to spite him. More than that, he allowed my mother and me to bypass the lines and meet in the cookhouse—if the adjutant would give his permission. I rushed to see the adjutant. He at first refused:

'If I allow this you'll complain afterwards that the visit took place on improperly equipped premises.'

I started to beg him and promised him that I wouldn't complain, having requested it myself. And in truth, I wasn't being visited by a wife—I was going to be with my mother in a room without bars; and if there was only one bed in it then I'd return to my hut every night. After I had written out an application in which I requested to be assigned a visit in the cookhouse and declared that I would make no complaints on the subject, the adjutant gave his permission. I went back to Ageyev again—his signature was the decisive one. He took my application:

'How many days shall I sign this for? Lubayev knows you better than I do, but that great cunt has fucked off somewhere, and I don't know a monkey's tit. Okay, fuck off with you, here!' And he handed me the signed application. It was for three days! Tremendous luck!

Several hours later I was summoned to the guardhouse, searched more carefully than ever before (I was about to mix with someone from Outside) and taken to the end of the corridor. The corridor was barred by a door with a peephole in it and the lock was on the guardhouse side. On the other side was the room for visits and adjoining it the cookhouse. They let me through this door and locked it behind me. I took one step along the corridor towards the cookhouse and stopped dead—I couldn't walk. I felt as if I would never ever be able to move from the spot. At last I forced myself to go up to the door and knock. I would never in any case have heard the answer from the other side; I waited for several seconds, then opened the door and went in.

Mother was standing at a table piled high with food of all kinds; she had evidently been waiting for me some time already and was aimlessly fiddling with the things and moving them around. I stopped in the doorway, she too was incapable of moving towards me. I don't remember how we came to be close to one another, how we embraced. Mother stroked me and kept saying over and over again:

'It's all right, son, it's all right, keep calm, son, keep calm.' Probably she wasn't so much calming me as attempting to calm herself, so as not to burst into tears on the spot, before my very eyes.

Then there came a knock at the door—not the one that led into the corridor but the one that linked the cookhouse with the visiting room. An extremely plump woman came through the door, still young, about thirty to thirty-three. She greeted me and said to my mother:

'There, you see, now you've met your son, and you were so worried the whole time.'

She was followed into the cookhouse by her husband. We were acquainted already and knew one another by sight, although, as so often happens in the camps, we knew no first names or surnames. Here I learned that his name was Alexander Klimov. Later, after the visits, we got to know one another better and I learned his story. At the time, though, we merely exchanged a few words, and the conversation with Klimov helped mother and me to compose ourselves. When they had gone back into their room we already found it easier to talk. Mother started to tell me all the news from home—about my father, my brother Boris, the neighbors, who had left Barabinsk, who had got married, who had had children. While she talked she kept trying to thrust into my mouth some of the food she had brought. But I could get nothing down, I was too agitated by our meeting. Mother talked very loudly to make sure I could hear, but not once did she inquire how bad my deafness was; obviously she wanted to avoid upsetting me with too many questions. I reassured her that I was feeling well, that I was fit and that everything was all right. It was only after several hours that I made out that she had aged considerably and looked exhausted; at fifty she looked like a real old woman already. That was because of me, grief had aged her prematurely. And then life in general had never been a bed of roses for her: hard work, three of us children (one brother had died while still small, Boris and I had remained), constant need, shortages. . . .

That night I went back to the zone to sleep. And at six the next morning I was back again. On the emergency gang we worked not on shifts but on call, and for those three days the ganger didn't call me and gave me the chance to spend the time with my mother. Klimov, however, was made to go to work every day and came to his wife only in the evening and then spent the night with her. One day he tried to take a piece of lard back with him from the meeting, hiding it under his belt. Sometimes it can be done. But he was unlucky: they searched him diligently, found the lard and threatened to stop his visit.

We and the Klimovs cooked our food jointly and ate breakfast, dinner and supper together. Klimov's wife told us about herself and her baby and what it was like living in Saratov. Mother talked about life in Barabinsk. It turned out that everywhere was much the same: people were barely able to make ends meet, hanging on from payday to payday. My folks had it a bit easier, it seemed, because they had their own vegetable patch and a cow. Alexander's wife, however, had a really tight time of it, what with the poor pay she got in the kindergarten and having to earn for herself and the child.

On the last day of the visit the door opened and in came Lubayev without knocking. It was obvious that he was in a filthy temper: he had failed to screw up my visit from my mother, the permit had been signed in his absence. When he came in I was sitting at the table, eating jam straight out of the pot with a spoon—mother knew what a sweet tooth I had and had brought loads of sweet things with her. I didn't dream of standing up when Lubayev came in—what a nerve, he keeps my mother kicking her heels for three days and then walks in on us uninvited. He gave me a sidelong look and greeted my mother. She invited him to sit down. The company commander started to complain about me: I was rude and insolent and behaved myself badly, and I obviously didn't want any remission so as to get out early. When my mother heard this her eyes opened wide with amazement: what, did I really not want to leave the camp?

'No, he doesn't,' said Lubayev. 'And it all depends on him, on the way he behaves.'

'Why, what's he doing,' said my mother anxiously, 'refusing to work?'

'Oh, he does his work all right,' began Lubayev, and then went on to explain how bad I was and how they were forced willy-nilly to punish me, to deprive me of shopping privileges and stick me in the cooler on starvation rations. At this I could stand it no longer, I didn't want my mother to get all worried and start weeping over my hunger and difficulties, I hadn't complained to her at all. I cut in on Lubayev and said, turning to my mother:

'And you ask the company commander what one has to do in order to be in his good books. He will tell you that you have to suck up to your superiors, spy on your comrades and inform on your fellow prisoners.'

'Oh my, there's never been any of that sort of thing in our family!' exclaimed my mother. Then I turned to Lubayev:

'You came here to this meeting even though you weren't invited, you came to distress an old woman with your tales. We've only got three days to meet in and we've got plenty to talk about without you coming in here. And it's not as if you're going to lengthen our visits afterwards, by the time that you're wasting. If you have to, call me out of the zone any time you like and talk away. But leave my mother alone.'

Lubayev left the room without a word, which was all I wanted—so long as he didn't have time to tell mother just how bad it was here. Mother looked at me in horror for talking to a boss that way. Throughout her whole life she had got used to the idea that bosses were to be feared, that it was better not to tangle with them, for you could only do yourself more harm. I felt very very sorry for her.

The visit came to an end and we parted. I was gladdened by our meeting and simply happy, I seemed to melt during those three days after all the years of loneliness. But I didn't want mother to come to see me again. I had three years to run to the end of my sentence, it was better somehow to be patient during this time, rather than for her to have to torture herself with travelling, to beg, to humble herself and to sit for three days behind bars—it was better not to see each other at all for three years than for her to see her son in those surroundings.

I was also glad again later that mother listened to my advice, and that she didn't come to see me in prison at Vladimir. Meeting there was even more painful. Once upon a time, about ten years ago, they used to have personal visits too, but what visits! In a cell-like room with bars on the windows and a peephole in the door. The light in the room used to burn all night and the wardress would patrol the corridor and keep peering through the keyhole, especially, of course, if it was a man and wife inside. Now even that doesn't exist any more, however, Vladimir has no personal visits. Sometimes they give you one or perhaps two visits a year—up to half an hour each; but even these can be taken away for the slightest excuse, or even without any excuse.

One day one of my cell-mates, Alexei Ivanov, had a visit from his mother—this happened quite recently, in the spring of 1963. She lives in Vladimir province and since she didn't have far to go she decided to take her little granddaughter along, Alexei's sister's child, who was five years old. Later he told us what had happened. A wardress sat in the room the whole time, listening and watching to make sure there were no 'infringements'. It is forbidden not only to embrace your family but even to approach them: you have to talk across a table. Alexei's mother had to wait a long time outside the prison, the little girl got tired and started playing up, so grandma bought her an ice cream. And so they went into the room still carrying the ice cream. The little girl held it out across the table for her uncle to have a try. The wardress swooped on her, ripped the ice cream out of her hand as though it were an atom bomb and at once put an end to the visit.

This story of Alexei's came back to me quite recently when I was listening to extracts from Svetlana Alliluyeva Stalin's memoirs over the radio. In one particular episode* she talked about meeting her brother in Vladimir prison. Why, those

* See Letter 19 in *Twenty Letters to a Friend*, Hutchinson (London); Harper & Row (N.Y.).

were the very years when we were there and not one of us had an inkling as to whom we had the honor of sharing the prison with! Powers we knew about, and 'Beria's generals', but not a whisper reached us about the 'heir apparent', Vasily Stalin.

I've no idea what conditions he was held in, or what soup they gave him in place of skilly; but how different was his meeting with his wife and sister from Alexei's meeting with his mother and niece. It's clear that not all citizens in our country are subject to the same laws and the same regulations.

The Suicide

... What if I go up the wire, okay?
Or onto the strip? If I wish
you to go, get lost, disappear—
will this favor make us quits?

Go on then, fire! You're also sick and tired
of Mordovia, godforsaken hole!
They'll give you leave for it, off you go
to your mother and sister waiting at home ...
... And you won't remember how I hung on the wire,
a semi-quaver on an empty stave.

Yuli Daniel: 'The Sentry' (1966)

THIS INCIDENT occurred on Sunday October 4, 1964. We came back from loading and unloading at five in the morning and went straight to bed. Round about eight o'clock I got up feeling extremely hungry. I was about to wake Valery, but he was sleeping so sweetly that I took pity on him: it was better to go short of food than short of sleep. I took my spoon, cut a piece of bread from my ration and went over to the canteen.

It was a clear, sunny morning and everyone was pleased that it would be warm by dinner time. Warm weather for the con is a gift of providence. I was also in a good mood as I walked to the canteen. On Sunday mornings the canteen stays open until nine, but almost everyone had had breakfast a great deal earlier and there was no more line, merely a few dozen cons sitting around on the benches and waiting for breakfast to end—perhaps the cook would have a few bowls of skilly left over and would give them second helpings.

I have a feeling that the breakfast on the menu that morning was called noodle-soup—and a few luckless noodles were floating inside the bowl. A spoon was superfluous here, so I stuck it in my pocket and emptied the bowl over the side—a few swallows were enough. All that remained to be done was to inspect the sides for any stray noodles that might be stuck there.

Suddenly a lone shot rang out. Everyone raised his head and kept perfectly still. Nobody dared clink a bowl. After about a minute, somebody said quietly: 'From the corner tower, by the bakery.' We listened and waited. There ought to be two more shots. A long minute passed and no shots were fired. What could it mean?

The shot had been fired by a tommy gunner in one of the watch towers, so a con must have climbed on to the palisade in order to put an end to himself. In such cases the sentry is supposed to fire two warning shots and aim only the third at the 'escaper'. But usually it is done in reverse order: the first shot is fired at the living target and then two shots into the air. Well, what difference does it damn well make—the con's bound to die so what's the use of fooling around? You let fly into the air and maybe he even changes his mind about it, and then goodbye gratitude, goodbye extra leave and a nice trip home. In short, none of us knew of a case where a sentry had fired according to the regulations—the main thing was to spend three cartridges.

One way or another there should have been three shots and we only heard one. What could it mean? We left the canteen to find out, but just as we emerged on the front porch a series of further shots rang out. The firing came from the same direction, near the bakery, but the sound was different from the first.

Cons from all over the camp were converging on the bakery. I was overtaken by a group of cons that included my old acquaintance from Vladimir prison, Sergei Oransky. As he walked past he called out: 'Somebody's been shot again!'

Oh, those 'agains'! How many of the 'escapes' had there been during my time alone at camp seven? The last time had been several months earlier, in June or July. Then, hearing the regulation three shots, we had rushed to the perimeter. The tommy gunner had shot the fugitive at the foot of the wooden palisade and he lay there with his nose digging into the warm earth of the softly raked strip. Evidently he was still alive: he was scrabbling at the soil with his hands and trying to raise himself on one leg. Some cons ran to the medical post and fetched the medical orderly. But what could they do? The wounded man lay on the raked strip, behind two rows of barbed wire, and the sentry wouldn't let them go anywhere near the wire: cons were forbidden to go on the strip and anyway the dead or the wounded con first had to be photographed on the spot, then a report had to be drawn up in the presence of several officers, and only afterwards could the body be moved and medical aid given.

The injured man lay there, jerking convulsively from time to time. The prisoners were noisy and shouting, paying no attention to the bellows of the warders and the bursts of tommy gun fire over their heads. So it went on for ages, at least an hour and a half. At last the officers appeared on the other side of the wire: Lieutenant-Colonel Kolomitsev ordered the palisade to be broken—it was forbidden to carry an injured or dead con through the camp. They made a hole in the palisade and two warders, taking hold of the man by his legs, dragged the body outside the compound. His head bounced up and down as it was pulled over the ground, leaving a bloody trail behind it. The cons roared and howled. Then Ageyev's face appeared in the gap in the palisade and he yelled:

'Well, what the fucking hell makes you go on the strip in the first place?'

Later, our medical orderly was called to the guardhouse 'to administer first-aid', and later a nurse and a doctor came. The orderly said that he was still alive and was dispatched alive to the hospital in camp three. But he didn't arrive there in time and died on the way.

I thought of this incident—and others like it—as I made my way with the others to the bakery. What happened this time? Who was the luckless con?

At the bakery a huge crowd had gathered, almost the entire camp. I found some of my gang-mates there. Kolya Yusupov pointed out the place on the palisade to me—there on the 'peak' (the inclined rows of barbed wire running along the top of the palisade), his clothing caught in the barbed wire, hung one of the cons. Only his legs could be seen from the side where we were, the rest of him hung outside—in freedom.

Kolya and I climbed to the roof of a low building nearby—the former parcel sorting office. From there we had an excellent view of the raked strip, the palisade and 'freedom' beyond. A crowd had gathered on the far side as well: officers, tommy gunners and free workers. Beside us on the roof sat a con who had seen the whole thing from the beginning. He was terribly agitated and shaken. And he told us how it had happened.

'I was sitting with Kiryukha in the stokehole,' he said, 'where I'd gone for a natter and some bread. All of a sudden

301

we heard this sentry yelling from his watch tower: "Get back, I'll fire! Get back you fucking idiot, I'll kill you! Where the fuck d'you think you're going in broad daylight?"

'Kiryukha and I ran out of the stokehole and saw this con. He'd already cleared one of the barbed wire fences and was tangled up in the other. And he was carrying a plank with him. I recognized him—we had been in the cooler together. He was sick, couldn't fulfil his norm and then stopped away from work: Kolomitsev himself had given him fifteen days. I called out to him:

' "Romashev, have you gone crazy, come back, they'll kill you."

' "I couldn't give a fuck if they do, it's all the bloody same to me. It'll be a quick release."

'He was in bad health all the time and the doctors wouldn't give him a certificate. Not only that but they insisted on driving him out to work and squeezing the norm out of him. I ran along the barbed wire fence, trying to persuade him to come back, but he waved me away, scrambled over the second fence and made for the palisade. He was almost directly under the watch tower by now. But the sentry, evidently, was a decent sort—the first one I've ever seen. He was swearing blue murder at Romashev, but he didn't fire. Then I heard him ringing the guardhouse:

' "There's a con here on the strip, tell the warders to come and get him."

'I couldn't hear what they said from the guardhouse end, but then I heard him yelling into the receiver:

' "He can be shot quick enough, but you can come and get him, he's still tangled up in the second fence."

'Then he added really harshly and angrily:

' "What the bloody hell are you sitting on your arses for? It's my job to keep a look-out and warn you and yours to pick

'em up, so pick the bastard up, you mother-fuckers! I'm
warning you, I shan't fire."

'And he didn't fire until Romashev was on the palisade.
Then the sentry fired once into the air and went on bellowing
to the con to get down and scarper back to the compound.
But it was as though Romashev couldn't hear. He was
crouched on all fours on top of the palisade, with his feet on
the "peak" and his hands resting on the points of the boards.
And it looked as though he had no intention of coming down.

'Then the sound of a motorbike engine came from the far
side of the palisade and it could be heard approaching Romashev and stopping just opposite him. Somebody shouted at
the sentry:

' "What the hell are you staring at? You've got a con on the
palisade!"

'We didn't hear the sentry's reply because the shout was
immediately followed by several pistol shots in succession.
Romashev took his hands off the palisade, stood up to his full
height and slowly tumbled backwards and outwards, towards
the farther side. Then his trousers caught on the wire and he
hung there, and was hanging there still. . . .'

Kolya asked the eye witness who had fired the pistol. The
latter replied: 'I can't say for sure. I climbed up here as soon
as possible to have a look, but the motorbike was already on
its way back. Judging by the voice and red kisser it was
Shved.'

While we were listening to this story a group of officers
appeared on the far side of the palisade, including Ageyev and
Shved. They walked up and down, looked, asked the sentry
something, and then Ageyev entered the compound while Shved
remained outside. Soon Ageyev reappeared on our side of the
palisade and walked through the crowd of cons accompanied
by officers and warders. He walked unhurriedly, paying no

attention to the indignant cries of the cons: 'Murderers!' 'Cannibals!' 'Go on, take him down, maybe he's still alive!' The officers went right up to the barbed wire and Ageyev shouted to someone on the other side of the palisade: 'All right, get cracking!' The photographer focused his camera and took several pictures from various positions. A few moments later the face of Shved appeared over the top of the palisade. He looked down at the cons and smiled. The cons went wild. From the crowd came shouts of 'Blood-sucker!' 'That's who the grave's waiting for!' and 'One day you'll burst with all the blood you've drunk!'

A warder then appeared beside Shved and without paying the slightest attention to the shouts, the two of them set about their work. First they disentangled Romashev from the wire, tearing his pants, it seems, in the process. The crowd fell silent and there was such a hush that I even thought I heard the sound of the material ripping. When nothing more held the body, Shved and the warder held the body still for a moment, head down, and then let it drop, and we heard Romashev hit the ground with a sickening thud. A low hiss, half sigh and half exclamation traveled through the compound. And then at once a dreadful din broke out—shouts, protests, hysterics almost. I myself saw several cons—old Kolyma and Vorkuta hands—break down in tears. Torture and starvation had never managed to squeeze tears out of men like this, but now they wept with mortification and impotent rage.

Meanwhile Shved stood on his ladder, looked over the palisade at us and smiled.

Later the nurse told us that Romashev had been dead when they took him down. Evidently he had been shot point-blank.

Friends and Comrades

DURING THE years I spent in Vladimir jail and in camps I got to know large numbers of prisoners and with some of them I became close friends. How many different stories did I hear! And I can't write about all of them. I will try, however, to describe just a few.

First, though, let me repeat what I have already pointed out before: people here vary, just as they do everywhere. You have marvellous people and you have rotten ones, you have brave men and cowards, you have honest men with principles and you have unprincipled swine who are prepared for any kind of betrayal. Here there are men who have been imprisoned for their beliefs, and there are more than a few who have come here by accident. Some stay faithful to themselves, serving out their entire sentence from bell to bell. Others disavow everything, and even publicly—themselves, their views and their friends. I can say absolutely categorically—and many will confirm this: the majority of the 'disavowers' (if not all) do it in order to ease their life in the camps and perhaps later outside.

Imprisoned in the political camps of Mordovia are writers, scientists, students, workers and semi-illiterate peasants. And also genuine 'politicians' with their own systematized views and criminal cons who have been transformed into 'politicians'.

I would like to talk about some of my friends and acquaintances without making any distinction among them, just as it was in real life.

One of my companions in the emergency gang in camp seven was Iosip Klimkovich, a fine, simple fellow. Later we were in camp three together, in hospital, and got to know each other even better. He told me what he was in for, why he had been sentenced to twenty-five years.

At the end of the 1940s Iosip had still been a young boy and lived in Stanislav county with his mother and sister. At that time armed partisan warfare was in progress over the whole of the Western Ukraine and many Ukrainian peasants had taken to the woods. Among them—with the partisans— was Iosip's uncle, or so they said at least. One day, when Iosip was sitting at a friend's hut, some canvas-covered trucks entered the village and disgorged a number of soldiers with tommy guns, who then proceeded to surround certain of the huts. Through the window they could see how a truck stopped at the Klimkoviches' hut and the soldiers surrounded it too. Iosip dashed to the door: his sick mother lay at home. But his friend's grandfather seized hold of the boy and prevented him from going out. And as he held him he said:

'What are you, weak in the head or something? Can't you see—they're sending them to Siberia. If you go out now they'll take you away too.'

He frogmarched Iosip from the door to the window: 'Take a good look, my lad, and take note.'

Iosip pressed up against the glass. He saw the soldiers running about his yard, looking behind the firewood and into the barn—probably for him. Then he saw them drive his sister out of the hut and tie her hands behind her back before throwing her into the back of the truck. His sick mother was unable to walk—she was dragged along by the arms and also tossed into the truck. Outside several other huts the same story was repeated. The scene was fixed in Iosip's memory for ever, but most clearly engraved of all was the face of the officer in command of the operation.

Afterwards Iosip learned that everyone taken away had been driven to the main town in the district and herded into a single barn. Iosip found the barn and prowled around in the vicinity, but couldn't bring himself to approach it: it was being guarded by soldiers. They said that the people inside were given nothing to eat or drink. Several days later Iosip learned that his mother had died and his sister, with the rest, had been transported to Siberia. Then he left his home, but not to go to the woods to join the partisans—he went to the town. He got himself a pistol (it wasn't difficult at that time) and started to hunt for that officer. For several days he drew a blank. People said that the officer was away at other villages doing similar work. But at last Iosip caught up with him when he was leaving the local military HQ in the company of a tommy gunner. Iosip followed them, made sure it was the same officer that had taken his mother and sister away, went right up behind him and shot him point-blank. The officer fell without even a cry. The soldier turned and jerked up his tommy gun, but had no time to fire—Iosip shot him too.

Iosip Klimkovich was subsequently sentenced as a Ukrainian nationalist and bandit and given twenty-five years. The trial was a closed one. That was in the late forties and Iosip is still doing time.

A similar story to this belonged to the man in the next cot to me at camp seven, Vladas Mataitis. He was a Lithuanian and also a peasant. He and his father and brother were with the partisans in the forest, while the third brother was a student in town. One day the student came home and the old man and his two other sons came out to meet him. Just then there was a raid, all three of them were seized, taken outside the village and shot. Vladas managed to escape. Later he learned that the three dead ones had been loaded on to a cart and brought back to the village. When Vladas's mother saw the three corpses all at once—her husband and two sons—she went mad. In this state, together with her daughter, she was transported to Siberia. He, meanwhile, was captured heavily wounded and sentenced (also behind closed doors) to twenty-five years.

He was still in Mordovia when his mother and sister were permitted to return to Lithuania.

Mataitis twice went before the courts to have his sentence reduced to fifteen years, but both times was refused because the camp authorities wouldn't give him a good character reference: he didn't want to become an 'activist' (serve in the IOS)! But he didn't want to stay inside either, so Vladas signed up in the camp sanitary section. That's what many people did to get a good reference for the courts: the older ones went into the camp sanitary section, while the younger and fitter ones went into the sports section. Although you were cooperating with admin, at least it wasn't at the expense of your fellow prisoners—all you had to do was observe the formalities and those alone, if the worst came to the worst, would be enough to satisfy the authorities.

Vladas went before the court yet a third time and at last got his sentence reduced. He was released. But he still wasn't allowed to go back to Lithuania.

In that same camp seven, in the finished goods warehouse, there was an old man who was also from the Baltic. I don't remember either his surname or his real first name—we called him Fedya, just as we used the Russian name Volodya for

Mataitis and Kolya for Yusupov. Fedya was also in for twenty-five years, just like all the so-called 'nationalists' from the Baltic states and the Ukraine who had been convicted in the forties.

Fedya spent all his free time writing petitions. This is a common disease in the camps—people write and write day after day: to the Central Committee, to the Presidium of the Supreme Soviet, to Khrushchev, to Brezhnev, to the Public Prosecutor's office; and Fedya wrote too.

He hadn't been sentenced alone—somewhere in Mordovia were his wife and son. I don't know what exactly he wrote in his petitions, but they all came down to the same thing: he had never been a partisan and a nationalist, he and his family had been wrongly convicted, by mistake. The cons used to laugh at him: 'Aren't you fed up with writing after eighteen years?' The company officer would hand Fedya the routine 'Application Refused' and start cussing him:

'All you do is write, write, write! Writers, the lot of you! Nobody's guilty, it's all been a mistake! Once you've been sentenced, sit it out and don't be in such a hurry. As if it's not obvious the kind of tree you were picked from!'

And all the answers came back the same: 'Correctly sentenced, there are no grounds for re-examining the case.'

And then one day the cons came running: 'Fedya, go to the guardhouse, they've come for you!' And in the guardhouse he found his wife and son—they had been released first and had come to find him, while he still knew nothing about it. It turned out that all three had been rehabilitated. After eighteen years justice had triumphed at last!

We had another similar 'writer', a country fellow known to the whole camp, whose name was Pyotr Ilyich Izotov. Both cons and officers called him simply 'Ilyich'. This Ilyich used to write several letters and petitions a day and used to receive

at least two replies daily in return. He had organized a whole
office for himself: copies of all his petitions were stored in a
special suitcase, later the answers were affixed to them, and
he kept a special exercise book in which he noted down when
he had sent out each petition and when he received the
answers. The answers that he got were identical with Fedya's
and the cons used to pull his leg in just the same way. But
now, whenever the company officer started his 'Write, write,
write, what's the use, none of you are guilty, but all this
scribbling won't do you a scrap of good, better join the IOS
instead'—the cons would stick up for Ilyich:

'You used to tell Fedya it was a waste of time and he got
rehabilitated'.

Although Ilyich used to make a point of sending several
petitions every day, he evidently had little faith in them
himself. True he didn't join the IOS, but he joined the school
instead, in class four, hoping no doubt that they would give
him a good reference for his pardon.

In the autumn of 1963 a new man was put into our gang—
Najmuddin Mahometovich Yusupov. I became very good
friends with him and we were together right up until my
release. We worked together, lived in the same section, slept
next to one another, kept our bread in the same locker and
shared all the victuals and money we had with the rest of our
group: whoever managed to get anything shared it around.
He was an extremely kind and loyal friend, ready to help
anyone. Our gang re-christened him Kolya—we couldn't get
out tongues round his other name at all. Kolya was young
and a fine figure of a man, well over six feet tall; he was built
like a giant, strong and handsome, with large regular features
and thick brows over big, deepset brown eyes. He arrived in
the camp beardless but once inside decided to grow one—
there were lots of men with beards in the camp. But some get

permission and some don't. Several times Kolya was forced to shave: for a beard they take away your parcel or shop privileges. And then sometimes they don't even do that, but the shop simply refuses to give you any food: you're clean shaven on this identity card, they say, and then you come to us with a beard. How do we know it's you? It was a very handsome beard, coppery chestnut and framed his face in such a way as to give it great expressiveness.

Kolya is now 37 or 38. He is an Avar, his old folk live in the mountains of Daghestan, where he too grew up. Having completed the teacher training college in town, he went back to his village as a teacher for a while and then into the army. He was in the paratroops, stayed on after his conscription time was up and did eight years altogether. During this time he saw the world a bit, tasted city life, and when he was demobilized was reluctant to return to his remote village. He decided to go for the big money and return to his family with full pockets, not as he was on demobilization.

The biggest wages are earned by miners, so Kolya decided to go down the mines. He worked away there like nobody's business. He liked work and knew how to go about it: all of us in the gang had seen him doing the work of three. But somehow or other he never managed to accumulate anything, he was always spending just as much as he earned, except, perhaps, for a trifle here and there. And no matter how hard he tried, he could never knock out more than 150–200 rubles a month. If he worked any harder the rates went down and the norms went up. Leaving the mine wasn't any better—not even one could live on a teacher's salary. And all the time food prices were rising. All the other miners were also discontented and used to mutter and grumble and curse, but always among themselves, in their own circles. And Kolya was just like the rest.

One Sunday he had been out drinking with his friends and was on his way back to the workers' hostel. He wasn't exactly drunk, but, as they say, one over the eight. He walked through the market and at every corner of the market place there were loudspeakers bawling out: 'Khrushchev, Khrushchev—a faithful follower of Lenin! The people's welfare, the growth of prosperity!'

Kolya got his dander up. He climbed on to some barrels and started spouting himself:

'People! Listen, they're babbling on the radio about us living better and richer every day. Have you noticed that you're living better? Nikita says that in Stalin's day things were bad. But in Stalin's day norms were lower and pay rates higher. In Stalin's day a miner used to get seven to eight thousand, and now under Nikita I can hardly scrape up 150–200. And what's it worth anyway? In Stalin's day butter was 2.70 a kilo, and now it's 3.60. Meat is dearer—who wants this sort of life? In the old days in the Caucasus, so the old men say, they used to eat mutton and there were mountains of mutton bones outside each village. But we hardly know what mutton tastes like. And instead of mutton bones we've got Khrushchev's maize.'

Kolya talked for a long time, stamping his foot so hard that he even broke the barrel. The barrel's owner came dashing over with fists ready to let fly, but when he heard him abusing Khrushchev and praising Stalin he stepped back again: 'All right, talk away, my lad.' (Many Caucasians idolize Stalin even to this day.) They let Kolya finish what he was saying and then several of the lads led him away. For a week nobody touched him, but then they caught up with him after all, jailed him and tried him for anti-Soviet propaganda and for slandering the Soviet system and state. The court, as usual, was closed, and they gave him four years. When

Khrushchev fell, Kolya, together with the others, was called
in and asked if he would like to apply for a pardon. He
refused, served his full term and was released some time after
me, on May 28, 1967.

Gennady Krivtsov had had an extremely turbulent and
adventurous life. He was, by the way, a countryman of mine,
being also from Novosibirsk county. He had completed the
Artillery College in Odessa at the end of the war and became
an officer just in time to take part in it. But when his unit
was passing through Czechoslovakia he deserted: he had fallen in love with a Czech girl. Then he married her and stayed
there. To avoid being hauled before a tribunal he later fled to
Austria; and on returning to collect his wife he was arrested.
Next, inevitably, came the tribunal, sentence, camps, exile.
Fleeing from exile he was caught, tried again and sentenced
to a new term. In one of the camps Genka wrote an article for
the camp newspaper and it was printed. Shortly afterwards
they decided it was anti-Soviet and added another term to his
previous one.

In general Genka Krivtsov was the sort of man who figures
in the prison song: '. . . Forever to you tied, my youth and
talent have died within your walls.' And he really did seem to
be in 'forever'. His whole life had consisted of camps and
exile and escapes and new terms. I can't even remember all
the camps he had been in, how many times he had escaped or
all the things he got 'supplements' for. And still he could
never manage to subdue himself, could never manage to come
to terms with his fate. Or didn't want to.

He was short and weedy and painfully skinny—even in
Vladimir jail I had seen few so far gone. But as belligerent
as they come. Already in the old camps he had been nicknamed 'Trotsky's Son'—for his flashing tongue. The company
officers were simply scared to cross swords with him: you

could never under any circumstances out-argue Krivtsov, only make a fool of yourself. People like him were to be avoided like the plague so far as they were concerned. But of course they wouldn't kick him out to freedom, only into the cooler or jail. I got to know him in jail and then we were together in camp seven.

In jail he had started writing a long story whose title I can remember—'In the Devil's Claws'. It was about life in the camps and prison. He had already written several chapters when it was taken away and he himself was thrown into the prison cooler for a start, with the warning: 'Krivtsov, you'll soon be earning yourself another term!' When his spell in the cooler was over the educational measures were continued. Genka was taken to an office where he talked with a poet from Vladimir named Nikitin. Nikitin tried to persuade Genka to repent and write on other subjects. He, Krivtsov, had an undoubted gift, he said, and if only he would change the tendency of his writings so that they could be published, he would probably be pardoned and could then stay on in Vladimir as a normal citizen and would be accepted into the Writer's Union. . . . These shining prospects failed to attract Genka. He remained 'forever tied' to the prison.

Krivtsov also had a married sister living in Novosibirsk. Both she and her husband were party members—he was Party Organizer at his factory in the ideological department of the town committee. The prison authorities found out about this and suggested to Genka that he enter into an open discussion with his sister, that is that he write to her as often as he liked and whatever he liked, expressing all his views. They promised him that there would be no comeback, that the censor would let his letters through. And so a polemic sprang up between brother and sister. Genka was a believer, she an atheist, and it was on this topic that their first exchange of views took place. It turned out that the convinced atheist was none too steady in her convictions, or at least not able to defend her views. So that the authorities very soon put an end to the dispute and brought Genka's correspondence back within the established limits.

Whenever a lecturer came from outside to give us a lecture in camp seven, Krivtsov, Rodygin, Nikols and others of that ilk were always locked up in the cooler for a day or two before his arrival. Thus we always knew: if Krivtsov and Rodygin were dragged off to the cooler, there'd be a lecture on the following day.

Valery and I were introduced to Rodygin by Krivtsov. Or rather, we had noticed him even earlier. We were walking past the staff offices one day when we saw the chief of the Dubrovlag KGB standing there, Major Postnikov, and some con arguing with him and trying to persuade him of something. We passed them several times and later Valery told me what they had been talking about. It seems the con had said to Postnikov: 'You say that Soviet power derives from the people, that in this lies its strength and its might. But if you, the representatives of that power, were truly convinced of your strength, you wouldn't imprison us. How many people are you holding in camps and jails? A simple peasant gets ten years from you for the merest word, that means you fear that peasant and are not at all sure of the people's support. . . .' What Postnikov answered to this Valery didn't hear. Later we asked Genka if he knew this fellow and Genka introduced us.

Tolik Rodygin was from Leningrad and was still very young—he was born in 1936. He had also been an officer, but whereas Krivtsov was in the artillery, Rodygin was in the navy. Krivtsov wrote prose and Rodygin wrote verse. In Leningrad he had published a volume of poetry and had become a member of the Writer's Union. When he first came to camp seven he found a copy of his book in the camp library and removed it, refusing to show it to anyone; they were bad poems, he said, and made him feel ashamed.

Somehow or other he left the navy and went to the Far East to catch fish as captain of a trawler. He was imprisoned in 1962 for the same thing as me—attempting to go abroad: he had tried to get away by swimming the Black Sea, either to Turkey or to some foreign ship. He was picked up and got eight years in Mordovia.

He and Krivtsov were good friends. When they got started on an argument, half the camp would come running, it wasn't like our 'political talks' or lectures. Rodygin was an atheist, Krivtsov, as I have said already, was a believer, and so they would have a debate. It was usually held in our section—the emergency gang's. Sometimes it went to the extent that the listeners would even miss their suppers. They didn't debate only religion, of course, but also politics, literature, art, the role of contemporary science, ethics, where do moral values come from, and then religion again. For the officers these debates were a thorn in the flesh: they were too frightened to join in because Krivtsov and Rodygin would pin them down in a flash from opposite sides, and so they would be furious. A company officer would come running into the section and say: 'What's this meeting about? There's nothing here worth listening to! Break it up! Obey your officers!' This last argument was usually conclusive.

In the autumn of 1965 Rodygin, Krivtsov, Mark Nikols and other dyed-in-the-wool arguers were clapped in the punishment block for six months. Valery and I saw them only rarely, when the punishment block was taken out for exercise. Soon afterwards I was sent to the hospital in camp three and while I was there camp seven was dispersed to other camps. Rodygin and Krivtsov went to camp eleven, but only stayed there for two weeks or so before being tried again and sentenced to three years in prison. So that when I came back from number three I no longer found my friends in the camp. But I remember one of the last conversations between Rodygin, Krivtsov and an officer shortly before they went to the punishment block.

Somebody came to give us a lecture—a Mordovian writer (for some reason they had failed to stick Rodygin and Krivtsov in the cooler beforehand and they were present too). The writer talked about some writers' congress he had been to or some conference or something—who had made speeches and who said what. Sometimes after lectures they allowed questions to be asked by the audience or proposed that anyone wanting to ask something should go up on the stage to 'chat among themselves', depending upon the subject of the lecture. This time those who wished to ask questions were invited to go over to the staff building. But Krivtsov, Rodygin and several others stopped the lecturer on the front steps of the staff building, so that nonetheless the conversation took place before a large number of people.

The lecturer was being 'assisted' by Major Postnikov, our top KGB officer. Krivtsov asked why at the writers' congress or conference no opportunity to speak was given to any of the more progressive writers, such as Nekrasov* or Solzhenitsyn.†‡ The lecturer replied that it was impossible for everyone to speak. But at this point Postnikov intervened (with him, as

* Viktor Nekrasov (b. 1915), author of 'In the Trenches of Stalingrad', 'Kira Gheorgievna' and controversial travel sketches on the USA and Italy (trans. as 'Both Sides of the Ocean').

† Alexander Solzhenitsyn (b. 1919), a former camp inmate and the Soviet Union's most controversial living writer. Author of 'One Day in the Life of Ivan Denisovich', 'Cancer Ward', 'The First Circle' and a number of short stories and plays.

with all the officers, warders and KGB men in the camp, to pronounce the very name of Solzhenitsyn was like waving a red rag in front of a bull—they literally foamed at the mouth):

'Get lost with your Solzhenitsyn! What makes you think he's a writer? He's nothing but a disgrace to the profession of writer!'

'Why don't you like what he writes?' asked Genka sardonically.

'Who the hell does like it? It's an insult to the Russian language! What about all this 'mucking butter' or 'muck all'* on every other page?'

At that moment some con asked the duty warder to let him through into the work zone to visit the dentist. He showed the warder his certificate, but the latter brushed him aside and yelled:

'Fuck off with your bloody certificate! Wait till the shift goes through, until then you can go and get fucking well stuffed!'

'And what words,' asked Rodygin, 'would you recommend to describe that little scene with?'

'There's no need to describe it at all. It's pointless and even harmful to draw attention to the dark side of life, to petty details and individual shortcomings,' replied Postnikov didactically.

'If Shchedrin† hadn't written about life's "petty details"

---

* A reference to euphemisms (for obscenities) used by Solzhenitsyn in his novel of camp life, 'One Day in the Life of Ivan Denisovich'. These words are never printed in the Soviet Union and appear only rarely, as in Marchenko's book, represented by the first letter followed by dots.

† Saltykov-Shchedrin, M.Y. (1826–1889). Political and social satirist who exposed conditions of his time in his novels and stories. He was in government service, was banished, and retired as vice-governor of a province in order to write.

and Ostrovsky* hadn't denounced the kingdom of darkness no one would remember them know; and it's impossible to fight against shortcomings, whether petty or major, when you sweep them under the carpet, keep quiet about them and draw some cheaply painted veil over them to hide them,' said Krivtsov, speaking not so much to Postnikov as for the benefit of the cons crowding round him. But Postnikov wasn't worried about Shchedrin and Ostrovsky, he still hadn't finished with Solzhenitsyn.

'Your Solzhenitsyn distorts life! My two daughters—at school both of them—went and read "Ivan Denisovich" and then imagined that they could start criticizing their father. Questions, reproaches, tears almost every evening! In the beginning I explained it all to them nicely, but later I had to throw the magazine† on the fire and that was the end of it.'

'Well,' said Rodygin, 'and did that convince your daughters? You always have one infallible argument: put the magazine in the fire and us in the cooler.'

* Ostrovsky, A. K. (1823–1886). Playwright whose works are concerned with the evils of Russia in his time.

† 'One Day in the Life of Ivan Denisovich' was first published in the monthly literary magazine, 'Novy Mir'.

Youth

THE CONS serving nowadays in the Internal Order Sections, prisoners' councils and other prisoners' organizations are for the most part old men. But even these old men finish their terms sooner or later and the camps are filling up with youth—students, workers, young writers, scientists. The camps are 'growing younger'.

But with youth the administration is having much more trouble in finding a common language, as the authorities like to put it. If they squeeze the young people harder, they only get angrier. They don't bend before the authorities and won't keep quiet—there's a continuous stream of protests in various spheres.

They tried replacing the stick with the carrot: youth gangs were formed, and huts only for youth. They hoped it would be easier to control them in this way. But the opposite happened. Finding themselves together, the young Ukrainians and Lithuanians, Estonians and Russians, workers and students, soon found that 'common language'.

And the warders complain: 'You should see the con nowadays! Say a word and you get two back again. You cuss him blind and he outcusses you. And he's not afraid of the cooler!'

320

The Bouquet

To MORDOVIA are brought political prisoners from all corners of the Soviet Union and from all republics. There are particularly many Ukrainians and people from the Baltic republics—Lithuania, Latvia, and Estonia. And it's not enough to bring them to a camp in Russia—they are even forced to speak Russian during visits from their relatives, so that the warder can understand. Between themselves, however, these prisoners speak in their own language, sing their own songs and organize secret celebrations in honor of their poets and writers.

Apart from this the camps are sometimes visited by representatives of the public of the various republics. These 'representatives' don't look to see what conditions their countrymen are being held in, they don't ask them how they are getting on and they even go out of their way to avoid any direct contact with the cons, fearing that they will be accused of interference in the affairs of the camp. All the conversations they have are conducted exclusively in the presence of members of admin or the KGB (sometimes the representative himself is a KGB man, and even in uniform). On the whole they don't want to know or hear anything at all about the camp, they would prefer to keep their eyes tightly closed and their ears tightly stuffed. They talk, on the other hand, about life in their republics, and this the cons don't want to hear: how can you believe a man when you can see his knees knocking in the presence of the KGB? And on top of all this he says how nicely everybody lives and how free they all are!

At first very few people went to these 'meetings with representatives', the cons had to be forced to go, just as to the political talks. Then the public representatives began to be accompanied by amateur artists. Now you could hardly get into the canteen at all for these occasions, not only Latvians or Lithuanians went, but all the other cons as well. Everyone liked to listen to the songs and poetry and look at the dancing. On the stage there would be people in national costume, not cons in their camp rags. They were given a very friendly reception (not like the speakers) and offered flowers and heartfelt thanks.

In the summer of 1965 we had an official visit at camp seven from representatives of one of the Baltic republics: after the speeches a concert was promised. The canteen was full to overflowing. At first, as usual, we had to listen to the 'representative'! When he had finished, the audience peppered him with questions—that was also quite usual. The speaker couldn't answer them, he was pinned to the wall—cons have no embarrassment and aren't afraid to ask questions that don't get asked outside. The discussions are usually ended by the officers: 'Comrades, pay no attention to provocative questions, we have plenty of provocateurs in here.'

And to the cons: 'Some of you are fed up with strict regime, it seems. Don't forget that special's just around the corner!'

Suddenly a young con made his way up on to the stage, a former law student from one of the Baltic republics. In his hand he held a bouquet tightly wrapped in paper. Evidently he wanted to present the bouquet to his countryman. And this was unprecedented: flowers were presented to the artists, but never to speakers.

There was a hush in the audience. The young man turned to the speaker: 'Permit me, in the name of all my countrymen, to present to our Homeland these flowers, which grow here so far away from her.'

He spoke with an accent, but in Russian, so that all could understand him. And while he was uttering this short speech, the audience began to show its consternation. From all sides came shouts of:

'Scum!'

'Arselicker!'

'Stool pigeon!'

I was boiling with indignation: to think that Krivtsov and Rodygin had been friends with this fellow! But the con had finished speaking now and was offering his bouquet to the speaker. The latter grasped it in his hand and at that moment the youth tore the paper off: it was a bouquet of barbed wire!

For the first moment everyone on the stage and in the audience just sat there rigid with mouths gaping, not knowing what to think. The speaker, holding on to his bouquet, shifted from foot to foot beside the table. A minute later the audience exploded. Never in my life, either before or after, have I heard such applause as I heard then. Literally every man jack of them was clapping, including well known stool pigeons and members of the IOS wearing armbands.

The KGB man on the stage regained his presence of mind. He ran over to the speaker and snatched the bouquet from his hand. But he himself had no idea what to do with it—he could hardly run through the audience in order to take it outside. He sat down in his seat again and laid the 'flowers' on the table in front of him. Then he snatched them off again and thrust them under his chair. The hubbub in the audience continued.

The young fellow who had presented the bouquet left the stage and made his way through the crowd. The warders made a dash towards him, but the cons fell to yelling and howling. The chief of political instruction gave orders to an officer and he dashed after the warders and told them something, after which they left the young fellow alone. We all understood that this would be only a short respite, while the visitors were here.

Somehow the audience calmed down. Another of the guests took the rostrum and started to say that this was merely a provocation 'as the comrade captain has just pointed out'. And he added: 'But we know that the majority of those present have correctly understood this incident and will condemn their comrade.'

Somebody shouted back in reply: 'You saw and heard the attitude of the majority. Don't pretend!'

The speaker fell silent. And then at once they hastened to begin the concert.

After the concert the performers were presented with flowers—genuine ones. And when the bouquets were handed over the cons and performers exchanged glances and smiled.

That evening the young fellow was thrown in the cooler and fifteen days later transferred to a restricted form of special regime.

Several days after the incident we read in the Dubrovlag newspaper, 'For Outstanding Labor' that '. . . in unit seven a meeting with national representatives was held in a warm, friendly atmosphere . . .'

Flowers in the Compound

THE THING that amazes the visiting stranger from outside most in the camps is that the compound is full of flowers and greenery. 'The territory of the unit is overflowing with flowers' as the camp newspaper puts it. And it is true.

The people who spend most time on the flowers are the old men and invalids, especially the ones who aren't driven out to work. There aren't many, but it is enough for the gardening. They are absolutely useless for work any longer, but they can't be let out till their time is up. Flower seeds are sent in by relatives—this is allowed. And many of the younger men help too. Everybody likes flowers.

The authorities don't order the flowers to be grown, but they don't forbid them either, and they don't trample on them like they do on carrots or onions. Let the visitors see them and say how well our prisoners live!

Quite often the officers and warders take flowers home with them to give to their wives. And on August 31, before the start of the school year, all free workers leave the compound carrying flowers: the following day their kids will be giving them to their teachers.

One day a speaker came to visit us and the cons got into an argument with him about conditions in the camps.

'Well, what are you complaining about?' asked the speaker in surprise. 'You've got a sports ground, volleyball court, library, and a camp full of flowers!'

'Don't you know,' replied Rodygin, 'that flowers also grow on graves.'

Hospital (Camp Division 3)

> And those whom the torturer cripples
> they patch up and darn and mend
> and back for more torture send.
> B. Brecht—'Song'
> (*The Fears and Miseries of the Third Reich*)

AT ABOUT eight o'clock on the morning of September 17, 1965, all of us who were going to hospital had to gather at the guardhouse with our things. Already the day before we had filled in our release forms showing that we had handed in all our camp equipment—mattress, pillow, etc., and had had our work payments settled. And now about twenty of us had gathered there: those who were able to came on foot, the more serious cases were brought on stretchers. Then the stretchers were placed straight on the ground.

We were waiting to be searched. The warders began to call us one by one into the guardhouse (those on the stretchers were carried into the guardhouse). Every single one of us, without exception, had to strip stark naked and then they examined and pinched us all over, pinched and felt every seam of our gear and took away everything that was forbidden to a con to possess: money, sharp or pointed objects, tea. Everything, in short, was as usual.

The main thing they were looking for was notes or letters: maybe a con would try to use the opportunity for dropping a few lines to a friend elsewhere, also a con, and correspondence between prisoners was strictly forbidden. When they finished one they would take him into the outer boundary zone, which was fenced off both from the inner boundary zone and the compound proper, and then call the next.

By the time they had searched us, lined us up in fives, checked our personal belongings against the documents and counted us again, two hours or so went by. Finally we set off: those who could walk went in formation, escorted by armed guards, while those who couldn't were transported in carts— also accompanied, of course, by armed guards.

We arrived at the station and waited for the train. It was the same small train that did the usual run from Potma to Barachevo—just a few coaches with a prison coach usually at the back, so that you couldn't enter it from the platform but had to do it straight from the ground. For us who could walk it didn't matter, but with the stretchers it was a hell of a job: the coach was terribly high off the ground, the doors were narrow and you couldn't turn in the corridor. The stretchers had to be turned from side to side and almost stood on end to get them in.

Luckily the stretcher-bearers had the knack of it through doing the job so often. Every Tuesday and Friday there was a convoy to camp three the whole length of the railway line, from every camp in the group; the other two days were reserved for civil prisoners. Here it is necessary to point out that although there are trains to the hospital every week, the number of the sick in the camp never decreases: almost half the inmates of every camp suffer from ulcers or stomach complaints alone, and there simply isn't room for them all in number three. In any case they don't cure patients in camp three, they merely examine them, get them back on their feet somehow or other and send them back to work in the camps again. Their places are then taken by new arrivals, and so it goes on in perpetual rotation.

In the prison coach it makes not the slightest difference that sick men are being transported, the crush is as bad as ever and there is nowhere to sit down. No sooner have the stretchers been put inside than the others have to crowd in as best they can. Never mind, you'll get there somehow, it's only a couple of hours till we arrive. And they don't give you any sort of toilet break either because again, as they say, it's only a couple of hours, you can wait. In actual fact we were chased out early that morning, so that it's not at all a case of waiting two hours but from eight o'clock in the morning. And sick men at that. But you can cry as much as you like, you still have to wait.

At every station they put more sick men on board and then lock everything up again.

At last we arrived. Here it was—number three—the hospital camp. And a camp like all the rest: palisade, barbed wire, watch towers, and a number of huts inside.

The distance from the station to the guardhouse was very small, about a hundred yards. But rules were still rules: the officer in command of the prison coach handed us over to the officer in command of the armed escort, just as he had received us, counting us and our files. The armed escort, having led us these hundred yards, handed us over yet again to the warder in the guardhouse, counting and checking each con against his photograph in the file. Then we had to go through another search. We were all gathered together into one big cell in the guardhouse and driven one at a time down a narrow corridor into another. In the corridor sat several warders; they ordered us to strip naked and pinched and felt every thread of our clothes and every hidden place on our bodies. However, they still didn't return our things to us but handed them all in to the stores. Then we were dispatched to different blocks—some to the surgical block, some to the psychiatric and some to the therapeutic—and once there we were issued with a towel, long underpants, an undershirt, and slippers for our bare feet. Now you were a patient and nothing else was prescribed, though you could also take with you a toothbrush, toothpaste, soap, a book or two and whatever food you happened to have. On the whole it was like when I went to hospital at home, the only difference being that I got no pyjamas and that the first 'examination' was carried out not by a doctor but by warders.

I was sent to block seven—the therapeutic block. A long hut with a corridor running its full length, on either side of the corridor small wards containing 12–20 cots, then the doctor's office, a treatment room, and a pantry (all the people who work in the block live here too—orderlies, food servers, and so on). The ward was clean, the cots, although close together, weren't arranged in double tier. White bed linen. Dressing gowns hung on one wall—about 5–6 per ward: whoever needed to go into the corridor took one down and put it on, though people also used to walk about in their underwear. It was all very similar, I must say, to an ordinary hospital. The difference was that whereas in an ordinary hospital the patients are always in a hurry to get out and go back home again, here it was the opposite: stay in as long as you can, for the way out of here lay not homewards but back to the camp, to those same officers, reformers, warders, back to parades, searches, and that hated forced labor. . . .

Then again, in a normal hospital you look forward to visiting hours, when your family will come to see you and bring you some delicacies to eat. Here in the camp hospital nobody comes to see you, your friends perhaps merely send you greetings via one of the regular convoys. And there are no parcels, no 'pick-me-ups', unless you happen to be due for a parcel in the ordinary way (and so long as you haven't been deprived of the right to receive one). Healthy or sick, a con's a con and should expect no extra privileges—God grant, only, that his lawful ones aren't taken away.

On the other hand the food in hospital is better than in the camps. Patients with ulcer or kidney trouble, post-operational patients and patients suffering from under-nourishment—each gets a suitable diet. For one man the food is strained, another gets a saltless diet. Even the general diet in number three is better than in the ordinary camps. In the first place, you really do get everything that is prescribed in the daily rations: if, say, it is 2 ozs. meat a day, you don't get a sniff of it in a normal camp, whereas in number three, even if you don't get the whole 2 ozs. you get one and a half in the form of rissoles or meat balls. The skilly for breakfast and dinner is the same, the gruel is the same and you get the same amount, but on the other hand you also get a dish of stewed fruit in the mornings, and half an ounce of butter. And every sick person gets a glass of milk a day. The bread ration is smaller: 18 ozs., but then 7 ozs. is white bread.

It may be that the calorie count of the camp hospital rations is no higher than a con's normal camp ration, but the quality of the calories is undoubtedly higher. Needless to say, such hospital delicacies as eggs, curd cakes, apples, are be-yond the con's wildest dreams, he'll die before he sees any. . . . But then there's the milk, the stewed fruit. . . .

For so long as you're in a serious condition or very weak, the hospital rations are fully satisfactory and sometimes there's even a bit left over, but once you start to get better the situation's grim, you feel hungrier than in camp. For in the camp, as I have said before, nobody lives on 'basic',

everybody contrives some way out of it: one man buys bread
with money smuggled to him from home, another speculates,
and even the man with nothing gets a part of somebody else's
rations—the leftovers of some more resourceful con. Here in
number three, though, you eat meatballs and drink milk, but
you can't for the life of you get beyond the authorized norm,
nor is there anywhere where you can get more than the prescribed 18 ozs. of bread. There is a shop in the camp, it's true,
but everything is done to prevent the con from using it.
You're transferred to hospital, for instance, and you've no
idea when the money from your own personal account will
arrive, and then while you're waiting you're discharged again
and when you get back to your own camp your money is still
traveling about somewhere, so that here too you have to go
without the shop. . . .

Free people can hardly comprehend all these problems and
what seem at first to be the petty practical complications
that fill a con's life. Take, for example, the question of whether to apply to go to hospital or not. On the one hand you
feel like death warmed up, treatment is absolutely essential,
you haven't the strength to work; on the other hand you will
lose your shop privileges, perhaps for two or three months, so
that if you go you'll have to live on an empty stomach for a
month or two. . . .

I felt that I was turning into an invalid, that I simply
wasn't strong enough to stay in the gang. Day and night we
would be ordered out—unload, push the wagon up, shovel
coal, shovel grit, haul logs. The work was enough to break
even a healthy man's back. And on top of this, autumn was
setting in, to be followed by winter—rain, cold winds, frost.
You'd get soaking wet at work, the autumn wind would blow
right through you while you waited at the guardhouse—and
by the spring you'd be either dead or a permanent invalid.

The lads advised me nonetheless to apply for hospital and to try and hang on there for as long as possible.

And so I had come to camp three. The ear specialist, with scarcely a glance at my ears, prescribed me some drops. The treatment was timed to last five days. That meant that in a week, when convoy time came around, I would be on my way back to camp, to my dearly beloved emergency gang.

Fortunately I met up with an acquaintance of mine in the surgical block—Nikolai Senik, a senior orderly working for the camp service. And there was a doctor's assistant too, also a con, who knew me slightly. They advised me to apply for work as an orderly: it was close to the doctors, just in case, and they would treat me a bit on the side. And the work too, although not easy, was at least indoors, out of the weather.

On the whole cons are unwilling to take work as orderlies and do so only in cases of extreme necessity or in order to get a good character reference. The point is that a hospital camp has no income, it is pure expense as far as the authorities are concerned, and so they do all they can to reduce this expense as far as possible. A whole block will have only two or three orderlies. And the work includes lighting stoves, washing and cleaning, laundering the doctors' white coats, serving out food, washing dishes and attending to the bed-ridden. What's more they ask far more of a camp orderly than one in a normal hospital: there, if you wear the orderly out with too many demands, she will simply ask for her cards and go elsewhere; and just you try and find another to take her place on the miserable pay she gets. That's why I have never seen a free hospital as clean as our camp hospital. Our doctor on his rounds used to take a piece of white cotton wool and rub it over the walls and window panes and even over the leaves of the flowers—and God forbid that he should find any dust! Thus the orderly has to dash about all day long. What's more, fifty per cent of his pay, just as elsewhere, is deducted for his keep, so that after deductions for food and clothing there is nothing left—not even enough to go to the shop. And so only cons like me used to volunteer for work as orderlies—in the hope of getting some treatment.

Here too, of course, the authorities tried to operate with administrative measures: once you were appointed an orderly, willy-nilly you had to work and knuckle under. If you refused—off to the cooler. But here in the hospital these measures didn't help. One con would be stuck in the cooler, another let out, again they would refuse and again go back to the cooler; but somebody had to do the work anyway. And so the authorities were forced to adopt an uncharacteristically liberal approach: the nurses or doctors would themselves pick suitable cons for particular kinds of work, or else interested cons would come to an agreement with them independently. Then, even though you were working unpaid in point of fact, at least it was voluntary.

I decided to apply for work as an orderly in the surgical block: here there were tiny rooms for two for members of the hospital service; and it was an enormous blessing, after living in communal huts, to have almost a separate room to yourself (actually we lived there 'illegally'; all members of the hospital service had a separate hut to themselves and whenever a commission came we were hurriedly evacuated there from our cubby-holes in the block).

Senik recommended me to the matron. She talked to the head doctor, the head doctor pleaded my case with the Chief Officer—and I became an orderly. My friends' advice turned out to be correct: I continued to receive treatment and was even given some sort of injections. The work too, although there was plenty of it, didn't bother me: my mother had been a cleaner and as a boy I had been used to helping her. The only difficult bit was lighting the stoves. The firewood they brought us was in such big pieces that it wouldn't go into the stove—and a chopper, of course, was not allowed into camp! Use your teeth, seemed to be the motto. As always, of course, I found a way out: I got myself a chopper. But I still couldn't chop anything outside, where it could be seen—I had the chopper, but had to pretend that I hadn't. And so I was forced to crawl under the front porch and there, bent double and practically on my knees, hack away at the billets in secret—as though I was gaining something for myself instead of providing fuel for the hospital.

Our complement for the surgical block was supposed to be two orderlies. I was taken on in excess of the complement and later they had to take two more: one assisted Senik in his duties and the other assisted me. We were registered officially as patients, so that no pay at all was credited to us and we worked solely in exchange for treatment. We were also fed as patients. The patients in our block also worked a bit: some volunteered to help with the washing up or to do some cleaning. As soon as their condition permitted they would ask for some little job or other. Not, of course, for lack of anything to do, but for an extra bowl of skilly or some bread: the orderly would go to the cookhouse and wheedle for some and then give it to whoever had helped him.

In our block we also had civil prisoners and cons from intensified* regime camps, and for a while they even brought women to us from the women's compound for operations, because their operating theatre was being renovated.

Patients from intensified regime camps were held in separate hospital cells, which were equipped with barred windows and sloptanks and always kept locked. After an operation, a

---

* Intensified regime is a penal arrangement between 'strict' and 'special' regimes.

'stripey' (cons on intensified have to wear striped uniform) was put into the general post-operative ward where he lay until he began to come round a bit from his operation, say for two to three days. Then, the moment he began to stir, it was off to the cell with him and under lock and key. These hospital cells were triple-headers, the keys to them were supposed to be held by the duty warder in the guardhouse. We tried to badger the duty warder as much as possible: at one moment we would be running to him to open up the cell for cleaning, the next it would be for treatment—injections had to be given or an enema administered; then the doctor's assistant had to check a patient's condition; then it was time to let the patients out for exercise (in hospital they were authorized to have half-an-hour's exercise in the corridor per day, but the time was determined by the assistant doctor). The upshot of all this was that the duty warder used to get fed up with this running back and forth and would give the keys into the safe keeping of the assistant doctor. The assistant doctor, of course, had no intention of holding convalescent patients under lock and key and allowed them to wander up and down the corridor—'they've just been getting their injections' or 'the orderlies are washing the floor'—there was no shortage of excuses.

Senik tried to feed these patients up as much as he could; and in any case we all knew what it was like on intensified regime and had seen what pathetic 'goners' used to come from there.

We used to scrounge left-over bits of black bread from the bread-cutting room and dry them out for the cons doing intensified so that when they went back to camp they could at least take these 'rusks' with them for themselves and their cell-mates. Whatever else they took back with them would be confiscated during the search, but rusks made of black bread were allowed. As for the other cons from strict regime camps, they could always shift for themselves in the matter of food, but on intensified regime, just as in prison, there is no way at all.

Surgical patients from among the civil prisoners also had separate wards (therapeutic patients had a separate compound altogether), but they were not kept locked in and used to troop down the corridor all together. On the whole the authorities try to separate the civil prisoners from political prisoners not because the latter have to be protected against bandits, but on the contrary—they are afraid in case the 'politicals' with their views and conversation might somehow corrupt these honest and respectable swindlers and hoodlums.

The women's hospital compound was just behind that of the civil prisoners. That winter the women were operated on in our theatre. Senik and I were usually sent to bring the patients who couldn't stand, and it was we who usually took them back again. On operation days we would be summoned to the guardhouse of the women's compound, where we would go under armed escort, put the patient, who had already been prepared by the women orderlies, on to our stretcher and carry her straight to our block. There we would place the stretcher in a narrow passageway in front of the operating theatre, undress the patient to her undershirt and then carry her in on our arms and place her on the operating table. Meanwhile the convalescent men would crowd at the door to the passageway just for a chance to set eyes on a woman, especially one that was almost completely undressed. It didn't matter that she was sick and wasn't even able to walk, but had to be brought in on a stretcher.

After the operation, while the patient was still under the influence of the anaesthetic, we would remove her from the table, place her on a stretcher, wrap her up as warmly as we could (it was wintertime, frosty) and carry her to our guardhouse. Here we would have to lower the stretcher and begin to beg the duty warder to get us an escort quickly—he always insisted on taking his time. Officers and doctors would walk past the stretcher as it rested directly on the ground and not one of them gave a damn for us and our patient—every free worker here had long since got used to the idea that cons aren't human beings. Then we would begin to lose our tempers and rush from one to the other: 'We've got a patient here fresh from the operating table, the anaesthetic will wear off in a minute and when she starts to move about she'll uncover herself and catch cold! Hurry up with the escort!'

The officers replied: 'We're not doctors, our job is to guard you. Anaesthetics and patients are none of our business.'

Just then an elderly, dignified lady in a light-brown overcoat with a fur collar would pass by. This was the hospital director, Shimkanis, a major in the medical corps. Without even a glance at the stretcher, she would reply: 'We're doctors, our job is to heal and perform operations. Escorts are nothing to do with us. What do you want me to do?'

We tried complaining about such inhuman methods. The Chief Officer replied by putting us in our place:

'It's none of your business! You've brought the stretcher to the guardhouse, now wait! People can only complain for themselves, not for others. Have you forgotten that?'

And the same reply was given to us by Major Petrushevsky, chief of the Sanitation Department of the Dubrovlag directorate: 'Why can't you mind your own business! The authorities themselves will answer for everything!'

Yes, and they do! A healthy man is sent to the camp and he comes out an invalid—will Major Petrushevsky or Major Shimkanis have to answer for that one day? And to whom? . . .

And so we stand and stand, wait and wait. At last the armed guards crawl out and lead us to the guardhouse of the women's compound. We walk slowly, fearing to fall: it is slippery, our boots skid on the frozen snow—and we are carrying a patient in a serious condition. Before we get there we stop several times to take a breather, obliged each time to lower the stretcher directly on to the snow. At the guardhouse we are received by two wardresses—coarse, fat women wearing greatcoats with striped epaulettes—who take us to the block. Here we are obliged to wait in the corridor while the women orderlies remove the patient and free our stretcher. That's another joke: we are one administration, in essence a single hospital compound, although divided up into a women's, political and civil prisoners' compound—yet each division has its own equipment, its own stretchers; and for the sake of these and in order that we should remain responsible for them, they allow us to remain for a while among the women prisoners. Although any contact between men and women is forbidden and harshly punished, nevertheless when it comes to even such a trivial piece of equipment as a stretcher, the rules can all go to hell!

While we are waiting for the stretcher we are surrounded in the corridor by women prisoners, both patients and orderlies. They are delighted just to see or talk to a man who is not a guard and not a warder. The majority of them are criminal prisoners—and the things you get to hear while you're waiting! Some of them have friends in the men's camps and these ask to see us to pass on greetings or notes to them—after all, patients come to us from every corner of Dubrovlag. And we also look around us as though in a different world. We don't notice either the skinniness or the pitiful clothing of the women surrounding us. Or rather, we notice it, we pity them for it, but in spite of their unfortunate appearance they seem terribly attractive to us. One door off the corridor opens into a small ward from where we can hear the sound of a sort of high pitched squeaking, like the miaowing of cats. We look in. Round the walls runs a double line of cots, just like the ones we have in the men's compound, and across the cots, several to each, lie little squeaking bundles: new-born babes.

'Who's are these?' we ask.

'Gulag's* children!' answers a cheerful young woman con.

There are quite a few women among the patients who have children born to them here in the camp. 'My Valery's two already!' 'My Nina's going on five!' Where there are no families outside to take the children, they grow up inside the camp and are brought up in the camp nurseries and orphanages. The mother stays in the compound behind barbed wire, while the child stays with her for a time and then goes into a special orphanage—but still not a free one. And so they grow up. . . .

Sometimes women used to come on their own for operations—under armed escort, of course, but not on stretchers. They usually didn't feel too bad and were awaiting some simple sort of operation. They would bring five to seven to the block all at once and take them to the treatment room, where they would undress (also to their undershirts) and wait to be called for their operation. In the corridor would be a crowd of convalescent men. The politicals tended to be more reticent, but the civil prisoners simply went wild over the women; and then the women were of different types too. Then one of the cons would start to beg Nikolai Senik:

'Listen, you bring her to the toilets and I'll already be there. Go on, just for ten minutes, eh?'

After the operations, of course, some have to be carried back on a stretcher, others shuffle back on their own. But

* Gulag is an acronym for Main Administration of Camps.

they're not up to anything by that time, least of all men. . . .

Our surgical block was also good in that our doctors were young, they hadn't yet been worn down by the system, hadn't become accustomed to it and hadn't adapted themselves to it. Having finished their studies they had been drafted here, and they were only waiting for the day when they could get back 'to freedom' again. From every one of them I heard the same:

'All I want to do is get these three years over with and then get away from here to wherever I can, even to the devil himself if necessary!'

On the other hand, the work in camp three was beyond even the wildest dreams of a beginning doctor: operations of all degrees of complexity, traumas, even bullet-wounds.

One day they brought us a young fellow from one of the civil camps—his chest had been shot away by a tommy gun. It had happened like this: a group of cons had been standing on a porch in the compound and having a slanging match with the sentry in the watch tower. The latter lost his temper and trained his tommy gun on them. The rest of the cons ran into the hut, but this one stayed behind—it wasn't conceivable for a sentry to fire into the compound. Well, the sentry did let off a burst. I don't know whether he was punished or not, but the con came to us in the surgical block.

So here was the chance to get experience and independent work and reasonable conditions (although, of course, it was a pretty poor hole to be stuck in)—and yet the young doctors were anxious to get away from this work to 'wherever they could'. One of the main reasons was that they were unable to help their patients properly—and all around them they could see injustices and hunger. Here they were undergoing a training in heartlessness and indifference: do what directly concerns you and don't interfere with anything. For a doctor, of course, it is difficult to reconcile this principle with the principles of his profession. But some accustomed themselves to it, remained there forever and themselves became like admin and the officers—like Shimkanis for example. But then there were lots more like her, especially in the camps themselves.

Our surgeons, however, were quite different, including both the chief surgeon, Zaborovsky, and the two other doctors, Kabirov and Sokolova. They used to talk to the patients and would turn a blind eye to us orderlies meeting late at night in the treatment room. How many times did our doctors go to the hospital director to ask for more firewood for our block! Sokolova was the sort of woman who would order me not to light her stove during the frosty weather and would sit in her office in her fur coat—so that there would be more firewood for the wards and because it was better for the patients to be warm. In actual fact, this was about all the doctors could do for us, apart from giving treatment. Another characteristic feature was that they lacked the arrogance with which most free workers regarded prisoners. Our assistant doctor, Nikolai, had a twenty-five-year term to serve, he had long experience, and our young doctors always sought his advice: his diagnoses were considered the best of all.

Here I again came into close contact with various 'self-mutilation' cases, tattooed cons and failed suicides. Almost every operation day included some sort of stomach operation, when they cut out whatever it was the con had swallowed. I won't talk about them all in detail, since this would only be a repetition of what I saw and described in Vladimir jail: barbed wire hooks, pieces of glass, bent kettle spouts. . . .

A young fellow from the Baltic coast was brought in one day from the psychiatric block. I had got to know him earlier when in hospital for the first time. Then he had just cut off one ear. They healed the wound and put him in the psychiatric block. And now, when he had only a few months to go till his release, he had cut off his second ear and swallowed a spoon and some pieces of barbed wire. He was operated on by Sokolova, but two months later came back again: this time he had swallowed a whole set of chessmen, both the black and the white pieces, with the exception of two knights. Only about forty days remained till his release. I don't know whether he was really crazy. I had often talked to him and he gave me the impression of being fully normal—far more normal, at any rate, than many cons in the camps who passed for normal. He was the son of a priest, a literate, well-read fellow. And he read a lot in hospital too. The second operation was also done by Sokolova: Senik asked her afterwards if he could have the chessmen from the stomach. He and I preserved this museum exhibit—we couldn't play with it, two of the knights were missing.

I also met another old acquaintance of mine here—Boris Vlasov, the one who had come into our cell at Vladimir on crutches. Soon after that, Boris had been taken out of prison and put on intensified regime, and all this time he had been doing intensified. He was brought in wearing a striped uniform and put in a cell with the other 'stripeys'. While in the intensified regime camp he had tattooed himself all over, including on the face and chest, and had all the usual slogans: 'Slave of the CPSU' and so on. In our block they cut out his tattoos and he didn't stay long with us. As soon as his wounds began to heal he was transferred to the therapeutic block, which he didn't like for one minute! Only in our block did the 'stripeys' live relatively freely, stroll up and down the corridor and talk to the other cons. In the other blocks they kept strictly to instructions: in the cell they stayed, under lock and key.

One day they brought a young fellow in from one of the camps. While doing intensified he had swallowed several rusty nails, two spoons and some pieces of barbed wire. He knew that as soon as he recovered from his operation he would be taken away again and put back on intensified regime. And so, immediately after his operation, before he had hardly come round, he tore off his bandages and split open the seam on his stomach. They were forced to sew him up again. And he lay there, tied down in his cot, until the scar healed. Naturally he was put back on intensified regime. There he got hold of a razor blade, ripped open his stomach again and again got sent to us; and again we were forced to tie him down in his cot. . . .

These are just ordinary, everyday stories of camp life to which cons, doctors and admin have grown fully accustomed. But one day one of our nurses (they were all free workers from outside) went on holiday to some nurses' holiday home. Once there she avoided telling her companions that she worked in a camp, no, she was just a nurse in a hospital. But, as happens on holiday, she got to telling them about the kind of things that happened at work: they took a spoon out of one patient's stomach, another one had nails inside him, or chessmen, or glass. . . . And lo and behold, after she had told these stories her companions at the holiday home decided that she was abnormal, that she was psychologically unbalanced, and they even began to be afraid of her. After her holiday she told us this on one of the evenings when we gathered in the treatment room. And all of a sudden we seemed to see properly for the first time everything that surrounded us, the whole savagery and fantastic incredibility of the situation we were in, of these ordinary stories of ours, and of this hospital behind barbed wire under the armed guard of tommy gunners in their watch towers.

Love

EARLIER THE men's and women's hospital compounds had been next door to one another, separated only by a wooden fence, some rows of barbed wire and a ploughed and raked strip. We were able not only to see the women but even to talk to them secretly and throw notes over. And even later, when the women's hospital camp was moved farther away, our orderlies and patients managed to keep contact with them, and this is how it was done. Sometimes we stretcher bearers would have to take the women to and from operations, while the nurses used to take our linen and sterilizer over to the women's camp, at which times a note could be passed over. Admin persecuted prisoners remorselessly for any relations with women and if a note was ever discovered and they succeeded in tracking down its author and the addressee, the cooler was a cert for all three of them, that is for both 'partners in the relationship' and the person who passed on the note. And if a nurse was to blame, she was dismissed immediately.

It is not quite clear to me why these platonic affairs should so arouse admin's ire and indignation. Was it that they imagined more in them than there really was? Sheer malice (not even the slightest pleasure can be permitted)? Or simply because the regulations were being broken? But no prohibitions or persecutions in the world could stop men and women who for years had been deprived of any natural relations with one another. And so these forbidden camp affairs would break out, a paper love that might last a week, but sometimes went on for years. They began always with introductions ('my name is so-and-so'—'and my name is so-and-so'; often the first note was sent completely at random). Well, and then—declarations of love, dreams of a meeting, and sometimes even a photo got passed. And so a con dreamed no longer of kissing a woman in the abstract but thought of his Nadia or his Lucy, and she would tell him that she loved him and write tender words, and he would wait for the next note and undergo agonies of uncertainty—did she still love him, had she found another? . . . Gone is the camp, the barbed wire, the loneliness; all that seems real is the separation from your loved one. . . . Sometimes, though very rarely, of course, this camp love survives even after release.

Nikolai Senik once had his own 'sweetheart'—her name was Lyuba and she was an assistant doctor in the women's hospital. Both Lyuba and Nikolai had been working in their respective hospitals for ages, for five years already. They had got to know one another when the women's camp was still next to ours and used to send each other notes and look at one another from a distance. Nikolai knew that Lyuba had a husband outside, some of the boys had even seen him when he came to visit her and said he was a nice sort of fellow. Nikolai himself was alone: his wife had left him and married somebody else. The fact that Lyuba was married didn't stop them loving one another. Anyway, they were two different lives: the outside world, a husband, visits once a year; and against this the camp, love notes and dreams of a meeting. I don't know which of these two lives was the reality and which of them existed only in imagination.

When the women's camp was moved away, Nikolai and Lyuba continued to correspond through the nurses. Now they even managed to see one another from time to time, for our orderlies used to take the women to be operated on. For the first time they were able to see one another close up, for the first time they were able to talk. Nikolai always tried to go himself with the stretchers to the women's camp in order to have an extra chance of swapping a few words with Lyuba. And we used to help him as best we could. We would either take over his duty in the operating theatre or try to fiddle about with the stretchers in the women's camp as long as possible, so as to distract the wardresses. Sometimes Nikolai and Lyuba even managed to be alone for a few minutes.

Not long before Lyuba's release she was operated on for varicose veins. She came over herself for the operation. The women orderlies had picked out the best smock they could find for her, with no holes and more or less the right size. And Nikolai himself had prepared for her in advance the most becoming dressing gown and the best slippers. He had also washed and ironed it himself. But he didn't go to the operation in order not to embarrass Lyuba, and asked me to go on duty instead. The doctors knew of their love and Kabirov, who was doing the operation, permitted Lyuba to keep her panties on on the operating table—usually the patients remained naked under their smocks.

When the operation was over, Nikolai helped me to carry Lyuba back to the women's hospital. They continued to write letters to each other as before, but it didn't last much longer. Lyuba was soon released. Nikolai and I wrote a last letter to her together—in farewell. . . .

I also had offers to introduce me to one of the women

prisoners—to 'get married', as they say—but I didn't want to. I knew that I wouldn't be here much longer and that soon I would have to return to my camp.

Paper love gets carried on not only in hospital but in any camp, particularly if there are men's and women's camps in the same settlement. In camp eleven a number of friendships were struck up when our construction gang was working in the women's camp. Knowing that their affairs would have to be broken up as soon as the construction gang finished its work, the women and the cons made plans in advance about how to keep in touch—through relatives and through the hospital. And what quarrels, scandals and even fights took place over love! Suddenly somebody would find out that one woman was writing to two or three at the same time, or on the contrary, a con would be writing to one and her friend would then start writing to him and 'steal' him—tears, despair, jealousy. . . .

There were also cases, of course, of more 'material' love, for there were women working in the camps as medical staff or teachers in the school. Many prisoners used to go to school only to look at the women teachers. But this in any event wasn't love—it was a case of many looking at one, and in a certain sense she belonged to them all. Well, and then there were instances of a con getting together with one of the un-skilled women working inside the camp. I've no idea, I'm sure, of where and how they managed it. Sometimes an affair was the result of mutual attraction, and sometimes because of some sort of present. One of our cons had an affair with a free worker after giving her a watch. And that's all there was to it. The most intriguing thing about this whole business was that most of the free women in the camps were the daughters and wives of the officers and warders.

But the majority of prisoners live all these years and the

whole of their sentences—five, ten, fifteen, twenty-five years—without any kind of love whatsoever, either paper or genuine. This is why in the ordinary camps, among the criminal prisoners, homosexuality is rampant. Practically one hundred per cent of them indulge in it, despite the fact that homosexuality is punishable by law. If they catch you out you can get a new stretch for it—but then they can't catch everybody. I remember when I was at Karaganda, in Stepnoy Camp, all the homosexuals there—the ones that were known, that is, and caught in the act—were herded into a single hut with 180 men in it, in an attempt to segregate them from the rest. 180 men—these were only the ones that got caught and the ones who played the woman in the couples. Those who played the men were not considered as homosexuals. The former were universally despised, while the latter went about like heroes, boasting of their masculine strength and their 'conquests' not only to each other but even to the guards. One day I heard Vorkuta, a famous pederast known to the whole camp, stand next to a company commander and say to him about another commander (who was just walking past): I wouldn't mind getting hold of him and doing this, that and the other to him; and the two of them lovingly lingered over all the details. That was not in a criminal camp, but a political one.

In general homosexuality is also spreading to the political camps, together with the criminals who find their way there. But the position of homosexuals there is far different from in ordinary camps. They are despised by the whole camp, but on the other hand are beloved of admin. If anyone is ever caught at this game, they don't send him for trial but merely threaten him with a trial and publicity. That way they blackmail them and enlist a whole army of stool pigeons and provocateurs. It's true, though, that admin don't get much use out of them: there are few homosexuals in the political camps, you can practically count them on the fingers of one hand, and the prisoners know who they are even better than admin and do their best not to mix with them.

I used to know several homosexuals: in Vladimir and later in Mordovia there was a certain Subbotin (the one who swallowed the dominoes), also Yuri Karmanov—nicknamed Lyubka—a homosexual since the time of the Byelomov Canal, and then the celebrated Vorkuta. They were all scum, the lowest of the low, cynical and foul-mouthed. As far as obscenities went, however, the officers and guards and all the members of admin could compete with them any time, and I don't know who would have won. Once Vorkuta got into such a competition with our censor. He was lining up for printed packets when, all of a sudden he let loose a terrific hail of curses. The censor evidently decided to show that he wasn't born yesterday either and also knew a thing or two—and sent back an even bluer reply. Vorkuta then started fucking everything up hill and down dale—his God, his soul, his mother, and the censor likewise. I was also in the same line and to stand by and listen to it was both comic and disturbing.

The married cons, of course, were a different matter entirely, they didn't need any paper love. They lived on memories of their families, letters, and their wives were allowed a visit once a year. But the KGB and admin tried to use the con's right to one visit per annum as one more means of exerting pressure, a means of enslaving the prisoner. At first, while a case is still under investigation and immediately after it's over, they endeavor to persuade the wife to disown her criminal husband. And a few wives disown them of their own accord: all the unpleasantness, the troubles, the journeying, bringing up the children on your own, and on top of that to wait for ten to fifteen years. The wife of one of my camp friends demanded not only a divorce from her husband but also that he give up all rights of paternity. The law went out of its way to satisfy such demands, even when a normal divorce in our country was complicated by all sorts of formalities—they just went ahead and divorced and took away paternity rights with no red tape whatsoever, and without saying a word to the convicted husband. My friend asked: how was it, then, that they had divorced him from his wife and taken away his children without any consent from him (in those days you still needed the consent of both parties for a divorce)? They replied that he had betrayed his country— that was the article he was convicted under—and by virtue of that very fact had obviously betrayed his wife as well, and that was why she was disowning him.

And if a wife doesn't disown her husband and travels to visit him, they call her in for a talk before the visit in the hope that she will influence her husband and persuade him to give up his beliefs and his friends in the camp and cooperate with the administration. In return they promise that he can have a visit lasting three whole days and have parcels, and that his lot will be improved. On the other hand 'obstinate' prisoners, who stubbornly maintain their convictions, have their visit shortened to two days, one day, or one day during which they have to work (in other words sixteen hours); and they dream up all sorts of excuses in order to deprive him of his personal (with no warders present) visit—his one and only visit a year.

The unmarried cons—and there are quite a few of them now in the political camps, more and more young people have been coming in in recent years—suffer badly from the lack of women. You get the following sort of thing. While outside, a young fellow lived with a girl as man and wife, only the marriage was never registered. And then suddenly he's put away and she can't come on a visit, not even a communal one, because the camp administration recognizes only legal marriages confirmed by the register office's rubber stamp. True, they might permit a visit if the unofficial wife gets a certificate from the district or village council testifying that she had in fact been cohabiting with so-and-so. And although it was humiliating for a woman to have to ask for such a certificate, still a great number used to accept the humiliation in order to be able to meet their beloved. And it even used to happen that unknown girls, after becoming friends through correspondence, would come armed with such certificates to see their pen pals—if they were lucky enough to get one from the village council (and what could the council do, how the devil could they know who was living with whom?).

They say that not so long ago, about two years before I came to Mordovia, the village council's confirmation or certificate of marriage was insufficient. Then, so the boys told me, a woman had to also have a certificate from the V.D. clinic that she wasn't suffering from any venereal disease. So a husband would end up writing to his wife: 'Darling, I'm allowed a visit. Please come, but don't forget to pick up a certificate from the doctor saying that you haven't got syphilis or gonorrhea. . . .' The wife, of course, would be in tears: 'We've got children, I'm waiting for you—and you don't trust me.' 'I trust you, my dear, it's my commandant who's so suspicious.'

Particularly amusing was the fact that if the wife was a party member, she didn't need such evidence—instead of a doctor's certificate she could show her membership card. This gave rise to a multitude of questions: did an applicant for a party membership need a certificate? Did you have to have a certificate from the clinic before being accepted into the party? If not, then had it been established by science that entry into the party would cleanse and cure you of syphilis that had been caught earlier. . . . In brief, there was no shortage of jokes on this theme.

I was too late to see this rule in operation. In my time it was sufficient to have evidence of marriage or a certificate from the village council. I wrote about this to a girl friend of mine and in 1964, having obtained the necessary certificate in her village, she came to pay me a visit. At that time I had no black marks to my name and they gave me three days; and the ganger didn't call me to work on those days. I was lucky: in six years of imprisonment I managed to spend three days with a woman.

After that I didn't ask her again. What was the point of her tying her life to a con, what fun was it for her to travel once a year just to spend three days with me? After all, she wasn't my wife.

The Loony Bin

APART FROM the therapeutic and surgical blocks in camp
three we also had a psychiatric block—everybody called it
the 'loony bin' (from 'lunatic asylum', I suppose; there are
other words for it too). What horror stories you hear outside
about madmen and about mental hospitals! I was overwhelmed with curiosity: although it was frightening, I was
irresistibly drawn to have a look at the madmen close up.
And the more so since everybody feels flattered by such a
confrontation: looking at lunatics you rise in your own
estimation—they are lunatics, but I'm clever. I had heard, of
course, that sometimes perfectly healthy people were incar-
cerated in lunatic asylums if they had displeased the authorities in some way. But still, a loony bin was a loony bin. . . .

I went on a visit to the orderlies in the psychiatric block.
The block was divided off from the others by a high fence. I
rang at the gate and it was opened for me. Cautiously I
entered the yard. All over the yard there were cons walking
up and down—patients who were quietly talking to one another. Maybe these were the mild cases, only slightly cracked?
I walked through the whole block and visited every one of
the cells—everywhere it was the same picture. Reading, playing chess, quietly talking together. The orderlies made fun of

me for trying to find the lunatics: 'Are you cracked yourself, or something? Don't you know where the madmen are? Didn't you see them in the camps?'

I recollected that in the camps and in jail—in the communal cells—I really had met cons who were genuinely mentally sick and in some cases even violent. Many of them absolutely poison the lives—which God knows are miserable enough already—of their fellow cons: they make a racket at night, shout things out, howl, steal food, create uproar, start fights; there are even those who defecate on the floor and then eat their own faeces. How often did we complain to the authorities and beg for them to be taken away and isolated from the healthy cons, but the answer was always the same: It's none of your business, you're not in charge here!' And at the best we might hear: 'What do you want us to do with them? We can't take them home with us!'

'Do you mean to say that everyone here is normal, that there are no genuine madmen here at all?' I asked an orderly one day. He explained to me that indeed there were a few genuine ones too, but these were kept there for a short time only and then sent back to the camps. Sometimes they would be sent to the Serbsky Institute in Leningrad for expert diagnosis. There, more often than not, they would be pronounced normal and admin would be given an authorization to treat them as normal. People under investigation for a crime are a different matter, of course: the Serbsky Institute can proclaim as mad almost anyone with even the slightest abnormalities in his psychology, or even completely normal people—if that is what the KGB wants.

Afterwards I often used to go to the loony bin, and in any case our 'lunatics', secretly from the administration, used to wander all over the camp, even though it was strictly forbidden. The orderlies weren't in the least afraid of letting them

out: they knew that they need fear no unpleasantness from
their patients.

Among the 'lunatics' I met several people I knew. On my
very first visit there I was astonished to recognize one of the
patients as a con I had known in camp ten—he was tha
same man who had tangled with Captain Vasyayev on the
memorable evening of our failure to dig a tunnel. I was told
by other cons that he used to enter into discussion not only
with the officers who were our 'teachers', but also with visit
ing lecturers—and always floored them with his questions
and arguments. The prisoners used to listen to these discus
sions with enormous interest, but admin used to get furious
How many times did they stick him in the cooler, but he stil
wouldn't let up? He and I talked together, recalled that even
ing and acquaintances we had in common, including Burov
whom he had known very well. I cautiously asked him how
he had come to land up among the 'lunatics'. He laughed a
my embarrassment and said that there were lots here like
himself: admin felt much happier with them in the loony bin
than in camp.

Kolya Shcherbakov was also there, minus both ears and
blue all over from the slogans and sayings that were tattooed
on his face and body. I also met a genuine madman, Nurm
saar, from the Baltic coast. I had known him earlier at camp
seven, we had lived in the same section. He was more or less
quiet in his behavior and caused more trouble to himseli
than others. Every now and then he would refuse to go to
work; when the time came to go on parade, he would walk off
in the other direction. We used to stop him: 'Nurmsaar
where are you going? It's time to go to work!' But he seemed
not to hear and would look straight through us. Several times
our company officer, Alyoshin, gave him two weeks in the
cooler for failure to go to work. And now he had been brought

to the loony bin—correctly in this case, you could hardly drive him out to work and demand a norm from him as if he were normal. I went over to him in order to ask about my friends in number seven, but it seemed he didn't understand me, and maybe he didn't even recognize me either. Thus, having got nothing out of him, I went away. Later, after my release, I learned that Nurmsaar was back in camp again and had also been stuck back in the cooler.

It was another meeting, however, that produced the biggest impression on me. I went, as was customary, to meet one of the regular convoys, to pick up patients and bring them back to the surgical block. And who should I see among the new arivals but a close acquaintance of mine, Mart Niklus. He had been a friend of my own friends, Genka Krivtsov and Tolik Rodygin. All three of them had been put into an intensified regime block (IRB) ostensibly for failing to fulfil their norms, but the whole camp knew that they had been put in the block for their 'obstinacy'—in other words because they stood up for their beliefs. I knew that their term on intensified regime wasn't up yet, so I was all the more pleased to see Niklus—both because he himself had managed to get out of the IRB (this happens very rarely, usually they say: 'Finish your punishment first, then you can go for treatment') and for the sake of news of my friends. Mart passed on greetings to me from Genka and Tolik and I told him a bit about life in number three—so as to help him orientate himself as quickly as possible. Then I asked him what had happened and how he had managed to get himself out of the IRB and into hospital. And although by this time I was used to just about everything, nevertheless I was stunned by his reply: 'Well, don't you see—I'm mad now, that's why they've brought me to the loony bin!' Somehow I just couldn't fit this news into my head. Mart explained that he had gone on hunger strike as a mark of protest against the starvation rations. They threatened that if he didn't call his strike off they would lock him up in the lunatic asylum—and here he was: 'Now,' said Niklus, 'I can live among the same sort of lunatics as me.'

Sometimes Niklus would come secretly to join us in our block. Four of us—he and I and two of our orderlies, countrymen of his, named Karl and Jan—used to spend our evenings in conversation. He stayed for about a month and then was sent back to the IRB—to finish out his term. When that was over, he and Krivtsov and Rodygin were 'tried' and sentenced to three years in Vladimir jail. Niklus was soon let out again, but Genka and Tolik are in jail even now.

What an interesting situation: the same man turns out to be normal at one moment and abnormal the next, and then normal again—all according to the whim of the authorities. Niklus, for instance, was considered normal—he was obliged to keep up with his work and observe all the conditions of the regime; he went on hunger strike, became 'insane' and landed up in the loony bin; then he went back to the IRB and was tried by a camp court as though fully normal (and on the same charge that had cost him six months in the IRB already—perhaps if he went on hunger strike at Vladimir he would be pronounced a lunatic again).

And here is another case: one day in camp three a warder detained a patient from the psychiatric ward outside the library—the patient was not supposed to go beyond the fence. This patient had been pronounced abnormal by the Serbsky Institute and I think he really was cracked. Nevertheless the warder started dragging him off to the cooler for breaking regulations. The patient broke away and made a run for it, the warder caught up with him and grabbed him, then the patient started to fight him off and in the ensuing struggle tore off one of the warder's shoulder-straps. The patient was put on a charge. But so long as a man's a lunatic, he cannot be tried. And so a few days later the madman was pronounced normal, tried for resisting a member of the security services, for causing him bodily harm and for tearing off one of his shoulder-straps. So they tried a sick man solely to frighten off the others, so that others wouldn't be tempted. His sentence was extended to fifteen years; and still he was lucky that he wasn't shot!

A Skirmish with Authority

On a normal convoy day at the end of February, Karl and I set off for the reception centre to meet the surgical patients. We travelled light: wearing just our mules, capless, without our oversleeves and not even wearing our padded jackets.

With our hands in our pockets and the stretcher tucked under our arms, we set off at a run. Although there was more than thirty degrees of frost, we weren't afraid of getting cold: the reception centre was about one minute's walk from our block.

When we got there we found two patients unable to walk—that meant we needed another stretcher. I dashed out on to the porch and hesitated: where was the best place to go? Our block had only one stretcher. As I looked around I saw some officer standing by the guardhouse and beckoning me with his hand. Just my luck, I thought, for him to want to see me in this frost. But I ran anyway, there was no question of not obeying. I kept my hands in my pockets, my bare feet flip-flopped in the mules and I could feel the frost already nipping at my toes. I arrived. The officer was wearing a warm great-coat with the epaulettes of a full lieutenant, the ear flaps of his cap hung down but weren't fastened, he had felt knee-boots, fur gloves and evidently was also wearing something warm under his greatcoat. His face was unfamiliar to me. Still, we knew very few of the officers and guards at number three, they rarely bothered us and we thanked God for it.

The officer moved his lips—he was saying something to me, but not very loudly. I said:

'Speak louder, please, I'm hard of hearing.'

He really bellowed then:

'Ah, so all at once you're hard of hearing! What's your name?'

'Marchenko.'

'What block are you from?'

'Number one, surgical.'

While this exchange was taking place I got thoroughly frozen: all I had on was a cotton tunic over a cotton undershirt—and I was practically barefoot. I was in a filthy temper. Couldn't he see that I was completely undressed? What was he keeping me out in this frost for? And he was shouting:

'Why have you got your hands in your pockets? Have you forgotten how to speak to your officers? That rule goes for the deaf as well!'

I was so taken aback that I couldn't even think of anything to say. And he went on shouting, without a pause: 'What are you bobbing up and down and jerking about for? Can't you stand still when you're being spoken to by a representative of the camp administration?'

I was silent. Then he started again: 'Why don't you say something? You are obliged to reply when asked a question by a representative of the camp administration! Take your hands out of your pockets, stand up straight as you're supposed to! Why won't you obey your superior? Why don't you answer any questions?'

'Because your questions are idiotic!' I replied bitterly, with my teeth already chattering from the cold.

His eyes popped. But at this point, remembering himself, he shouted to two warders in the guardhouse to come and cart me off to the cooler. 'I shall sort you out a little later, we will finish this talk elsewhere,' he snapped threateningly. I was at least glad to be able to move at last and go indoors, even if only to the cooler—it was better than standing out in the frost.

While I stood with the warder by the gate in the fence surrounding the cooler, waiting for it to be opened, I thought I would freeze solid. We went inside. The usual procedure followed—I was stripped to the skin, searched, ordered to dress and thrust into a cell. It was a small cell for two, about a good pace wide and eight feet long. From wall to wall and not very high off the floor stretched a row of continuous boards; there was a tiny window and in one corner a sloptank. Over the door a hole in the wall held an electric light bulb.

It was so bitterly cold in the cell that you didn't dare sit or lie down—you'd freeze to death. The glass in the window hadn't been puttied and a draught was blowing through the cracks. I started to stamp about in the small space left free at one end of the boards: one step from the door to the boards, one step along the boards from wall to wall and then round again in the same little circle. Soon I noticed that the draught got stronger from time to time, just like that, and an icy wind would chill me to the marrow. This would happen when a door was opened in the corridor—the wind came through all the cracks in the window and the hole for the bulb went right through from cell to corridor. Because of my deafness I couldn't hear the door being slammed, but I could see the glass shuddering in the window frame.

For dinner they gave me a bowl of luke-warm skilly and about two hours later a warder came to take me to the chief officer's office. Behind the desk sat that same lieutenant. His

cap and gloves lay on the desk. He invited me to sit down
and invited the warder to leave the room.

'Why are you behaving in this way?' was his first question.

'What way?'

'You behave like a scoundrel.'

'And you behave like a fascist!'

The officer leapt from his chair: 'I am a Soviet officer! How
dare you call me a fascist! Do you know what can happen to
you for that?'

I said that only fascists would make a point of freezing
people to death. He himself (and I pointed to his cap, gloves,
boots and greatcoat) had been warmly dressed, while I, with
almost no clothes on, with no cap or jacket and only mules on
my feet, had been made to stand there and be questioned in
the frost, what's more he had forced me to take my hands out
of my pockets and stand to attention without moving. After
all, it was only because of the frost that I had been shifting
from foot to foot.

The officer calmed down a bit after this and even seemed to
excuse himself.

'You should have done as you were told and taken your
hands out of your pockets. Now you've got three days in the
cooler. And you can thank your lucky stars you're in a hospital—in a normal camp you'd have got ten to fourteen days!'

After that he began to ask what I was in for, how long my
sentence was and where I had been tried.

'Probably a student, eh?' And without waiting for an
answer he went on didactically:

'You young people, why do you always have to get mixed
up in politics? You don't understand a thing about it, yet you
insist on going ahead. You should get on with your studies,
but no, you have to poke your nose into everything! . . .'

I didn't bother to enter into discussion with him on this point, but merely asked:

'Why did you call me over to see you in the frost? Specially to find fault with something and put me in the cooler?'

'There you are again, behaving provocatively,' said the officer sadly. 'I called you over because prisoners are not authorized to come near the guardhouse when a convoy arrives.'

'But I'm an orderly, I was near the guardhouse on business, it's my duty to receive patients.'

'Well, why didn't you tell me that?'

'But you never asked.'

'Oh well, it's too late to sort it out now. While you're doing your three days in the cooler you can think things over a bit. Maybe you'll pipe down a bit next time, and won't be so impertinent to a representative of the camp administration.'

I was led back to my cell and immediately set to work. Pouring the rest of the water from my soup bowl into the sloptank, so that just a tiny drop was left on the bottom, I picked some plaster off the wall, crumpled it up in the water and mixed a thick paste. Then I stuck this home-made putty over all the cracks in the window frame and round all the edges of the glass. It was a good job the cell window was small! By evening the work was finished. Now there was no draught from the window, not even when the corridor door was opened. And later it became completely cosy: a con came and lit the stove in the cooler. I was warm, there was no draught and I could sleep right through until the next morning, until the stove went cold again. Even on the bare boards I didn't freeze. It got colder towards morning, however, and I froze all day until the following evening: then they lit the stove again.

There was no getting away from it, the hospital cooler was far better than any of the coolers in the camps!

Back to the Compound

WHILE I was in camp three they transferred the politicals from camp seven, where I had come from, to camp eleven. And they filled up camp seven with criminal prisoners.

Soon we began to hear reports about various scandalous incidents in number seven. The criminal cons raped several of the women working there, including a cashier and the daughter of one of the company officers who had a job in the camp. Two cons also came to number three from camp seven—they had drunk huge quantities of acetone. Three other cons had had their stomachs pumped out in time, while these two were dispatched unconscious to the hospital. They didn't get there, however, but died on the way, so that two corpses arrived. Now the officers began to moan: how nice it had been, and how quiet, to work with fifty-eighters (we politicals are still usually referred to as being under article 58, although a new criminal code has been in force since 1961).

When I returned to the camp from the hospital compound I didn't go to number seven, but to camp eleven. There were lots and lots of cons here from camp seven and I was delighted to meet some of my friends again. How lucky to be with Valery, Kolya Yusupov, Burov and other old acquaintances of mine! Another awful thing about the camps is that close ties of friendship are always being broken. Once admin learns of any friendship between prisoners, it hastens to split them up into different compounds. And then you can't even exchange letters, for correspondence between prisoners is forbidden. But this time we had been lucky: we were together again.

Camp eleven was crammed to overflowing, there were even cons living in the attics for a while, for there was no more room in the huts. But my friends helped me to find a place—and in any case I was no novice in camp. I was assigned once again to the emergency gang. I didn't even try to explain to them that with my health and hearing it was impossible for me to work at unloading—you could explain until you were blue in the face, it still wouldn't do any good. Admin knows best. On the following day, February 28, 1966, I was already supposed to start working.

Meanwhile Valery, Kolya and I got together to exchange our news. What were their families writing, how were things outside? In eight months' time my term was due to end and from my first day in camp eleven we started discussing my release and what I would do outside. It was no easy problem: where would I be allowed to live, what work could I get? Because of my deafness I would never again be able to work at my trade as a drilling foreman. And in the camp there was no hope of getting a different profession. Evidently I would have to sign up as loader outside as well, there was no other course open to me. But what about my health? Valery insisted that I should first concentrate on getting cured. Well, never mind, I still had eight months to go—plenty of time in which to think things over. And who knew what else might turn up in the meantime?

Yuli Daniel

WE TALKED about one event that interested all of us politicals at that time—the trial of the two writers, Sinyavsky and Daniel. The first news of them had reached me at camp three already, but now that the trial was over they would soon be coming to Mordovia. One of them was bound to join us in camp eleven: they always separate co-defendants, stick them in different camps and employ different tactics in working on them. For the time being we knew neither of them.

The cons in the camps quarrelled a lot about this trial and also about the two writers themselves. In the beginning, after the first newspaper stories had appeared and before the trial began, everyone agreed unanimously that they were either scum, or cowards, or maybe provocateurs. After all, it was absolutely unprecedented—an open political trial, an open hearing of a case brought on Article 70. We still didn't know that the whole world was talking of their arrest and that this was the only reason the case could not be hushed up. Anyway, these two were bound to weep and recant, and to confess that they had taken their orders from abroad, that they had sold themselves for dollars. How many more of their like were already in the camps, and not one of them had been tried in open court. That meant we were in line for the standard sort of show trial where the accused would play their parts without a murmur.

But then we began to read the first accounts of the trial itself. The accused were not admitting their guilt! No admissions of guilt, no pleas for forgiveness—they were even arguing with the court, standing up for their right to freedom of speech. This was clear even from the accounts in our own press, just as it was equally obvious that our newspapers were distorting the heart of the matter and the course of the trial. This last detail, however, did not bother us: soon we would be hearing it all from the writers themselves. Bravo, Sinyavsky and Daniel! For the first time the KGB was openly trying someone other than scum—and how they were catching it! But what was at the bottom of it? Why an open trial, why were the newspapers writing about it? Some prisoners guessed that the West must have somehow got to hear of it. Oh well, we would soon know.

As for the sentences, we fixed those at once, on the very first day: Sinyavsky would get seven years and Daniel five. Say what you like, but we were men of experience. A few predicted prison at Vladimir, but the majority was confident they would come to us. Everybody, though, agreed unanimously on one thing: whatever the sentence might be, this time the KGB had suffered a crushing defeat. And it wasn't just because the accused had behaved honorably. The main thing was that now the whole world would know that the Soviet Union had political prisoners. Khrushchev had bayed to the whole world that there were no political prisoners in the Soviet Union, that people were not imprisoned for their beliefs. What would he do now with these two? Build a special camp for them?

Valery, Kolya and I discussed the trial. What did they think in camp eleven? And what about number three? We decided that to begin with we would help whichever of the two came to us; and if we couldn't then others would, somebody could always be found. The young people in particular were the first to show admiration for the two writers.

On my very first day back in camp eleven I had a meeting with our section boss, Captain Usov: 'Well, Marchenko, I hope you've had a change of heart and are starting to mend your ways. Why don't you join the IOS, help the administration, and we'll see to it that you get packages and can see your family.' I replied that I had almost finished my sentence and that I could easily manage the remaining eight months without any packages. Then, when free again, I would still be able to look my fellow prisoners in the eye if we met outside.

'Marchenko, you have a false conception of honor and conscience. How will you be able to live outside with the views that you hold?'

'Oh, I'll manage somehow.'

The following day the captain summoned me again to read me a homily about attending political indoctrination sessions. At the end he said:

'You young people are all the same, always dissatisfied with everything, nothing ever suits you. You should get down to some hard work here, but no, you want to run abroad instead.'

'All right, so I did. But even if people ask you openly you won't let them go.'

'I should think not!'

'Well then, why did the Soviet Union sign the Declaration of Human Rights? It says there that every man has the right to live where he wants and to choose the country that he prefers. They signed it all right, but they haven't the least intention of carrying it out.'

'How do you come to know what's written in the Declaration, Marchenko? Where did you read it? Who gave it to you? Who told you what's in it?'

'It's been published in the UNESCO "Courier". And although not many people in our country get a chance to look at that journal, you, sir, can get hold of a copy if you wish to. Incidentally, perhaps you can explain to me why the contents of this Declaration are never mentioned in our press?'

'I don't know. I work for the Ministry of the Interior, not External Affairs'—the abbreviation he used (MVD) was the old Stalinist one, not the new name; even the younger officials still use the old name. 'But you are wrong to think that the workers in America live better than ours. Why do they go on strike if they're living so well?'

'Do you mean to say that the reason ours don't go on strike is because they live so well?'

'Of course. It's beyond dispute.'

At this point I made a comparison between the wages of our workers and those in America. He knew how much our construction workers earned because he himself signed the wage sheets: if there was no faking it came to 70 rubles a month. But in America it was 500 dollars!

'How do you know that, Marchenko? Who told you? I've never read it anywhere.'

'I have, though. And you can too if you like, in "An International Comparison of World Economics".'

'But dollars are worth less than rubles!'

'According to the official exchange rate they are. But in real value? On a wage of 500 dollars an American worker can buy a television set like our "Radius B" for 99 dollars. Five television sets out of a single month's wage! And how many television sets at 360 rubles a time can you buy out of one month's wages here?'

'Marchenko, you've been reading too much bourgeois propaganda and now you've been led astray!'

'And where could I get it! I don't know about bourgeois propaganda, but your camp censors stop even letters from my own mother.'

'Don't you lecture me, Marchenko. I'm here to teach you, not you me.'

'All right, then, teacher (here Usov grimaced), convince me that I'm going astray. Go on. Convince me that our workers live better than the Americans and that that's why they don't go on strike—that's where you began, I believe.'

'According to you our workers don't earn very much and live poorly. Okay. But what about those two', he pointed to an old newspaper with an article about Sinyavsky and Daniel in it, 'what was the matter with them? They also didn't earn very much, I suppose? They both had cars, you bet, just like ministers! But still that wasn't enough, so they sold themselves for dollars and francs, working for the CIA. Men of conviction! We know their sort!'

'Are you sure about their connection with the CIA, sir? There's been nothing in the newspapers about it.'

'Not yet, but there will be! There's bound to be.'

'Well, we'll see. And we'll get to know them ourselves. They're coming here, aren't they?'

'Knowing them's got nothing to do with it, I'm telling you straight, they sold themselves. And you, Marchenko, had better think about your own position a bit. Come to your senses. We can't let you out, you know, with your ideas about life in the Soviet Union.'

On this note the conversation ended. Usov had similar talks with Valery and Kolya and with many other cons.

A couple of days after these pep-talks I came back from working in the zone and looked for Valery in our block. He

wasn't there. I went to the changing room to change. Just
then Izotov poked his head round the door and seeing me
yelled:

'He's come! He's come!'

'Who?'

'The writer.'

'What? Well, where is he?'

'He's been put in our gang and he'll be living in your block.
Valery's taken him over to the canteen.'

I didn't ask which of them it was. So long as Valery was
with him it was all right—he would show him and tell him
everything.

Valery came back while I was still changing. With him was
a fellow of about thirty-five to forty. The new man was wearing his own clothes still, but had clearly made preparation for
camp life: a quilted jacket with buttons, kneeboots and a
ginger fur cap with ear flaps. The jacket was unbuttoned and
beneath it could be seen a heavy sweater. His general appearance struck me as funny: the collarless jacket somehow didn't
fit with the expensive cap, he was bandy-legged when he
walked, like a bear, his back had a pronounced hunch to it
and his whole bearing was somewhat embarrassed and uncer-
tain. We introduced ourselves. It was Yuli Daniel. When we
talked he turned his right ear to me and asked me to speak
louder. And since his own voice was low I too turned around
so that my right ear was towards him and cupped it in my
palm. So we were two of a pair—he was just as deaf as I was.
And both of us found it very funny.

Others of our gang mates came up, surrounded the new
man and began to ask him what was going on outside. Every
now and then people would come running into the hut from
other huts to stare at Daniel—he was a celebrity! Questions
were showered upon him from all sides. We learned that the

trial had been open in name only, and that only people with special passes had been allowed inside. Of his friends and family in the court he had seen only his own wife and the wife of Sinyavsky. He was sure his friends would have come, he said, but they weren't allowed in. The majority of the people in the courtroom were typical KGB stooges, but there were also some writers there, some of whom Yuli had recognized from their well known pictures and others whom he knew personally. Some of them had lowered their eyes and turned away; two or three had nodded to him in sympathy.

'Yes, but why do you think there was so much publicity?'

It turned out that Yuli thought the same as some of us: they must have kicked up a big fuss in the West. Sitting under arrest in the investigation prison he could know nothing, of course. But he had deduced a thing or two from what the judge said and the answers of the witnesses under cross-examination.

'Were you wearing your own or did they put you into prison clothes while you were under arrest?'

'My own, of course. Both during the investigation and during the trial.'

'And alone in a cell?'

'Only for the first few days. The rest of the time there were two of us. A good companion he was too, we played a hundred games of chess together. . . .'

'Good God, another Powers. We were all stuck into prison clothes from the day of our arrest. I was kept in solitary for the whole five months, and others were too. Whereas these two—oh well, they were being kept ready for their "open trial".'

'What did you and Sinyavsky write?'

'What sort of car have you got? One of ours or a foreign model?'

'The same as yours.'

Captain Usov passed through the room where we were talking. As he went by he said:

'A new man? Hand your cap and sweater in to the quartermaster's today—they're not allowed.'

Yuli started to ask us about the work. We did our best to reassure him, the way we did all newcomers:

'It's hard work, but don't be scared, you soon get used to it. You're not the only one, we've got plenty of others who've never held anything heavier than a fountain pen before and now they're experts with a spade. Cheer up. You'll come through!'

Yuli talked more about Andrei Sinyavsky than about himself:

'Now there's a man for you! And as a writer there can't be more than maybe one or two to equal him in the whole of Russia today.' He was extremely worried about his friend, how he had settled down in camp, what sort of work he would be put on and whether it would be too hard for him or not. And this, of course, pleased us all very much.

Although Daniel was supposed to go to work the next day, our brigade decided not to take him on assignments for the first three days, just as they had done with me when I came back from Vladimir prison. Let him look around the zone first. Furthermore we knew that he had a broken right arm that hadn't knit together properly—a legacy from the war. So it must have been on purpose that they put him on the heaviest kind of hard labor in the camps. How with his crippled arm, would he be able to lift logs and shift coal? The bosses knew what they were about: smother him in this hell until he could bear it no longer and begged for some sort of lighter work. Then they would have him right where they wanted. First let him write to the camp newspaper and go on the radio, in return they'd make him a librarian and the doctors would certify him for third category work only. If not in a week then in a month—it was all the same, this intellectual was sure to cave in. No submission in court—all right, let him submit here. He'd soon learn what trouble was.

We advised Yuli to hold out, no matter how hard it would be for him, and not to ask the bosses for anything. But he wasn't thinking of it anyway, he was prepared for hardship.

Far from all the cons reacted to Daniel favorably. Some of them waited suspiciously to see how he behaved in the camp. And some gloated openly: 'Let him knuckle under with the rest of us! We know these writers, they're all corrupt, they live off the fat of the land themselves and then write about our heavenly conditions. These two have been caught, so now let 'em redeem their real sins.'

Cons usually detest all writers. How many times have they read in books or newspapers about 'reforming criminals with honest labor' or the stern but just reforming governor. But where does anyone ever write about our starvation, about the brutal tyranny that drives so many cons to suicide? Only Solzhenitsyn has dared to write the truth, and then not all of it. All the rest are scum, and because of those bastards they stiffened the regime in '61. Made a pretty picture of the camps they did—thanks very much. 'Send them to us in the emergency gang, governor,' yelled our criminal cons, Footman and Vorkuta, before Yuli arrived, 'and we'll find the biggest coal shovels we can for them!' While others said: 'And what makes you think Daniel's going to stand at a machine or handle a shovel? He'll find himself a cosy little nook here too, the Jews always get away with it everywhere.' We already knew from the newspapers that Daniel was a Jew. In the camps, just as outside, there is no lack of anti-semites, even though here too some of the Jewish cons pitched in on the same terms as the rest of us, while others looked for a cushy number—in this too differing in no way from the cons of other nationalities.

The administration played on these feelings in their little 'chats', fully aware that the majority of the cons were well disposed toward Sinyavsky and Daniel for their honest behavior at the trial. And they also stuck Yuli into the emergency gang so as to compromise him in the eyes of the hard workers, so that his authority would be undermined by his physical weakness.

'Hold on, Yuli, hold on for all you're worth,' said Valery to him, 'show them all that they haven't succeeded in breaking you.'

Footman's and even Vorkuta's attitude to Daniel changed after the first few days. It might have been that the admiration of the others rubbed off on them, but more likely he won them over himself. For he was a simple and straightforward fellow, fame and celebrity had not turned his head in the least. His own view was that he had become famous by accident, that he had simply had the luck denied to others just like himself. And it also meant a great deal that he deeply sympathized with the others around him and didn't remain indifferent to their troubles. Soon everyone was sure that Yuli was not looking for an easier life than the rest of us. When unloading he would pitch in as best he could, but of course he did less than the others: what chance did he have of keeping up with people like Kolya Yusupov? Yet at the end of it all he was more tired and worn out than anyone. He also suffered from being unused to physical labor—he had not had to do any physical work since being wounded in the war— and from his arm. Very soon he began to get pains in his shoulder, in the spot where the bone had been shattered. But even then Yuli didn't ask any favors of the administration, and we in our gang decided to pick out for him the sort of work he could manage. We had such jobs, for instance, as cleaning up the timber sheds. After the timber had been unloaded there was always lots of litter left behind—boards of various kinds, sticks, small logs and the straps that held the timber tight in the wagons. There was enough work for the whole shift, but it didn't require much strength. The hardest part was rolling the logs away with crowbars, but then they were never very big. And at night-time they are just left there: once you've done your shift it's straight off to bed. Anyway we insisted that the ganger put Yuli on to this work, but it only lasted a few days. Admin found out about it and the camp KGB immediately insisted that he be transferred back to unloading again, although nothing came of their plans even then. Daniel absolutely refused to ask for any concessions, and all the cons helped him as best they could. Kolya Yusupov asked the ganger to let him take Yuli's turn but the ganger was afraid of admin and refused. When coal was unloaded, however, Footman, Yusupov and Valery used to finish their own hatches and then go over and help Yuli.

Our gang started to be called in by the KGB.

'Who's helping Daniel with his work?'

'All of us.'

'Why? Can't he do it himself? He's shirking! Maybe you'd like to serve his sentence for him as well?'

One talkative fellow had the presence of mind to answer back: 'And what does it say in your moral code? That mutual help should be the rule among comrades, that man should be a friend, comrade and brother to his fellows.'

There was nothing the KGB could do with this sort of thing. Then they took Daniel away from our gang and transferred him to the machine shop, making out that they were doing him a favor on account of his crippled arm. The point was, though, that he hadn't just crippled his arm yesterday; they had known about it from the very beginning and still they had assigned him to the emergency gang and forced him to work at unloading. We all got the point: it wasn't a question of any sudden generosity on admin's part, but simply that they didn't like the other cons helping him out. And in any case, where was the generosity? In the machine shop the racket of the lathes would set even a sound head ringing and Daniel suffered with his ears, a fact that was just as well known to admin as the business with his arm. What's more, lathe work also puts quite a strain on the arm, though not as much, of course, as shovelling coal. Still, nobody could help here, because each man had his norm to fulfil.

Yuli continued to stay friends with us. Although we lived in separate barracks now, we kept up our old ties and whatever one of us got was divided among all. Footman too became one of us now. He grew fonder than anyone of Yuli, protected him in various ways and was even jealous of the other cons. How many times did the following little scene take place? Yuli would be lying on his upper bunk, reading or writing a letter or perhaps writing poetry. Someone who was not in our circle would come in and ask: 'Where's Daniel?' Every now and then somebody would come along to ask him something or tell him about their troubles, or else just to chew the fat. They didn't even give him time to rest in the early days. Footman would be there every time: 'Whoever disturbs Daniel is going to have to deal with me.' Needless to say, there were no takers.

The one thing Footman didn't like was to hear references to one of his first conversations with Yuli. The whole group of us were standing in the corridor one day, by a window, and every now and then first one con and then another would come by and stare into our hut. They just wanted to see and get to know him, and kept coming along. So Footman said:

'Hey, look at those whores of Jewboys come running and hanging around.'

'Don't forget that I'm a Jew too.'

'Ha, I couldn't give a shit who you are.'

After this conversation, however, Footman never again spoke disrespectfully of the Jews in Yuli's presence.

Footman in general, after making friends with Daniel, underwent a significant change. Beforehand he had been the criminal to end all criminals, a permanent con, as they say. He had fallen foul of politics in the same way as other criminals. He didn't give a damn about anything or anyone—he cursed the lot of them, admin and cons alike, he was scared of nothing. In some situations he wouldn't have hesitated, in my opinion, to use a knife as well. And he didn't expect ever to live outside. Now, however, Footman grew much quieter, started to read a lot and to think seriously about his future. Perhaps for the first time in his life he was experiencing a human relationship with someone. Admin didn't like this at all. They called in first Yuli and then Footman and attempted to set them against one another, telling each of them disgusting stories about the other. And when they failed to smash the friendship, they transferred Daniel to another camp. That was after I had already been released and I heard about it outside.

Of course, it wasn't only Daniel's friendship with us and Footman that annoyed admin. Daniel was liked, I should think, by everyone in the camp. He involuntarily became the centre that united diverse groups and nationalities. One day it would be the Lithuanians inviting him in to their circle to listen to their songs, another it was some young people from Leningrad inviting him for coffee, or else the Ukrainians would read their poetry to him. One day one of the groups offered him some 'Mordovian special', in other words the varnish that cons drink in place of vodka. Valery advised him against it. 'Earlier,' he said, 'you could have drunk yourself silly on it, but now you don't have the right. What's more there's no point in giving admin an excuse to get at you.' Yuli had great respect for Valery and always listened to his advice.

A certain amount of time passed and everyone got used to Daniel, he became just another con among cons, like the rest of us. He told us how it had been on his way to the camp: 'Where were they taking me, I wondered. Just like in the song: *Oh, where, oh where am I going? Who will I be meeting there?* All the political prisoners had been released ten years ago. True I had heard of some Kiev Jew being sent down for having a connection with Israel, was it, or something of that sort. He and I and Sinyavsky made three. Well, and maybe there were a couple of dozen more of the same kind as this Jew. Probably they would stick us in with the criminals. I had already worked out how I could get on with them. I remembered the war—there were some convicts in our unit. Then in Ruzayevka I was told about the thousands of politicals. There's no doubt about it, they certainly know how to pull the wool over our eyes.'

And there were also lots of laughs when we heard what he had taken with him.

'My wife,' he said, 'brought along enough things to clothe an army just before I was due to leave. Warm stuff it was—evidently all my friends had collected it up, each one giving me what he had. There were my father-in-law's fur mittens—from his own days in the camp; the quilted jacket, I remember, had been tried on for size by one of her friends; and there was warm underwear—which I had never had in my life before. Well, and then there were a few things of mine: a sweater, a cap, my one and only suit and a white shirt. And she also gave me some new felt boots and leather knee boots—what was I to do with it all? I picked out some of the warm stuff and also took my suit, best shoes and a shirt. During their time in the camps the cons still used to wear their own clothes. These best clothes, I thought, might come in handy for group activities, reading poetry at a camp show. And what do I find? Warders on stage warbling 'The Party is at the helm.' And every damn one of us in prison togs. . . .'

We all burst out laughing, and Yuli too. Now he sports a camp beaver to cover his shaven head. Once he tried to compensate for the lack of hair on his head by growing a moustache, but it came out a sort of splotchy ginger colour. He didn't like it and shaved it off again.

Occasionally it still happened that some unknown con would pester Daniel about having his own car. But we all knew now how writers like Sinyavsky and Daniel lived. Sometimes on nothing more than bread. And Sinyavsky, according to Daniel, wrote all his articles and stories in a basement because there was nowhere else for him to work. Perhaps it was this that helped Yuli to endure the deprivations in camp; his life had never been a bed of roses.

Unable to bully Daniel one way, admin decided to try another tack. In June 1966 they gave him fifteen days solitary for 'malingering and failing to fill his quota'. Both the cons and admin knew that his old wound had turned septic and that a splinter of bone lay at the root of the sepsis. But the doctor wouldn't let him off work and then Yuli refused to go out, so he landed up in the cooler and spent fifteen days inside. Coming out the last evening he was sent straight back in again the next morning for another ten days, and again everyone knew it was for nothing, they simply wanted to give the poor fellow a roasting. Some of the cons made an official protest about it. I know, for instance, that a prisoner named Belov sent protests to the Central Committee and to the Presidium of the Supreme Court, demanding that an end be put to the victimization of political prisoner Daniel and that he be granted medical aid. These protests brought no results, of course, they never did in such cases. They continued to bully Daniel right up to the time I was released; never once did they let him have a full meeting with his wife and he was not even allowed to take any cigarettes back with him after a meeting. But then it was all done on instructions, so that there was no point even in protesting.

We were all pleased to see that Yuli was made of too stern a stuff to be easily broken. Never for any reason did he complain, nor ask for anything for himself, though he was always ready to stick up for someone else.

Ears

In CAMP eleven, as in all the other big compounds, we had
our own medical post: a doctor's office, dispensary and
laboratory. If you fell ill you could go to the doctor. In the
beginning there were up to four thousand of us cons in the
camp and the office was manned by one woman doctor. If she
were to fall ill or for some other reason was unable to come to
work, patients were received by the husband of the medical
post's director—a surgeon from the local civilian hospital
nearby. Attached to the medical post was a small infirmary
with twenty-five beds in it. Eight to ten of them were more or
less permanently occupied by motionless paralytics
(nowadays they are not 'signed out' any more, so they stay
cons until they die). The remaining beds are usually empty.
To get into the infirmary you have to be carried in practically
unconscious on a stretcher. That's the way I got there too.

On March 17 they brought up three wagons of sawn-off
birch trunks for us to unload—the wagons were full of huge
blocks about five feet in diameter. We had to unload them by
hand—the crane, as usual, was out of action—the blocks were
wet and we worked in the rain and the snow. And when we
had finished the work we stood about for another hour or so
in the wind outside the guardhouse, waiting for them to

provide us with an escort. I got so chilled that even in my cot under the blanket I was unable to get warm and I shivered the whole night long. During the night they also brought up two wagons of coal and a further three wagons of birch logs. The ganger started to rouse me, but I was unable to get up. Valery said: 'Leave him alone, he's ill, can't you see?' And the ganger left me in peace. In the morning, though, I'd have to have a meeting with the company officer and it was quite possible that I had already earned myself a spell in the cooler.

I could hardly wait for the morning in order to go to the medical post. My head was splitting apart. I attempted to rise from my cot, but my head spun and I felt horribly sick. I lay down again: doubtless it would pass and I would be able to go. But it got worse and worse with every moment. I could no longer even move my head. The slightest motion brought on giddiness and vomiting. Footman ran to the medical post and fetched the doctor. She examined me and ordered Footman and Valery to carry me to the infirmary. The lads placed me on top of a padded coat and carried me away.

On the first day no one came to examine me. On the second the rounds were being done by the surgeon from the local hospital. 'Where does it hurt?' I even had difficulty in speaking. The con who worked as medical technician in the infirmary explained that I had been brought in with giddiness and vomiting and when the surgeon had gone he told me that they were calling in the ear specialist from camp three because the surgeon could do nothing, it wasn't his specialty. Two days later on his rounds the surgeon repeated that I needed an ear specialist and that the specialist had promised to come as soon as he had some free time. 'And what if the specialist doesn't have any free time?' cracked the con in the next bed to me sarcastically. For five days I had been lying here, and there was no thought even of giving me some treatment.

In the meantime I was still getting worse, I could no longer move my eyes from one object to another. So long as I kept looking at a single point it was all right, but the moment I moved my eyes—more giddiness and vomiting. There was a basin by my bed all the time—I was vomiting very, very frequently. Every time he came round the surgeon would say: 'There's nothing I can do, I'm not a specialist, wait for the ear specialist.'

At last, on the sixth or seventh day, the ear specialist came, it was the same one who had examined me at camp three. He behaved in a friendly fashion to me, questioned me and prescribed some injections. I asked him:

'Doctor, what is this I've got?'

'It's nothing serious. Just take it easy for a while and it will pass.'

In the evening the technician came to give me an injection. It turned out that the ear specialist had prescribed penicillin. At camp three, however, I remember him telling me that penicillin had no effect on me.

For three days I had injections and my condition still didn't get any better. All this time I was unable to eat, the very sight of food would turn my stomach. In a whole day I would get down a few swallows of hospital stewed fruit, and that was all. The rest of my rations I gave to the con lying next to me.

On the fourth day after the ear specialist's visit my temperature rose still higher—103.6. The technician told this to the surgeon on his next walk round and the latter suspended the injections, since they didn't seem to be helping. I asked them to call in the ear specialist again, but he never came and after a while they told me that he never would come either. He had gone away for four months on some course or other.

And so I threshed around in my hospital bed for about three weeks or so, and in all this time the only one to help me was the con in the next bed—he gave me water to drink and changed the cold compresses on my head. I felt so ill that I was sure I was going to croak there. Then everything would be all right—the con had died in hospital and not out working, what could we possibly do? Medicine is not yet infallible. And the fact that I had received no treatment, that the ear specialist had examined me only once, that for nine days they had been unable to get the results of my blood analysis—who cared about that? In any case nobody would ever find out about it!

After about twenty days or so my condition began to ease and I gradually started to come round: at first I was able to turn in my bed without giddiness or vomiting, then I began to get up and even to walk about a little, holding on to the wall. Only the sight of food continued to disgust me. At last I managed to crawl outside. It was already the middle of April, sunny and warm. Valery dragged some doctor along to see me, a prisoner. Outside he had been a doctor, here he was a construction worker. He questioned me closely and was amazed: 'Well, well, well, now you'll live to be a hundred since you haven't died already. You had meningitis!'

My temperature fell and, although unsteady, I was able to stay on my feet. Now the surgeon on his rounds used to look at me with suspicion and would say:

'Marchenko, you've got no temperature. It's time to send you back to the compound.'

'But doctor, I can hardly walk, how can I possibly do any work? And my ears are still painful just the same.'

'I know nothing about ears, there's nobody here to treat

your ears and I can't keep you in hospital any longer. For two more days, okay, you can bum around a bit, but that's all. In two more days you go back to the compound.'

I looked at his tattooed arms (the same old thing, I had seen it a hundred times already: 'life is full of sorrow') and I thought: 'It is you who's a bum, you skunk, you bastard! Call yourself a doctor! You know what condition I'm in and you're sending me back to shovel coal. You're no better than the officers!' I was afraid that after a few days of unloading I would be carried back in again on a padded jacket, and I didn't want to die, especially when I had only six months to go until my release.

That same day I wrote a long petition to the Central Committee. I complained that I was ill and that I was receiving no treatment even though I had twice been held for a while in the hospital in camp three and once in the camp infirmary in camp eleven. I wrote that although a sick man and deaf, I was constantly being obliged to work in the emergency gang, doing the heaviest camp work there was. Also that the camp doctors always gave the same recommendation: 'Prisoner Marchenko has no need of medical treatment and is fit for all kinds of work'—and that as a result of this I had narrowly avoided a trip to the next world. And if they continued to refuse me medical aid here I would be obliged to turn for assistance to the International Red Cross.

I knew in advance that this petition would do me no good and might even do me harm. I knew that I would never be allowed to turn to the Red Cross even if I were free, let alone as a prisoner in a camp. But let them at least have it as a document—I was keeping a copy for myself anyway.

Two days later I was discharged and sent back to the compound—and straight out to work again. It was a good job I had friends. Valery and Tolya Footman now helped me the way they helped Yuli Daniel. I went out on calls day and night, but they wouldn't let me do a stroke of work. The only thing was that it worried Yuli and me to be an extra burden to the others—it was hard enough for them without us on top. Better to spend the rest of our days in the cooler! But the lads talked us round and reassured us: our turn would come to help the others one day.

Two weeks afterwards we received a visit from a Medical Board commission—it had come to interview the cons and re-define work categories. Two strange men in civilian clothes, three women and our surgeon with his arms tattooed like a jailbird: all of them clean, well dressed and well fed. Doctors! When they asked me I told them about my condition.

'Where do you work?'

'In the emergency gang.'

'What sort of work do you have to do?'

I explained.

'When the ear specialist comes he will examine you. Now you may go. Category A1.'

I went out of the room gritting my teeth with rage.

After about another two months I was summoned to the infirmary: 'You wrote a complaint? An answer has come. Sign here to say it's been read to you.' (They never give you a copy to keep. All you can do is write down the number and the date). I read: 'Your complaint has been received and forwarded to the Medical Board of Dubrovlag for consideration.' Well, of course! It's them I'm complaining about, so let them decide. That's the answer they give everyone. I read further: 'It has been established by the medical unit of camp division eleven that Prisoner Marchenko, A.T., is in no need of treatment. Signed: Chief of the Medical Board of Dubrovlag, Major Petrushevsky (Medical Corps).'

Four months after this reply, after I had been released, I went to a doctor. Doctor G. B. Skurkevich, MD, examined me and gave the following verdict: the left ear must be operated on immediately, after that the right ear will also need operating on. He himself did the operation and afterwards he told me that he had rarely seen a patient in such a neglected and dangerous condition. Dr. Skurkevich did everything he could to return my hearing to me, but with no success, it was too late. On the other hand he did clean out all the pus that had accumulated in my suppurating ears: he said that when he cut open the vestibule the pus came squirting out, as though under high pressure.

It was lucky that I was released in time, otherwise I would almost certainly have kicked the bucket in the camp from suppurant meningitis, still, of course, 'in no need of medical treatment'.

Mishka Konukhov

In THE spring of 1966 a new man came to camp eleven and was assigned to us in the emergency gang. This was Mishka Konukhov, a stevedore from the port of Arkhangelsk.

Mishka was a young man of about twenty-five. His childhood had been difficult, he grew up without parents. He became a stevedore and worked at unloading foreign ships; and although the pay was better than if he had worked on our ships or, say, in some railway warehouse, nevertheless he could only just manage to get by. For he was all on his own, with no one to help him: usually, if there are young people in the family, the parents provide board and lodging and your pay goes on getting some gear together and amusements. Mishka, moreover, had married early so that he also had a family to support. True, his wife also worked—in a laundry— but on her miserable pay (fifty rubles a month) she barely had enough to buy food for herself. Well it's clear, in other words, what sort of life they led: you worked in order to eat and ate in order to work.

But in the port and on the ships he worked on Mishka used to see the foreign sailors—they were well dressed, and although they spoke no Russian it was clear they hadn't much to complain about and were in no hurry to dash over to our side, to live in the homeland of the world proletariat. Not even the Negroes. Of course all this was bourgeois propaganda, but Mishka didn't understand. He merely became terribly enraged—and, evidently remembering something from his orphan childhood, found the sole form of protest open to him: across his chest he tattooed the words: 'Victim of communism.' And then stevedore Mishka Konukhov became the focus of political passions.

Someone among the foreigners photographed him stripped to the waist and this photograph appeared in the newspapers over there. Then the KGB started to pull Mishka in: let him make a statement, they said, pointing out that he was a victim of the underworld, that he had let himself be tattooed because of his youth and foolishness, and that now the gutter press was exploiting this without his knowledge. Mishka refused. Then all sorts of strange incidents started happening to him: one day some characters he didn't know would tag on to him in the street and start calling him names and insulting him; another day a brawl would suddenly break out right beside him and the participants would try to involve him in the melee; or else some 'hooligans' would fall upon him all of a sudden and beat him up in some dark alley. Mishka didn't respond to these provocations and kept out of brawls and didn't drink in company, and after every incident he went to the police station, made a statement and signed a charge. But the police somehow had no success at all in finding the culprits and in the meantime he continued to be called in by the KGB, who warned him on several occasions that anything might happen to him, that our patriotic-spirited youth was up in arms over his conduct and might easily take the law in to their own hands and make short work of him, and the police, of course, would be powerless to protect him against the wrath of the crowd.

Konukhov finally got tired of this comedy and took a train to Moscow. He wandered round the streets looking for the British embassy. He had already worked out how to get in. He knew that if he hesitated he would be stopped by our policemen on guard outside the embassy. Therefore he walked swiftly past the front of the embassy, as though hurrying somewhere on business, then directly opposite the door, took a sharp ninety-degree turn and ran into the vestibule. The policemen didn't realize at first what was happening and they were well behind him when he heard them shout: 'Where are you going young man? Halt!' But he was already inside.

In the vestibule he was detained by some employee or other—the doorman or a guard. Mishka explained that he absolutely had to see the English ambassador. 'The ambassador is engaged at the moment, but you may speak to one of the embassy secretaries; perhaps your business can be settled without the aid of the ambassador.' He was ushered into an office and invited to sit down.

An interpreter remained present during Mishka Konukhov's chat with the English embassy secretary, but he was being paid, it seemed, for nothing—the secretary himself spoke perfectly good Russian. To begin with he offered Mishka some dinner. Mishka politely declined: he had just had a meal in an eating house, he was full. Then the secretary ordered coffee for the two of them—chatting over coffee was somehow easier. Well, coffee was all right, Mishka wouldn't say no to a coffee. He explained the nature of his request: he was asking for them to assist him in going to England, he no longer wanted to live in the USSR. They asked him who he was, where he worked and why he wanted to leave the country. And the secretary listened very carefully to all his explanations. Then he began to speak himself. He said that in order to leave the country, Mister Konukhov would first have to renounce his Soviet citizenship. Then he would be able to take any nationality he liked, including English, and the embassy would assist him in this. But the secretary advised him to think his decision over once again. It happens quite often, said the secretary, that a Soviet tourist or member of a delegation remains in England, asks for political asylum, and then realizes that he finds it hard to live away from his homeland, his family and his friends—for a very long time, for dozens of years, your government doesn't allow such people to return and visit them. Some emigrants decide sooner or later to return to their homeland. We understand their feelings and our government places no obstacles in their way. However it happens quite often that upon their return to the USSR these people explain their decision not by homesickness and a desire to see their country and family, but by the bad living conditions in our country. What is more, they make it sound as though they were obliged to remain in England almost by force or by trickery, and as though they were not allowed to go home. Statements such as these, quite naturally, are extremely distasteful to us, they impugn our honor and cause diplomatic friction. Therefore we are obliged to be extremely cautious in approaching requests such as yours. And in general, Mister Konukhov, perhaps you don't know our country and are idealizing it? We have our problems and our difficulties, you know, and when you run up against them you may, perhaps, regret your hasty decision.

In short the Englishman was politely dissuading Mishka from fleeing to England, rather than luring and decoying him and Mishka was taken aback. In conclusion the secretary explained to Mishka that if, on mature consideration, he did not wish to change his mind, he should go to the Ministry of Foreign Affairs and renounce his Soviet citizenship. Thus, although the embassy did not refuse to accept him as an

English citizen, the business would obviously take some time.

Mishka resolved to carry it through. But when he left the embassy he noticed three unknown men following closely at his heels and beside him, in the street, a slowly moving car. Mishka tried to merge with the crowd, but he knew it was useless, that he wouldn't be able to get away. At one of the crossroads the three men came right up to him, laughing and joking, embraced him tightly, like an old friend and bundled him into the car. It all took place in a moment and probably not one of the crowd on the pavement either saw or understood what had happened.

They drove him—it goes without saying—to the KGB. There they threw him into a cell and began to question him. Why had he gone to the embassy? With whom had he talked? What about? Had he not left something there? Mishka told them everything as it had happened—he had nothing to hide. While he was there he also wrote an application to the Ministry of Foreign Affairs informing them that he wished to renounce his citizenship and requesting permission to go to England. Both the KGB officials and representatives of the Ministry of Foreign Affairs came to talk to him, persuading him to withdraw his application and write that he had changed his mind. Well, what sort of 'persuasion' did they use? 'Anyway we'll never let you leave, do you understand?' Mishka insisted on having his own way. Three days later they let him go, ordered him to return to Arkhangelsk and made him sign that he wouldn't leave without permission.

In Arkhangelsk, of course, he was no longer permitted to work on foreign ships and he was transferred to a different sector. Here his pay was lower too. They continued hauling him in to the KGB and trying to provoke him into 'hooliganism' on the street. But Mishka didn't fall for the provocation and he didn't give up either. Several times he wrote to the Foreign Ministry and in the end received a questionnaire. In answer to the question: 'Why do you want to leave the USSR?' he wrote: 'Because I don't like its political system and ideology.'

And why should he lie—say that he wanted to visit a second cousin or something? They still wouldn't have let him go.

And so they kept pulling him in to the KGB, to the party committee, working him over at meetings—all the stevedores had long known that Mishka was trying to go to England and wasn't being allowed. The time came round for his annual holiday and although he couldn't go anywhere because of the undertaking he had signed, Mishka handed in an application: 'I wish to be granted a month's holiday.' A month, and the regulation holiday was twelve days! Konukhov was interviewed on this subject by the first secretary of the regional party himself, and Mishka again dug his heels in and insisted on having his own way. 'The workers in Sweden, by striking, have long since obtained a month's paid holiday during a year, and I demand the same.' To the astonishment of all the other stevedores he got his month's holiday and even got the same for his wife. What the devil next and what if they up and send him to England—what will he be telling them about life over here!

Shortly after this a letter came from the Foreign Ministry: Konukhov was required to pay a duty of 90 rubles for the drawing up of his renunciation of citizenship. Mishka sent off the money. Three days later they came for him at home in a car, took him away by force and drove him somewhere. He ended up in some camp or other, in the camp hospital, with a ward to himself. The surgeon came and said: 'Konukhov, do you agree to an operation to remove this embellishment from your chest?'

'And what happens if I refuse?'

The surgeon laughed:

'Sooner or later you'll agree, it's better not to drag it out.'

And Mishka agreed.

After the operation, however, he was sent not to Arkhangelsk, but to solitary confinement in a KGB investigation prison: 'You see, Konukhov, we warned you we would put you inside, that we would find a way if you didn't pack it in. Now you have only yourself to blame.'

He was tried for possessing foreign currency and some sort of printed matter—God knows if he really did have a few dollars or whether it was all trumped up from beginning to end. The court, as usual, was closed and Mishka was not given a copy of the sentence.

And so our gang acquired a practically fully qualified Englishman. He looked around him with the same lively curiosity as he would have done had he landed up in England. He was particularly interested in cons who had come back from abroad: what was life really like there, why had they come back, how had they landed in Mordovia? He remembered his conversation with the secretary in the English embassy and was checking both him and himself.

We had plenty of such cons in the camp and there were several in our gang alone: Volodya Pronin had come back from West Germany; Anton Nakashidze, a dancer in the Georgian State Song and Dance Ensemble, had stayed on in England and then returned; Pyotr Varenkov, Budyonny, Bessonov and the Ossetian, Pyotr Tibilov, had all come back from abroad. All these 'returnees' said that the material standard of living in the West was far better than in our country and everywhere, of course, there was freedom: nobody forces you to do anything. 'Then what the bloody hell brought you back if life was so good over there?' They replied that they felt homesick for their country and their families—one would have a mother here, another a father, a third a wife (the biologist Golub, for instance, about whom so much was written in the newspapers at one time, returned because his wife implored him; when he was jailed she renounced him). They came back free men as far as the frontier and from the frontier on—under armed guard to prison and then to camp for a stretch of 10–12 years. Golub, it is true, and other such 'celebrities' are not jailed right away, but 6–12 months afterwards when their stories are forgotten. 'Well, now you should be pleased,' say the cons to those who have come back, 'here's your homeland and this is your family—Mordovia and the fraternal collective of the camps!'

Maybe if these people would agree to appear in public and announce how badly they had lived in the West, how they had been recruited as spies or something of that sort—maybe a few of them wouldn't have been jailed or would have been pardoned and released. But even then not all of them: it is easy enough to get into a camp, but few manage to get out again before their term is up, even at the price of a public recantation.

Mishka Konukhov no longer dreams of going to England and they haven't even returned his 90 rubles to him, although the official act never took place. Now he dreams of something else: how to train to be a medical technician, at least he would have cleaner work. And greater respect.

In the summer of 1966 a routine 'accident' occurred—our hut was burnt down. They tried Yurka Karmanov for it, an old friend of mine from Vladimir and camp seven. There were different accounts of how it happened. Some people thought it was a routine provocation on the part of admin in order to have an excuse for tightening up the regime still further. They alleged that the sentry in the watch tower had stated during his evidence: 'I was instructed to sound the alarm as soon as I saw the fire.' I don't know. I think that Yurka Karmanov was indeed capable of setting fire to it out of despair and helplessness. Just as Romashev and many others deliberately put themselves in the tommy gunners' sights; as Sherstyanoy in camp seven set fire to the machine shop; as men slash, hang, poison and tattoo themselves. Whoever hasn't been in a camp can never understand the actions and behavior of a con.

Release

Two or three months before I was due to be released I was called into the KGB office for a chat. There were three people there: our KGB officer, the chief of the Political Education Unit and company officer Usov. I remember that conversation well: it was their last attempt to convert me, to re-educate me 'by peaceful means'.

'Marchenko, you're due to be released soon. Do you realize that, once back outside, you will have to behave and think like everyone else? It's not like in camp, where everybody has his own opinion.'

'Citizen officer, even outside I doubt if everybody's thinking alike. Times have changed. Even the communists have fallen out among themselves.'

'Don't speak such slander, Marchenko! Communists form a united front.'

'What about the Chinese? And the Albanians? And the splits in all sorts of communist parties?'

'What about the Chinese! There's a black sheep in every family.'

'Citizen officers, you are all communists, aren't you? But what sort of communists are you—straightforward or parallel?'

They looked at me hard, as much as to say—are you cracked or something? Usov said: 'I've heard all sorts of rubbish from prisoners in my time, but this is the first time I've heard that one. What are you babbling about?'

'In yesterday's newspaper I read that the government of India had released 30 communists from jail—members of the parallel CP of India. So I'm asking you what sort you are: parallel, perpendicular or oblique?'

The KGB officer took a file down from the wall and began to leaf through it. From where I was sitting I showed him the place where it was written. After that they changed the subject, going back to the beginning again:

'Take thought, Marchenko! With your beliefs you'll be coming back here again.'

'You can say that again, I know that already. The moment someone disagrees with you—to the camps with him. Tomorrow you'll be singing a different tune and again you'll all be unanimous about it. In six years, thank God, I've had time to see plenty of traitors like myself—your camps are full of them. But what I don't understand is how can you communists put me in jail for my beliefs? In other countries whole opposition parties exist quite legally, including communist parties dedicated to changing the system. These communists, when they go back home from a routine conference in Moscow, aren't then tried for betraying their country. But me, a worker who belongs to no party whatsoever, you have been holding behind barbed wire for six whole years and now you're threatening me with more.'

'What's the point of you telling us about other countries! They have their own laws and we have ours. You people are always throwing America in our faces—a fine country you've picked to show us freedom! If they had freedom there, why

would all the Negroes be rebelling? And the workers striking?'

'Lenin said that strikes and the Negroes' struggle in the
USA were themselves indications of freedom and democracy.'

When I said this my educators literally leapt up from their
seats and all three of them pounced on me together:

'How dare you slander Lenin!'

'Where did you hear such a lie?'

'Repeat what you've just said!'

I remembered this passage word for word and repeated it,
even naming the number of the volume it was in. The PEU
chief went to the door: 'What volume did you say? Just a
moment, I'll be right back.' He returned from his office carrying the book with its dark-blue binding—the latest edition, I
had seen the whole set in his bookcase, pressed tightly together, cover to cover, behind the glass doors. He handed it to
me:

'Go on, show us where it contains what you've just said.'

While I was leafing through the tightly pressed pages the
three of them waited like hounds on the leash: now they
would catch their game, now they would catch me out. They
were convinced that Lenin never said any such thing, that he
couldn't have said such a thing. An important consideration
here was that their minds couldn't contain the idea of an
uneducated fellow like me actualiy reading Lenin—or anything else for that matter. They themselves had read only 'from
here to here'. They tried not to argue with a con who was a
historian. But when somebody like me referred to an article
in a magazine or a document, in short any printed source,
they were convinced he was repeating it from hearsay, that
one of the cons in the camp was spreading hostile propaganda, and that's why they always pounced: where did you
hear that? Who told you that? And now it would turn out

that I was talking through my hat and these questions would rain down on me.

I handed them the open book. The political education chief read out the lines I had indicated. Usov gazed at him in perplexity. The KGB officer went over to him:

'Here, give it to me.'

Together they turned the pages over, hoping, no doubt, to find some appropriate explanation or refutation of the passage they had just read. But nothing was to be found there and the KGB captain said to me, not in the least put out:

'Marchenko, you must have misinterpreted Lenin. With your views you interpret him in your own special way, and that's bad. You won't last very long outside.'

'But how else can these words be interpreted? After all, it's really true that strikes and mass disorders occur only in democratic countries, whereas totalitarian regimes repress the people with terror. Under Hitler, for instance, there were never any strikes in Germany.'

Then it began again: 'How dare you! You ought to be stood up against a wall for saying that!' Then, cooling off a little, they again set about 'educating' me: 'The peoples of the whole world are moving towards communism, every day it is winning more and more followers. . . .'

'If these followers knew that they were leading their peoples towards prisons and camps they might, perhaps, think again. But you usually don't mention these things aloud, except when you start scrapping. One day almost every newspaper was full of: "China on the path to communism!" or "The successes of socialist construction in China!" And what is it now? A hundred million Chinese in concentration camps—what do you think, that they imprisoned them all in a single day?'

'Did you read that in Lenin as well—a hundred million?

Where on earth do you get this rubbish from, Marchenko? A hundred million—why, that's one seventh of the entire population! These are the ravings of a madman!'

'Then it's not me who's mad but that lecturer who came to camp seven last summer. But why ravings? Didn't we have tens of millions in camps ourselves? If it were me alone, perhaps, I wouldn't believe it, I'd think I misheard about China. But I'm not the only one: all the cons heard it and laughed to think that the pupils had outstripped their teachers.'

'A hundred million—that's slander! Here, take a pencil and paper and write that there are a hundred million prisoners in China. You know what will happen to you if it's untrue, don't you?'

I took a piece of paper and wrote: 'I, Prisoner Marchenko, A.T., heard during a lecture on such and such a day and at such and such a place that there are now a hundred million prisoners in China. During a talk with representatives of the KGB and PEU I mentioned this fact and referred to the lecturer, but was told that it was untrue. I would like the truth or falsity of this statement to be investigated and to be informed of the answer.' I wrote the date and signed it. Then I asked:

'When will I know the answer?'

'We'll check everything and when the time comes we'll call you in. You may go.'

I know that when people outside read of this conversation they will say to themselves: 'What the devil, there's more freedom in the camps than out here! Even at home I'd think twice before saying what Marchenko gabbed to his officers! And all they say afterwards is "you may go"—why, here I'd be clapped in a cell immediately if I talked like that!'

Of course, if I'd taken it into my head to talk like that to strangers in the compound, the stool pigeons would have squealed on me and I'd have my sentence extended for 'agitation among the prisoners', but an officer in his room is bound to convince me with his arguments and if the opposite occurs, what's it to do with me? He can hardly nail me for agitating among himself!

Nevertheless they might still have drummed up a charge and slung me into Vladimir jail—but only if it had been just me, whereas it was everyone, the entire youth. So that it couldn't really go beyond the cooler and the cooler in camp is in any case inevitable.

I landed up in the cooler almost on the very eve of my release, on September 30. The day before we had worked through the entire day, from eight till five, then during the night we had been called out to unload cement and the following morning were pushed out for a third time. But I was suffering from chills and giddiness again. I didn't go, I refused. Anton Nakashidze (the one from the Georgian Ensemble) also remained behind, he was too exhausted to get up.

In the morning I dragged myself over to the medical post, registered and settled down to wait my turn. The doctor handed me a thermometer, I thrust it under my arm and sat there thinking: 'I probably don't have a temperature, it was a week before it went up last time. But they won't put me in the infirmary anyway: I came myself, on my own two feet. So what was to be done?' The doctor took the thermometer:

'Almost normal. What's the matter with you?'

'It's still the same as before—giddiness, headaches.'

'Well, why have you come here to me, Marchenko? You know very well that it's the ear specialist you need! Take some pills for your headache, that's all I can do for you.'

I got some pills at the hatch and went back to the hut. Our

gang had already returned from work and were sleeping, except only for Anton. The company officer had already given him fifteen days in the cooler. Soon afterwards our orderly, Davlianidze, came in: 'Marchenko, the company officer wants to see you!' Well, I'd better go.

'Why did you refuse to work last night?'

I explained why and it seemed to me that Usov believed me.

'All right, you can go.'

Back in the hut Anton asked me:

'How many? Ten or fifteen?'

'Well, nothing it seems.'

Anton couldn't believe me:

'Get away with you! I wouldn't have expected it.'

I climbed into my cot and endeavored to go to sleep. But I had only just dozed off when somebody dug me in the ribs and started pulling on my leg. I opened my eyes and saw a warder.

'Come on, get ready!'

'What for?'

'Don't you know where shirkers go?'

Oh well, to hell with it, if it was the cooler, so be it. I still didn't know which was worse—the cooler or unloading timber. Anton and I started to get ready, putting on as many warm things as possible, but the warder warned us: 'You're wasting your time dressing up, we shall take it off you just the same.' Of course they would. It was so long since I had been in the cooler that I had forgotten. We picked up our padded jackets, our toothbrushes, some soap and a towel— and we were ready. I didn't even ask how long I had got. When we arrived they told me it was fifteen days.

Anton and I were separated and put into different cells. Mine turned out to be tiny, six feet by nine, but I was the

only one in it. This is what they always try to do: either
you're alone or they cram about twenty people into one small
cell. I was pleased to think that at least I could sleep peacefully, but I was in too much of a hurry. Instead of cots the
cell had two wooden shelves, as in a railway compartment,
and both of them were folded flat against the wall and padlocked. You were able to lie down only between lights out
and reveille. Still, it was a good thing I was alone, for at least
I could sit down. But when there are two of you, one sits on
the small block of wood that is fixed to the floor and the
other has to stand: there is seating only for one. Unless you
sit on the sloptank.

At night they brought the padded jacket that had earlier
been confiscated and unlocked one of the shelves. I lay
down. At first I had the jacket underneath me. But soon I
was frozen stiff. It was bitterly cold, October was only one
day away and the stoves weren't lit until the eighteenth. I
dragged my jacket out from underneath me, huddled myself
up and tucked it in around me. Now the cold began to come
from underneath: the shelf was made of boards with cracks
several inches wide between them, and the floor was the
same. In short, I was unable to sleep for the cold and spent
the whole night tramping about the cell in an attempt to get
warm. Yuli had been lucky, it was summer when he was in
here—in June!

In the morning my couch was locked up, the padded jacket
was removed until the following night, and I myself was led
to a small yard to work. It was old woman's work—the whole
of the intensified regime block and the cooler was put on knot-
ting shopping nets. The norm was seven or eight nets a day.
Nobody, of course, ever got anywhere near the norm, or even
half the norm. Once we tried an experiment: we worked one
whole day without a breather. And nevertheless, even the

hardest workers got stuck on the third net. When I first went in they didn't insist on us fulfilling the norm: so long as we didn't refuse to work we at least got our basic. But after a week they announced that anyone who finished less than three nets would be put on a reduced food intake. Nobody could manage this target and we were all put on 1,300 calories a day. For us in the cooler it wasn't too bad—a week or two of starvation was nothing; but what about the men in the IRB? They had up to six months to do—and all that time on starvation rations! No parcels, no shop, not even allowed to buy smokes: you had to make a special application to the camp commandant. Then some would get permission, others not. In the cooler, of course, smoking was completely forbidden, tobacco was confiscated if they found any on you.

As in all prisons, the toilet break here was misery. There was no time even to wash, let alone clean your teeth. And there was one latrine for the whole jail, with only two holes. Two cells would be led out at a time, consisting of 12–15 men, and there was no chance of them all having time. When they put you in the cooler they search you down to the last stitch of clothing and any paper is taken away; and they don't give you any paper when you go for your toilet break:

'Think you're an intellectual, eh? Well, you can wipe your arse with your fingers, it won't hurt you.'

It's a wonder no one's thought of keeping the sloptank locked and bolted.

In these conditions deceiving admin is a matter of life and death for the con. 'They know how to search and we know how to hide' is what they say in the camps. The compound even manages to get help to the IRB and the cooler. Friends who are 'free'—the compound, of course, is free compared to the cooler—manage to get smokes over to them, a bit of bread, sugar and margarine. And to do this the cons have invented the 'pony'.

What is a pony? The lads in the compound wrap some tobacco, bread or something else of that sort in a bit of rag, roll it into a tight little bundle and then wind it round a slender thread in which they make dozens of little loops. Then, at a convenient moment, they lob it over the fence so that it lands under the cooler windows. Meanwhile the cons inside are already prepared. They bend a piece of wire to make a hook, get hold of some thread—one usually sacrifices a sock—and they throw this line out so that the hook lands on the far side of the packet. Now they have to pull it slowly towards them. As it slides over the packet the hook is bound to catch in one of the loops.

If the bundle with the pick-me-up inside is too big and won't go through the bars on the window, they unwrap it right there on the far side of the bars, separate it with their hands and pull it into the cell bit by bit. So long as somebody manages to haul the pony in and once the pick-me-up is inside the prison walls, it is bound to go to whoever it is intended for; the cons pass it over either during the toilet break, or else at work or somewhere. Passing things from the compound to the cooler or from cell to cell is severely punished, but nobody takes any notice of that. If you were to fear punishment and obey all the regulations, you wouldn't last a year in there. And we all had terms of five, ten, fifteen years.

The pony was used right up until the summer of 1965. They had become so clever at it that the whole operation took no more than a minute: in a single moment the pony would be lobbed over and already inside the cell. But word got round to admin. The chief officer took steps to intensify vigilance and to put an end to this lawlessness. And so they welded extra steel bars on to the windows. Now the openings were three times as narrow and the bars formed not so much a grill as a net. Not only could you not get a hand through any more, but you could barely get two fingers in the hole.

When I was in the cooler that autumn the pony was already a thing of the past, it had served its turn. And the cons still hadn't found a new trick to replace it. But they are bound to think of something soon, I'm sure of it. For how could it possibly be otherwise?

On October 15 I left the cooler to go back to the compound; I was staggering like a drunkard after those scientifically calculated 1,300 calories. Till the end of my term, till the time of my release, I had precisely seventeen days to go.

Just as before I went out to unload, lifted tree trunks, shovelled coal and cement. I got up at night when called, went with the others to the guardhouse, waited for the armed escort. Just as before I still suffered from giddiness, but I no longer refused to go to work: I didn't want to spend my last few days shut up in the cooler, I wanted to spend them with my friends.

We were together for every free moment we had. The subject of conversation was always the same: where would I go, where and how would I get myself a job outside? The head of the records office had already warned me that 'on account of the passport regulations' I was forbidden to live in the districts of Moscow or Leningrad, in ports or in frontier regions. Besides these there were restricted access towns where I also wouldn't be allowed to register.

'What does that mean, restricted access towns, which ones?'

'If you're not allowed to register there, that means it's a restricted access town.'

'Okay, where can I live then?'

'You'll find out when you're released. Just tell me for the time being where you want your ticket and certificate made out for.'

'Well, what about Kalinin?'

The major grinned:

'You can't register in Kalinin.'

'Make it Kursk then.'

'I can give you a certificate with Kursk on it. But let me tell you straight, Marchenko: it would be better for you to go to the far north or Siberia through a special recruitment office, so as not to waste your time chasing about.'

'Go from one camp to another just like this one, only without the barbed wire? No thanks. Anyway, they wouldn't take me in a special recruitment office with this health of mine.'

'Do as you like, but if you insist on having your own way you'll end up by coming back here again and we'll register you for another five to seven years in Mordovia without the least trouble at all.'

The thing that concerned my friends most was whether I would manage to get myself treated by a decent ear specialist. They also made more distant plans for my future. Valery insisted that I should definitely go to school: 'Finish night school and you'll be able to go to a research institute. It's not too late.'

'Valery, what kind of a pupil do you think I'd make? I'm as dumb as an ox at mathematics.'

Valery began to demonstrate that nobody is incapable of learning, except for congenital idiots. It was just that maths was always taught badly. 'You can learn if you want to.'

'But I'm deaf, I won't even hear the lessons.'

Yuli said that in Moscow you could buy a hearing aid. They cost a pretty penny. But on the other hand the girls would never notice you were deaf. All you had to do was let your hair grow long—to hide the loop that went over your ear.

We discussed something down to the smallest detail: how I would dress outside, where to buy what so that it was both cheap and practical. I would have to travel in my camp reefer jacket, since it turned out that all that was left of my clothes was an old skiing suit and a pair of boots. What a hurry I was in to strip off that reefer jacket, how sick and tired of it I was by now!

The lads started bringing me clippings from various magazines: fashionable men's wear, what tie to wear with which suit. One might have thought that I was going to have at least three of these suits, that I would be spending my time rushing from the concert hall to a diplomatic reception.

My last days in the camp were particularly painful: they dragged on and on until it seemed they would never come to an end and I could hardly believe that the day of my release would really come, and I didn't know what to expect afterwards.

Already on the day before my release I had handed in my regulation equipment and overalls and early on the morning of November 2 my friends and acquaintances on the first shift came in to say goodbye: they were going off now and we wouldn't be seeing one another again. Among them were Burov, the two Valerys from Leningrad—Ronkin and Smolkin, Vadim, and also a number of others that I knew. They all hoped I would settle down all right outside, gave me their families' addresses and asked me to call in if it was on my way. They asked me not to forget them—those who were sitting in Vladimir prison as well as those remaining in Mordovia. When they left for their shift only my closest friends stayed behind—Valery, Yuli, Kolya, Tolik, Footman, Anton. Yuli presented me with Lebedev's book on Chaadayev—he knew that I was very fond of it. And on the fly-leaf he had written:

> Not bad on the whole
> Your fate is amusing:
> Your ears here were closed,
> Your eyes here were opened.
> Be proud of your uncommon feat—
> Not everyone seeing sees.

> To Tolya Marchenko with respect and affectionate best wishes, Yuli Daniel.

Footman and Valery presented me with Prévost's 'Manon Lescaut', probably as a hint. At ten o' clock the whole group of them accompanied me to the guardhouse. Here we again embraced and said our farewells. It is impossible to convey my feelings. All my joy evaporated, a lump rose in my throat and I was afraid of bursting into tears. I deeply regretted parting from my friends, leaving those who had become so dear to me behind barbed wire. For a moment I wanted to return.

'Go on, Tolya, you'll miss the train!' they said, hurrying and encouraging me at the same time.

I walked through the outer zone—a barbed wire fence already divided us. Waving my hand to them one last time, I entered the guardhouse and the door banged shut behind me. Now I faced quite a different sort of leave-taking.

I was taken into an office.

'Strip! Stand over here! Knees bend and hold out your arms! Go into the corner!'

After this they began to feel and examine my clothing. Every seam of my shirt, then my underpants, then all the rest. One warder examined the shirt before passing it to another; he then felt it and passed it on to an officer, who passed it to a second who passed it to a third who passed it to a fourth and then on to me. I then put it on. Present at the search were: the chief officer, the chief of camp security and the chief of the camp KGB.

Next came the turn of my suitcase. There was practically nothing in it: towel, soap, toothbrush, a few handkerchiefs, some exercise books with my study notes and some books. Everything was inspected just as painstakingly as my clothes, every object was poked and felt by five or six pairs of hands. The exercise books and books were checked with particular care and leafed through page by page. What were they looking for? The warder opened Chaadayev and saw Yuli's inscription. He immediately showed it to the KGB man who took it and left the office with it. They also kept taking my exercise books out into the corridor, showing them to someone and getting advice. Returning with my copy of Chaadayev, the KGB man put it to one side.

As I watched them rummaging through my things I suddenly remembered something. Not long before me a Muscovite called Rybkin had been released. As soon as he came to the guardhouse they had pounced:

'Come on, give us Daniel's poems! We know all about it!'

Rybkin was astonished, he had never exchanged a single word with Daniel, he didn't even know him. They set about searching him and when they reached his papers one of the warders dragged out a notebook with some verses: 'Here they are, we were right!' Their triumph was shortlived however. These verses were not by Daniel but by Ryskov (a former medical orderly in camp three). One of the stool pigeons had seen Ryskov giving them to Rybkin and had squealed. Therefore they knew in the guardhouse that Rybkin was trying to take some verses out of the camp, a whole notebook-full. But whose verses? No one was in any doubt—they must be

Daniel's! And it turned out they weren't Daniel's at all, but a collection of love lyrics! What a disappointment! And now they must be looking for Yuli's poems on me. Let them look! They had already found his inscription in the book.

Meanwhile they had already finished turning my gear upside down and the chief officer was examining, poking, tapping and thrusting a steel spike clean through my suit-case, which had in any case already been examined by the others. Then he set about a toy I had been given—a plastic fisherman with a fishing rod. The fisherman was completely soft and all but transparent. Only the head was hard, having been stuffed with something. The chief officer squeezed it and squeezed it, pinched it and pinched it, but was evidently unable to make up his mind and took the fisherman out into the corridor. A little while later he returned and tossed the fisherman back into my case—failed again!

Into the office came Major Postnikov himself, head of the KGB for all the camps in Mordovia. They showed him Chaad-ayev. Postnikov turned the book round in his hands, read the inscription and commanded:

'Cut it out and make a record of it.'

I asked him to explain what was wrong with the inscription and why they were confiscating it.

'You see, Marchenko, in my opinion Daniel was expressing his views in that verse.'

'Well, of course he was, you wouldn't expect him to express someone else's. But what's subversive about them?'

Postnikov didn't reply. He started to look through my exercise books.

'I see, Marchenko, that you've been reading the whole of Lenin. On the whole that's a good thing, of course, but . . . I fear that with your views we shall be seeing you back again.'

With this farewell ringing in my ears and having received

back my case, my mutilated Chaadayev, my internal pass-port and my certificate of release, I walked to the exit, accompanied by the major in charge of the records office. We passed through several doors. At each one the major handed some documents through a tiny window, after which the door would open and then close after us again. At last the last door opened and banged shut behind me and I walked out into the street.

Past the guardhouse and down the road between the living and work zones, past the festive posters and slogans, came a column of women prisoners. I could hear the rough shouts of the armed guards with their tommy guns: 'Stop talking! What did I tell you!' The women were walking slowly, drag-ging their feet in their clumsy felt boots. Dark gray padded jackets, padded trousers, grayish-yellow faces. I gazed at them—that one, perhaps, I had carried in for an operation; perhaps that one over there had said: 'My Valery's a year old already!' No, I didn't recognize any of them. They were all exactly alike in this column—cons.

The column passed. I filled my lungs with fresh air—although Mordovian it was unguarded and free—and walked away from the guardhouse. It was snowing. Big snow-flakes settled and immediately melted on my still warm clothing, which had not had time to cool. It was the latter half of the day of November 2, 1966, five days to go to the forty-ninth anniversary of Soviet power.